Death in Classical Hollywood Cinema

Death in Classical Hollywood Cinema

Boaz Hagin

First published 2010 by
PALGRAVE MACMILLAN

Palgrave Macmillan in the UK is an imprint of Macmillan Publishers Limited, registered in England, company number 785998, of Houndmills, Basingstoke, Hampshire RG21 6XS.

Palgrave Macmillan in the US is a division of St Martin's Press LLC, 175 Fifth Avenue, New York, NY 10010.

Palgrave Macmillan is the global academic imprint of the above companies and has companies and representatives throughout the world.

Palgrave® and Macmillan® are registered trademarks in the United States, the United Kingdom, Europe and other countries.

ISBN-13: 978–0–230–23622–6 hardback

This book is printed on paper suitable for recycling and made from fully managed and sustained forest sources. Logging, pulping and manufacturing processes are expected to conform to the environmental regulations of the country of origin.

A catalogue record for this book is available from the British Library.

Library of Congress Cataloging-in-Publication Data
Hagin, Boaz, 1973–
    Death in classical Hollywood cinema / Boaz Hagin.
        p.   cm.
    Includes bibliographical references and index.
    ISBN 978–0–230–23622–6
    1. Death in motion pictures.   2. Motion pictures—United States—History—20th century.   I. Title.
    PN1995.9.D37H34 2010
    791.43′65480973—dc22   2010002689

10   9   8   7   6   5   4   3   2   1
19   18   17   16   15   14   13   12   11   10

Printed and bound in Great Britain by
CPI Antony Rowe, Chippenham and Eastbourne

For Oded

Contents

Acknowledgments

This book is part of my ongoing work on death and moving images, which was made possible by scholarships from the Cohn Institute for the History and Philosophy of Science and Ideas, the faculty of Humanities, a fellowship at the Porter Institute for Poetics and Semiotics, Tel Aviv University, a Wolf Foundation scholarship, and a Dan David Prize postdoctoral scholarship. I am grateful to the Anda Zimand Film Archives at Tel Aviv University, to its manager, Liviu Carmeli, and to its staff, for their assistance and recommendations over the years.

Many of the films dealt with in the following pages were first viewed with others and frequently followed by lively discussion. For the countless hours, before, after, and in movie theaters, I am indebted to my parents and sister, to Itay Harlap, Lihi Nagler, Dana Zimmerman, Doron Galili, Asher Levy, and Ron Tirosh.

I would like to thank Christabel Scaife and the team at Palgrave Macmillan for their help in preparing the manuscript. I have benefited greatly from the stimulating discussions and suggestions by teachers, colleagues, and students at the Department of Film and Television at Tel Aviv University, particularly, Judd Ne'eman, Ilan Avisar, Alina Bernstein, Nurith Gertz, Odeya Kohen-Raz, Sandra Meiri, Gal Raz, Inbar Shaham, Yael Ben Tzvi, Pablo Utin, Raz Yosef, and Anat Zanger. The patience and knowledge of researchers at the Cohn Institute were of great help, and I am particularly indebted to Snait Gissis, José Brunner, Eva Jablonka, Leo Corry, and Miriam Greenfield. For reading previous versions of this text and for their very generous comments and advice, I would like to thank Alexandre Métraux, Thomas Elsaesser, Philip Rosen, Tony Kaes, Orly Lubin, and Adi Ophir. I cannot express in words my debt to Régine-Mihal Friedman, who is a great source of inspiration and support. Finally, for being there with me daily, as I was writing and rewriting, I would like to thank Mika and her friends, and above all Oded.

1
The Meaning of Death in Classical Hollywood

Practicing Film Theory

In this book, I would like to examine ways in which death is made meaningful in classical Hollywood films. The question of whether death is, or should be, meaningful in general is far from settled. It has frequently been argued that death ought to be meaningless to us. Some philosophers have claimed that as an ungraspable nothingness, which is beyond our lived experience, death should not concern us. So long as we exist, death is not with us; and when death does come, we do not exist. Death is, or should be, nothing to us.[1] As the universal fate of all mortals, it reduces difference between humans;[2] and as inevitable from the moment we are born, it is a matter that, regardless of what we do, has always already been settled and cannot be caused or avoided.[3] Yet, in fact, Western thought has always been occupied with death and its meanings, and death has been used to account for, to question, and to justify art, philosophy, religion, entertainment, political formations, violence, life as we know it, and our various ways of being.[4]

Death has certainly not been absent or meaningless in film studies. There have been various claims about an essential connection or disjunction between death and the cinematic medium as such (the single frame, the finite or infinite shot, a sequence or entire films, pre-cinema and post-cinema) by writers such as André Bazin, Edgar Morin, Susan Sontag, Roland Barthes, Pier Paolo Pasolini, and Laura Mulvey.[5] In some cases, it is argued that cinema is essentially related to death, in others that it vanquishes death and enables immortality. In the course of two adjacent paragraphs, Friedrich Kittler manages to tell us both that "[w]hat the machine gun annihilated the camera made immortal" and that "[i]n the principle of cinema resides mechanized death," that film "is an immeasurable expansion of the realms of the dead."[6]

My focus in this book is not on the cinematic medium as such, but on classical Hollywood cinema. I would like to ask how death is meaningful in these films in a way that is integral to them. I will not be adopting one preexisting claim about death in our culture and claiming that it can be sweepingly applied to American or classical films. Thus, I will not characterize death as having one specific social function, such as being sacrificial and serving to affirm "the values of the larger society."[7] I will not employ as an overall organizing principle commonly accepted taxonomies of death, such as "natural death," "violent death," or "executions." I will not argue that "there can be no serious representation of death and dying when the characters are African Americans"[8] or that "whiteness *qua* whiteness [...] is often revealed as [...] a kind of death"[9] and that if "whiteness and death are equated, both are further associated with the USA."[10] I will not claim that death as a result of violence between men is "designed to minimise and displace" an undercurrent of male homosexuality, "to disavow any explicitly erotic look at the male body."[11] There will be no necrology to prove the deadly fate of non-repressed homosexuals in Hollywood.[12] I will not be looking for films that take for granted or expose "the enmeshment of femininity and death,"[13] the way our culture "can repress and articulate its unconscious knowledge of death" because it dreams "the deaths of beautiful women" given that "the feminine body is culturally constructed as the superlative site of alterity."[14] In short, there is no postulation in advance of a special correlation between mortality and femininity, homosexuality, the working class, degenerate nobility, people of color, insipid whiteness, non-humans, being markedly young, old, handicapped, intellectual, American, Jewish, ethnic, Southern, Eastern, communist, sexually active, inactive, hyperactive, or any other other or non other. No one underlying "deep" rule will be unearthed in the films and no one insidious ideology exposed and therefore rendered defunct. These readings of Hollywood films are in many cases apposite, and I have used many of their insights in my analysis. However, my interest here is different.

I would like to use classical Hollywood films in order to think of different ways in which death can be made meaningful. This is methodologically similar and inspired by Gilles Deleuze's understanding of a philosophical theory of cinema. For Deleuze, philosophy is a practice that entails "creating or even inventing concepts."[15] A theory of cinema, or at least what Deleuze calls a "philosophical theory," is a practice that creates "the concepts that cinema gives rise to."[16]

How does cinema give rise to this creative and inventive practice which theorists carry out? Deleuze argues that a creator works only when she or he absolutely needs to, that there must be necessity, "which, if it exists, is a very complex thing."[17] Jacques Rancière claims that Deleuze belongs to philosophers for whom "thought abdicates the attributes of will and loses itself in stone, in color, in language, and equals its active manifestation to the chaos of things."[18] As I understand it, films can serve as part of the complex necessity that forces us to proliferate concepts, that is, in my case, to create and invent ways of thinking about how death can be meaningful. Cinema can be that chaos in which thought loses itself.

I particularly believe that Hollywood's films can be useful as a venue in which thought is lost. Deleuze suggests that cinema advances an "impower" of thought, a theft or "unlinking" of thinking, from which thought is brought face to face with its own impossibility and draws a higher power of birth.[19] The place which art and philosophy might share is such a "nonthinking thought."[20] By the standards of analytic philosophy, popular films do not think very well.[21] Classical Hollywood is an incoherent corpus of films which reason badly, do not make much sense, and elaborate illogical thought. They offer us "nonthinking" or "unlinked" thought. By preferring the spectacular to the rational, by structuring ludicrous plots, and by exhibiting outstanding absurdity, popular films might be that force which cannot mesh very well with existing ways of thinking about death and might necessitate the creation of new ones.[22]

Death on the Line

How exactly can such concepts of the meaningfulness of death in films be invented? One way in which death has been meaningful in philosophy is by making a connection between mortality and time. In the twentieth century, for example, Heidegger's *Being and Time* argues that the phenomenon of temporality is related to our Being-towards-death.[23] In what he insists is a different "modality" from that of Heidegger's work, Emmanuel Levinas has also sought "the connection between death and time."[24]

This book offers a variation on this philosophical theme by using Hollywood films, not the Being of humans, as its ground. I have defined classical Hollywood as feature films made or distributed by the

Hollywood studios between 1925 and 1955.[25] I have chosen a small sample of films from four genres, which have frequent and structurally recurring deaths: the Western, the crime or gangster film, the melodrama (in the strict sense of woman's film and family melodrama), and the war film.[26] I will use these films in order to construct the various concepts, or ways of thinking about death as meaningful in classical Hollywood.

In order to allow thought to lose itself in films, my starting point will not be known social biases and functions, but rather the classical Hollywood narrative, which, according to David Bordwell, already possesses several characteristics that constrain the ways in which death can be meaningful in these texts. The Hollywood narrative is character centered and is based upon "causality, consequence, psychological motivations, the drive toward overcoming obstacles and achieving goals."[27] Although common, these characteristics are not universal, necessary, or obvious.[28]

The Hollywood narrative, according to Bordwell, consists of two or more storylines involving the same group of characters. Each storyline is linear, causal, and character centered. One storyline is typically a heterosexual romance, and the others might also involve romance or another sort of activity, such as "business, spying, sports, politics, crime, show business."[29] Note that Bordwell is referring to the story, *fabula*, the events in their presumed spatial, temporal, and causal relations, which he distinguishes from the plot, *syuzhet*, the totality of formal and stylistic materials in the film, which might not be, for example, in chronological order.[30] Events in each storyline follow each other in a cause-and-effect logic, which considers the traits and goals of individual characters as causes. It is based upon their drive toward overcoming obstacles and achieving these goals. Coincidence, natural or social causes, and impersonal determinism, are not common factors in these narratives.[31]

How death is meaningful within the classical Hollywood narrative so characterized will be the problematic which this book deals with. I will discuss—while borrowing and distorting concepts from heterogeneous sources—various ways in which death is rendered meaningful within such storylines. In other words, how the event of death meaningfully functions in relation to events that come before or after it in a personal linear causal storyline.

There are three roles that death can have within a linear causal storyline. It can be an *initial death*, which begins a storyline and is a cause of subsequent events; an *intermediary death*, which is both an effect and a cause within a storyline; and a *story-terminating* death, which ends a storyline and is an effect of previous events. There are three aspects in which death can be meaningful within such a cause-and-effect chain of events: Story-terminating and intermediary deaths can be meaningful *in relation to the past*, by being results of previous events. Initial and intermediary deaths can be meaningful *in relation to the future*, by being causes of subsequent events. Death can also remain part of an ongoing event with no end in sight, which might be thought of as a type of intermediary death that is *meaningful in relation to the present*.

In relation to the past, the event of death can be meaningful by having epistemological value; it manifests a truth that is already there. The meaningfulness of death in relation to the past is that it reveals, clarifies, at most realizes what has already existed, at least potentially, in the situation which caused the action of death. We will look at death's relation to that which preexists in Chapters 2 and 3.

An intermediary death and an initial death can be meaningful by having an effect on the future. For example, in stories where a relative or a friend revenges a murder, the initial/intermediary death (the murder) motivates the action (revenge) later on in the storyline, in the future. We will look at how death is meaningful in relation to the future in Chapters 4 and 5.

The third aspect in which death might have meaning in a Hollywood film is by being a component of meaningful action. It is the meaning of that which is still taking place, an impossible attempt to look back upon something that is still occurring, to reveal a becoming. In its present-oriented aspect, an intermediary death has the most difficulties being meaningful, giving sense to that which is still senseless, attempting to envelop with significance an absurd death that has not yet ended, to guarantee that a possible failure be rendered successful. We will study this aspect of intermediary deaths in the strange world of the Hollywood war film in Chapter 6.

The same event of death can play a part in separate storylines in the same film, being, for example, a story-terminating death that is meaningful in relation to the past in one storyline and an intermediary death that is meaningful in relation to the future in another.[32] In addition, even within the same storyline, an intermediary death can be meaningful both in relation to the past and in relation to the future.

Classical Hollywood can offer us a whole array of different ways to render death meaningful within these constraints of the individual-driven linear causal storylines of which its narrative consists. Unlike reductive interpretations that claim that cinema as such has one essential connection to death or to immortality, or that death in classical

American cinema has a privileged relation to one specific social group or function, this book shows, in a concrete and systematic way, that there is a variety of options for making death meaningful.

Death is meaningful in a pragmatic, or performative, sense, by being a link within a linear cause-and-effect chain of events that considers the traits and goals of individual characters as causes. But the classical Hollywood narrative is not just an exercise in linking together events in a causal way. While according to Bordwell narrative causality "operates as the dominant" and is served by the other systems at work in the film,[33] there are additional constraints and demands, motivations and conventions. Various forces are at work, tugging at the fabric of the Hollywood text, pulling it in different directions. There are narrative strategies that increase the cohesion of the text and are not merely causal. Narratives can employ foreshadowing (planting elements in advance that will only be useful in the plot later on) and motifs (repeated object or dialogue line), which can create a sense of providence guiding the world of the film.[34] In addition to these cohesion devices, there are generic conventions and various non-narrative or counter-narrative components, such as "spectacle," "attractions," "melodrama," and "graffiti." These might work independently of, or even against, the causal storylines and the ways in which death is meaningful within them.[35]

There are other, extra-textual factors that can influence the way death functions in a film irrespective of the linear causal narrative. The star system, for example, might characterize certain actors, such as John Wayne and Gary Cooper, as particularly invincible and keep their characters alive throughout the film.[36] There are additional ideological, or overtly propagandistic, constraints, that require that death be meaningful in a moral or political sense. It has often been claimed that Hollywood frequently follows a hypocritical "moral compensation" strategy according to which evil is depicted as attractive and in loving detail, but its perpetrators are then punished—made to suffer and sometimes perish.[37] "Any man who broke the laws, man's or God's," wrote Ben Hecht of Hollywood's films, "must die, or go to jail, or become a monk, or restore the money he stole before wandering off into the desert."[38] Demands were, implicitly or explicitly, made by various institutions, such as the House Un-American Activities Committee, the military during World War II, and the Catholic Legion of Decency. Hollywood's own Production Code also constrained how death could be meaningful in classical Hollywood. It was adopted by the Motion Picture Producers and Distributors of America association in 1930 and more rigorously enforced by its Production Code Administration from 1934 until its gradual demise after World War II and formal replacement by the rating system in the late 1960s.[39] According to the Code, for example, there must "be no scenes, at any time, showing law-enforcing officers dying at the hand of criminals."[40]

Death, then, needs to be meaningful not only by being a cause and/or effect within a linear, individual-driven storyline. It also needs to be "justified" according to various other criteria such as what is considered morally decent by the Production Code, devices of narrative cohesion, the need for spectacle, and the star system. These various factors can be in tension with the causal linear storyline and with each other. Death might thus be *badly* integrated into the classical narrative; or it might be integrated into the narrative well, but not successfully justified by other criteria.

Hollywood can therefore not only pluralize the ways in which death can be meaningful, but can also problematize them according to various criteria. Each of the following chapters will thus discuss a specific way to make death meaningful within the linear causal personal storyline followed by some of the ways that the films indicate to question this meaningfulness, by showing that death is insufficient, superfluous, has deleterious effects, creates a sense of discomfort, or thwarts any attempts to link it to a certain goal.

The concluding, seventh, chapter demonstrates how the concepts elaborated in the previous chapters can be useful for analyses of films in specific historical junctures. In particular, it looks at historical situations in which it might be difficult to think of death as meaningful, notably the Holocaust and during periods in which the understanding of the self and human behavior were shifting. These limit or "pathological" cases can help us to think about, and beyond, our usual ways of making death meaningful.

Although making use of of the past, this book is not a standard historical study. Its method of creating and inventing concepts does not claim to reveal the "true" meaning of the films, to place them in context, to reconstruct how they were understood at the time they were made, or empirically by certain spectators at a specific time.[41]

I am also not claiming that the ways of thinking about death as meaningful suggested here are the only ones that can be created using these films, or that they can only be reached by encountering films. Indeed, although my starting point, and organizing scheme, is that of classical Hollywood cinema, at various points throughout my discussion I will refer to a wide variety of other texts that deal with ideas, which are, at least in some cases, similar to the ideas that the films give rise to. In these instances, I could be accused of offering no more than "applications" or "illustrations" of preexisting ideas by means of films. But as Stanley Cavell writes, "to know what the illustration illustrates," for example, in the case of a Heidegger–Keaton connection,

> is to know what makes Keaton Keaton, something that requires knowing what makes Chaplin Chaplin and Griffith Griffith and Brady Brady and film film; just as to know what makes Heidegger Heidegger requires knowing what makes Nietzsche Nietzsche and Kant Kant and Hölderlin Hölderlin and philosophy philosophy.[42]

So even when the films "simply illustrate" an idea that has already been formulated in the past, perhaps as part of a philosophical work, the discussion could be of value both to those who would like to better understand classical films and to those who would like to better understand philosophy. Applying philosophy to film means "a realisation" or "a rediscovery of philosophy" by the film.[43]

A Politics of Death

I have another interest in this work, which is more clearly political, or ethical in a certain sense.[44] As an Israeli and a moderate news junky, I am constantly told what death means. While most deaths are kept private and personal, some, particularly violent ones that are related to the Israeli–Palestinian conflict, are taken up by the media which will not easily let go. I am told by politicians and pundits that these deaths prove that peace is impossible, that they are part of an endless cycle of violence in which Palestinian terror kills us and our army kills them, and that the dead leave a legacy of more violence, which must be obeyed. Repeatedly, the Israeli media inserts death into an economy of debt and retribution, loss and gain, crime and punishment, judgment and proof, and sacrifice and reward—the building blocks of a circle of hopeless misery from which we cannot escape. Deaths are not traumatic in my culture; the cycles of violence do not derive from a senseless repetition compulsion. Rather, they are over-narrativized; they have been worked through, too much, through and through, worked over to a pulp. Death is meaningful, too meaningful, too easily. We are too much at home with death.

My aim in the following pages is to resist and question the ways in which death is instrumentalized in my culture. I do not believe that merely unveiling that the current meanings attributed to death are ideological, that is, that they serve certain clandestine interests is enough. The critique of ideology certainly seems to promise an immanent relation to political praxis. It exposes the particular interest of those who rule in what masquerades as a universal interest and it thus, as Jürgen Habermas notes, "unsettles the normative structures which keep the consciousness of the suppressed imprisoned" and so terminates "in political action."[45] Unfortunately, such an account of unmasking as a political force is no longer convincing. Peter Sloterdijk describes our period as one of modern cynicism, an "enlightened false consciousness," a "modernized, unhappy consciousness," which "has learned its lessons in enlightenment, but it has not, and probably was not able to, put them into practice."[46] Slavoj Žižek has gone so far as to characterize ideology as this very cynical split. "The fundamental level of ideology," Žižek argues, "is not of an illusion masking the real state of things but that of an (unconscious) fantasy structuring our social reality itself."[47] In the late capitalist mode of cynical ideology, "the emperor is naked and the media trumpet forth this fact, yet nobody seems really to mind—that is, people continue to act as if the emperor is not naked."[48] Revealing to the Israelis that bombing Palestinians is mere habit or racist cruelty, that it ensures continued hatred and violence, and that it will in no way end terrorism, might expose nothing that was not already known and bring about no change. The media has probably been "exposing" that for a long time now. I am not saying that an ideological critique is necessarily and in all cases futile. As one bright student of the past noted, all too often "we know the good but do not do it," yet "here and there a victory is nonetheless achieved."[49] It does not, however, promise an immanent relation to liberating political praxis. What modern cynicism, a knowledge that does not make a difference, does do, at least for me, is arouse apathy and despair, a feeling of indifference, and loss of hope.

My aim in elaborating ways in which death is rendered meaningful in classical Hollywood is to offer concrete tools for re-narrativizing the images and fragments of information I am exposed to in the media which can differ from the prevalent ways in which death is instrumentalized in my culture. My attempt in finding ways to problematize these meanings is to offer concrete options for questioning such narratives and meanings. The claim that death can reveal a hidden truth is dealt with in Chapter 2. It is frequently used in politics, for example, when a violent attack by one of the sides is claimed, by the other side, to reveal the truth about the perpetrator's desire for violence and that "there is no partner for peace." Chapter 3 discusses the claim that certain people are immutably bad and will never change as a justification for their inevitable demise, an idea which appears in current Middle Eastern politics when each side claims the other is not ready to alter its violent ways ("the Arabs are the same Arabs" in Israeli parlance). Chapter 4 deals with cases in which death is said to set a goal or remove an obstacle, for example, when it is said that a certain person or group must be killed in order to enable peace. Chapter 5 wonders how we remember the dead and what demands they are said to make upon the living. Chapter 6 deals with the view that war is an inevitable evil that can nevertheless achieve certain political ends. Each chapter offers ways to problematize such meanings of death.

How these ways of thinking and challenges will interact with other practices cannot be determined in advance. As Deleuze claims when discussing the relation between human struggle and art, it is "the strictest and for me the most mysterious relation."[50] I cannot pretend to control how these might be used, if at all. Unlike ideological unmasking, I cannot predict whether and in what fashion these ways of thinking might relate to other forms of praxis, to politics; if and how they will be cashed out. They might remain at the level of thought or lead to unexpected places.

For me, as already stated, the need to think about death in other ways is an attempt to flee from either apathy about death or from being immersed in a media environment that instrumentalizes violent deaths, particularly those that are the result of Palestinian terrorism, in order to justify an endless cycle of destruction and death, prove that there is no solution, and demand revenge or additional violence to fulfill the legacy of those who have died. It stems from the feeling that an ideological critique, merely exposing the particular interests, futility, and pain in such a "situation," is insufficient, and that other forms of theoretical practice might be more helpful and are a chance worth taking. When intercourse with one's environment can only offer hopeless cycles of perpetual violence, running off into the onanistic darkness of movie theaters of the past is also a turn away from despair and indifference; it is escapism in all its redeeming glory. Going to the movies is an engagement and disengagement with a politics of death.

2
Two Platos: Death, Truth, and Knowledge

Because Hollywood's storylines are linear and causal, an event in them can only directly affect the future. None of the classical Hollywood films I will be discussing involves time travel,[1] and so I believe it is not trivial to ask how an event in them can be meaningful in relation to the past, which cannot now be altered, that is, in relation to that which already exists and to that which has already taken place.[2] I would like to propose two ways. One, which I will discuss in this chapter, is by serving an epistemological or cognitive function, by enabling fuller access to knowledge of what was already there. And the other, which I will be discussing in the next chapter, is an ontological one, in which the past truth is embodied in the character who dies. In each chapter, I will also show some of the problems to which each method of rendering death meaningful can lead.

A Rehearsal for Death

How then can death be meaningful in relation to the past if the past has already taken place and if it can no longer be altered? Several Western thinkers might point the way. They associate death with gaining access to preexisting knowledge. Death is meaningful not by changing what has already happened, but by revealing it.

This idea is famously elaborated in Plato's *Phaedo*,[3] where Socrates suggests that since philosophers strive to release their souls from the prison of the body,[4] they would be happy to die.[5] The object of the philosophers' desire, which is truth, cannot be obtained because the body contaminates the soul, distracts it from pure thinking by cropping up at every point, "causing chaos and confusion, unsettling us, and so preventing us seeing the truth."[6] It is only in death, if anywhere, that the soul is free to reach "what is pure, always existing, immortal and unchanging." When the soul is allowed to be in contact with these constant and unchanging things it is in a state called "wisdom."[7] It is in this sense that philosophy, the pursuit of wisdom in the right way, could be considered practice or a rehearsal for death.[8] Death, then, is the key to gaining knowledge, to the soul finally reaching the unchanging truth of the Platonic forms—that which philosophers love.

Plato is far from being the only Western thinker to make a connection between death and knowledge.[9] In *The Birth of the Clinic*, Michel Foucault argues that the new medical spirit of Bichat and his disciples in the late eighteenth century was linked, according to historians, to the rise of pathological anatomy, the opening up of corpses as a source of knowledge.[10] External symptoms alone could no longer provide sufficient information, and the medical gaze was now required to simultaneously penetrate inside the ailing body. It was death, because it could occur at any stage of the disease and then enable an autopsy, which was now "endowed with the great power of elucidation that dominates and reveals both the space of the organism and the time of the disease." Death turned "into a technical instrument that provides a grasp on the truth of life and the nature of its illness."[11] As Bichat wrote, "Open up a few corpses: you will dissipate at once the darkness that observation alone could not dissipate."[12] For Plato it was the philosopher, the knower, who had to die in order to gain knowledge of the preexisting truth; Foucault's medical gaze, in contradistinction, required that patients die at various phases of their disease, so that the (living) knower could learn of the nature of their illnesses.[13]

In his 1936 "The Storyteller," Walter Benjamin claims that "not only a man's knowledge or wisdom, but above all his real life—and this is the stuff that stories are made of—first assumes transmissible form at the moment of his death." It is death, according to Benjamin, which gives a person the unique authority, which is at the very source of the story, and which the storyteller has borrowed.[14] In his case, death does not allow one to know, or to become an object of knowledge of the living, but rather endows the dying person with authority and makes that person's life transmissible.

Access, Authority, and Tests

Taking our cue from these thinkers, we can now ask whether death in Hollywood has a similar cognitive or epistemological function, which can make it meaningful in relation to the past. In classical Hollywood films, death can bring about a shift from ignorance to knowledge. It can be a discovery of new information or the disclosure of a secret. It can also be more of a change in attitude than in the actual information that is known, the complex epistemology of growing up or coming out, a shift from falsehoods to honesty, from self-delusion and childish lack of responsibility to acknowledgment and accountability, and from disavowal, avoidance, belittling, make-belief, playing, joking, pretense, or "passing" to a call for authenticity and genuineness.

In some cases, death can simply be the fatal result of acting in a way that enables one to gain knowledge. In *A Walk in the Sun* (Lewis Milestone, 1945), the men in a platoon that lands in Italy and is ordered to take over a farmhouse are constantly occupied with attaining knowledge about the fighting on the beach, the situation ahead, and particularly the farmhouse.[15] Quite early on, Mac the medic exposes himself in order to go and "take a look" to see if more forces are landing. He is gunned down by a passing enemy plane and is one of the first of many soldiers to pay with their lives for gaining knowledge in this film. Later on, a reconnaissance scout on a motorcycle drives ahead to the farmhouse to check if the road is clear but never returns. Presumably, he was killed. When the platoon does finally reach the farmhouse, they send a patrol—four soldiers and a sergeant—to go first and see what they should expect. They soon learn that they can expect the Germans to be quite alert and armed with machine guns, which kill some of the men in the patrol. In many war films, dying is the result of being in a situation in which one has access to information: the patrol knows the Germans have machine guns by being shot at and killed. The soldiers gain knowledge as they die; the two acts occur simultaneously.[16]

Death is also related to knowledge by being the possible result of a (sometimes-implicit) test. In this case, death functions as an index which points to the correct or incorrect hypothesis. Talking of a risky decision in battle, the protagonist of *The Desert Fox* (Henry Hathaway, 1951), Field Marshal Erwin Rommel, explains: "if it doesn't work, we'll know better than to try it the next time." In other words, some forms of knowledge could best be discovered through practice, even, or especially, if that might have deadly consequences. Similarly, Hynkel, the genial Phooey of Tomania in *The Great Dictator* (Charles Chaplin, 1941), is interrupted in his hectic schedule by Field Marshal Herring to test new and wonderful inventions. One professor presents a 100 per cent bullet-proof uniform. This turns out to be "far from perfect," in Hynkel's words, as the inventor falls flat on his back after the Phooey shoots him. Shortly after, another inventor jumps out of a tower, most likely to his death, in order to demonstrate the most compact parachute in the world which is worn like a hat and, moreover, does not work. Death, in these experiments, indicates that the hypotheses presented by the inventors are false. Indeed, they were already false in the past, before their falsehood was discovered by the tests.

The deadly demonstration of talent and imperfections is not limited to inventions and military strategies. We can consider a battle to the death as a way to determine which side is better. Individuals or groups can thus reveal their capacity and inadequacy at fighting by dying or remaining alive. Hollywood films are strewn with countless dead characters—some minor and nameless—to prove the superior killing skills of their rivals. Will Kane defeats Frank Miller and his gang in *High Noon* (Fred Zinnemann, 1952), Vienna defeats Emma in *Johnny Guitar* (Nicholas Ray, 1954), Shane defeats Jack Wilson in *Shane* (George Stevens, 1953), the Ringo Kid defeats the Plummer brothers in *Stagecoach* (John Ford, 1939), and the Earp brothers and Doc Holliday defeat the Clantons in *My Darling Clementine* (John Ford, 1946).

"The Western hero," writes Scott Simmon, "is always the best fighter, a principle whose inviolability is impossible to overstate."[17] To prove this point, or perhaps merely to underline a predictable truth, the films flood the screen with numerous victims of the hero who cannot lose. In *Red River* (Howard Hawks, 1948), for example, Tom Dunson kills seven people while taking over the territory of "his" ranch, several Indians who attack him, and three more men during the cattle drive up north. He, of course, remains alive to the end.

A similarly predictable outcome has to do with obviously inferior fighters losing, such as James, the youngest and most naïve of the Earp brothers in *My Darling Clementine*. As the film begins, we learn that his elder brothers think he is "pretty," a good cook (but not yet as good as their mother), and the marrying type. He is characterized as insecure about the worth of the metal pendant he bought his fiancée ("that chingadera" as one of his brothers calls it) and is left behind to watch their cattle while his brothers go to town to get a shave (he does not appear to need one) and a glass of beer. That he is shot in the back, their cattle rustled, and the pendant stolen seem like no big surprise given his tender age, lack of ruggedness, and gullibility. His death merely reaffirms this preexisting truth.

A predictable inferiority can also be noted in the typical en masse slaughter of unindividualized hordes of "Indians" which confirms the racial superiority attributed to whites in many classical Westerns. Accompanied by a very small inventory of clichéd "savage" music,[18]

Indians are "gunned down with godlike accuracy from long distance in uncountable numbers" by whites.[19] In *The Naked Spur* (Anthony Mann, 1952), three armed white men protecting the lives of an additional unarmed and handcuffed white criminal and his unarmed girlfriend kill a much larger group of Indians (there are "about twelve of 'em" they earlier explain). During the complete annihilation of the entire group of armed Indians, only one of the white men is injured. In *Stagecoach*, the small group of white men who fight is substantially outnumbered by the attacking Indians whom they nevertheless manage to fend off.[20] By the time the cavalry comes to the rescue, few Indians are left, and, moreover, there is no reason to assume that the superior marksmanship of the white men could not have allowed them to destroy each and every Indian warrior had they not run out of ammunition.[21] Dozens if not hundreds of Indians are killed, but only one single white man perishes—and this also occurs in the short period between their running out of bullets and the arrival of the cavalry. In *Red River* the cowboys come to the rescue of a wagon train with "a bunch of gamblers and women" and manage to slaughter "a few past a hundred" Indians that are attacking it. Matt, the leader of the cattle drive, tells his men not to "leave any of 'em alive" so they do not come back and "hit the herd." Here too, none of Matt's men is hurt, but one of the women in the wagon train is injured by an arrow. Matt pulls it out, she slaps him, and they fall in love. We hear nothing more of the "few past a hundred" dead Indians. No one is surprised by the ability of the cowboys to defeat the Indians in these battles. It merely reconfirms the racist beliefs underlying these films, proving them to be true in the racist worlds depicted in the films.

Battles can be fought without guns and in the domestic sphere as well. In *Mildred Pierce* (Michael Curtiz, 1945), the youngest daughter Kay demands less attention than her older sister Veda. She can be heard making statements like "Oh, you don't have to worry about me," while making a fuss about her sister. "Kay doesn't need so much thinking about," explains her mother, and indeed does not notice the persistent cough her little daughter is suffering from. Only when their father, who is separated from their mother, takes the girls for the weekend is it discovered that Kay suffers from pneumonia. Her inadequate ability to fight for her mother's attention ends in her death in the next scene, emphasizing and confirming a truth that could already be discerned—that Mildred Pierce is spoiling Veda in an unreasonable way that is harmful and even deadly to others.

Domestic or not, it is, of course, the better fighter who is victorious in these showdowns and battles. "Better" could mean just about any skill, such as, calmer, faster, craftier, more accurate, confident, or experienced. Yet this is not enough. The logic by which the winner is determined is not always limited to shooting skills. In fact, there are many cases in which knowing who the better fighter is does not suffice to explain the outcome. The final showdown—the climax the film has been building up to—is fascinating precisely because in the causal-linear narrative the results are unclear. In the "eroticized antagonism"[22] at the center of *Johnny Guitar*, is the desperate Vienna fighting for her life a better shot than the fanatically determined Emma? Even if the Ringo Kid does shoot Luke Plummer, how will he avoid being killed by one of Luke's brothers? Will he, could he possibly, defeat all three? What chance does Kane—now that the townspeople and his wife have forsaken him—have against the insane and enraged Frank Miller and his gang? Why should the remaining Earp brothers with the ailing and decadent Doc Holliday defeat the deadly Clanton brothers and their ruthless father who are expecting them? The opposing forces in the final confrontation have more-or-less equal strength, and no previous test has revealed to us which force is stronger. Here, and finally, death, cavalry-like, rides to the rescue with its traditional powers of exposing the truth and determining the victor.

What is this truth? Presumably, as already noted, someone was more skillful—calmer, faster, craftier, more accurate, confident, experienced, and so on—but the film did nothing to point out this fact. Not only do we not know for certain who should win in advance as far as shooting skills are concerned, we are often denied any explanation during or after the shootout: no running commentary from one of the characters, no revealing close ups or slow motion, and no after-the-fact verbal analysis. It happens so fast! How did Shane defeat both Wilson and "Ruf" Ryker? We have no idea. "The hero," explains John Cawelti, "never kills until the savage's gun has already cleared his holster. Suddenly it is there and the villain crumples."[23] This is not an exaggeration: in *Jesse James* (Henry King, 1939), for example, the editing literally elides Jesse picking up his gun when challenging the railway men after his mother's death. It is just, suddenly, there. Even worse, in some cases, the opposing forces were not even. Rather, the weaker side won, and we have no idea why. We never even see how the Ringo Kid alone managed to defeat three other, skillful, spiteful, and better-armed men in *Stagecoach*. Despite our ignorance, if not incorrect assumption about who is more skillful, in a classical

Hollywood film, we have no doubt who will win—it must be the "good guy."

No physical, physiological, or psychological explanation seems to be enough to explain why one side wins in many of these battles. Perhaps, as Kant suggests, if our explanation does not belong in the realm of the sensible world, it will come from a different, supersensible, realm, from morality.[24] The shootout's result can in some cases be a sign of whom the film approves morally, and not unlike Max Weber's protestants, for whom profitableness was seen as a sign that one is in a state of grace since God blesses his own.[25] The victor in the shootout, then, is not the most skillful (although sometimes nothing contradicts this), but the one who has followed the correct path and was the most "moral." This is the "reigning religion of Hollywood cinema," which according to Scott Simmon ensures "the survival of the decentest."[26] It is the superior decency of one of the sides that the film reveals to be true.

What might this "decency" actually be? Perhaps the one possessing the character traits the film appears to value more. Perhaps it is merely the character whom we have been following and with whom we have been sympathizing. Perhaps the victor is the one played by the more powerful movie star. Perhaps it is a question of what each force represents and best explained as a variation on the Nietzsche-à-la-Deleuze theory of forces and *ressentiment*.[27] Do they want what they are doing or are they merely hired guns? Are they affirming their freedom to go on with their lives as they choose or fighting in the name of asceticism and fear of dealing with their own passions and wills? Is it any surprise, then, that Kane in *High Noon* and Vienna in *Johnny Guitar*, who just want to live their lives as they choose and love whom they wish, ultimately defeat those they face? Frank Miller wants to kill Kane for sending him to jail—in revenge. Emma, who according to Vienna, hates whomever makes her feel like a woman, presumably Vienna herself, is a self-hating ascetic. It is the life-affirming protagonists who defeat the reactive antagonists who embody *ressentiment*. It is the gunfighter— Shane, Wyatt Earp—who can outshoot all others because he is back in his element, no longer trying to split who he is (a violent gunfighter) from what he does (peacefully working on a ranch or raising cattle).[28] The truth that death shows down or shoots out in these concluding gunfights, then, might be "supersensible," moral, or best explained by a battle of qualitatively different forces, but it is no less a death that is meaningful by revealing a preexistent truth.

For characters in classical Hollywood films, the link between truth and death seems to go beyond causality and reasonable inferences not only in the assured moral victory of the "decentest," but in other cases as well. Mortality seems to purify falsehoods of the past. It is as if the arrival of death itself, the real event, somehow puts an end to games, illusions, and lies. The importance, the grave seriousness, of death could allow no more of those deceptions. As Schopenhauer says, "the sight of a corpse suddenly makes us serious."[29]

A simple example is the mysterious Southern gambler Hatfield, who is "no gentleman," in *Stagecoach*. Only when he dies does he admit— we have been led to expect for some time that he is related to Judge Greenfield—his true identity as Judge Greenfield's son. For whatever reason—perhaps he did not want to taint the name of Greenfield with his present being as "no gentleman"—he has kept his identity a secret, but could do so no longer now that he is dying.

Death can also endow a person with the authority to be heard and therefore to convey information that remained unnoticed in the past. In *Letter from an Unknown Woman* (Max Ophuls, 1948), Stefan is a shallow and selfish pianist whose hobby seems to be making cuckolds of Vienna's husbands. As he is about to flee a deadly duel, his butler hands him the letter from an unknown woman. It begins with "By the time you read this letter, I may be dead," and ends with a note from the hospital that indeed she has died. The author of the letter devoted her life to him. She did all she could and sacrificed everything—even, albeit not deliberately, her son's and her own lives—for a chance to win his long-lasting affection and love, or, at the very least, have him remember her each time they meet again. After reading her letter, Stefan finally asks his butler what the dead woman's name was and decides to go off to the duel and almost certain death, while the unknown woman's image is superimposed next to the door, where she first saw him and fell in love. Perhaps, he finally remembers what she looked like.[30] It is death that has given her the authority to speak and to be heard by him. It is death, as Maureen Turim writes, that "allows the secret of a female's desire to be told."[31]

In *Letter from an Unknown Woman*, death also seems to change her object of desire, Stefan, and turn him into a serious man who accepts the values of turn-of-the-century Vienna as imagined by mid-twentieth-century Hollywood. At the beginning of the film, he was about to flee the Austro-Hungarian capital so as to avoid a duel at dawn that would surely end with his defeat. "I don't mind so much being killed, but you know how hard it is for me to get up in the morning," he explained to his friends. Her death seems to have made the frivolous woman-izer, finally, into a serious, committed man, willing to die for love and honor. This too, however, might be a form of truth, if we understand it as Stefan becoming what he always truly was, or should have been, in the eyes of the unknown woman. As Stanley Cavell argues, she claims, throughout the film, already to know his inner life,[32] and in the end he "internalized" her image, "a fixated image of his past, of what might have been."[33] Her knowledge of him has, in retrospect and with death, become true.

The Superfluity of a Truth-Revealing Death

My goal in this book is not only to show ways in which Hollywood makes death meaningful, to pluralize the options we have for making sense of death, but also to show how Hollywood offers ways to challenge and subvert these, how we might problematize the specific meanings death has. One critique of the use of death to reveal a preexisting truth is to ask whether a death that possesses this type of meaning is actually necessary.

Some Westerns, for example, manage without the brutal slaughter promised throughout the film.[34] In *Apache* (Robert Aldrich, 1954), Massai, the last Apache warrior, kills quite a few of his military and civilian pursuers. This indicates that he is indeed a very capable warrior who out-battles all of the other characters in the film. In addition—and unlike other Hollywood Indians—he manages to stay alive until the end. It is clear to him and to his squaw, Nalinle, that when the time comes and he is forced to fight his enemies, he will kill many of them before he too—being overwhelmingly outnumbered—will die a glorious death. There is no doubt that he is a particularly gifted and brave warrior. This has been shown by the numerous deaths he did cause during the film and by his obvious courage and determination. This truth is by no means challenged when, at the end, the white men who are hunting him down realize that he really does want to become a farmer and when he (literally) drops his rifle and goes home to his newly born child. That his one-man war against the world was discontinued is of little importance—his capabilities as warrior and determination to fight to the end have already been proven by the deadly fate of rivals throughout the film. The final showdown, his own death, is superfluous. It is mentioned throughout the film, generically perhaps required, and then denied.

She Wore a Yellow Ribbon (John Ford, 1949) similarly tricks its viewers out of a war promised throughout the film. One of the storylines begins with the news of Custer's defeat at Little Big Horn and with

assorted Indian tribes uniting against the US cavalry following that successful battle. A narrator explains that another defeat would mean that a
wagon train would not dare to cross the plains again for a 100 years. The
newly united Indian warriors prove their deadly capabilities in a series
of deaths throughout the film: an army paymaster, a cavalry trooper
who was shot and died, another trooper and two civilians at a post the
cavalry patrol never managed to reach on time, a gunrunner, and his
interpreter. These slayings in addition to their killing of Custer and his
troops prove that in the upcoming war they will either be triumphant
and defeat the US military, or will be, eventually, overcome, but at a
heavy price. As to the soldiers of the American cavalry, the film devotes
considerable screen time to showing their way of life. Their capabilities
and expertise are clearly displayed, as is the experience of the commanders who trained them. The potential loss of lives is so clear that the film
does not need to actualize it in war, and indeed does not. Mere hours
before his retirement, Capt. Brittles tries to stop the grim war that lies
ahead. He goes to the Indian camp to talk with Pony That Walks, an old
chief, who says he no longer controls the young braves and that many
will die. Finally, 12 minutes before his official retirement from the cavalry, Brittles leads his men to chase away the horses of the Indians. No
man is injured and the war is prevented—"no casualties, no Indian war,"
he explains to his successors. Brittles orders them to follow the hostiles
all the way back to the reservation, but to keep a mile behind, because
walking on foot will hurt the pride of the Indians, and being watched
will "hurt it worse." Order has been restored with no additional violence beyond that which was needed to reveal the deadly abilities of the
belligerent forces without actualizing it any further.

Here, and in other cases, it is not only that the outcome is obvious,
but also that all of the sides seem decent; it would prove nothing, even
in the moral sense, if they died. They are all equally decent (or indecent), so "survival of the decentest" means survival of them all, never
taking the battle to the end, never actually reaching death. Hence, the
generically surprising fact that *Red River* dispenses with an ultimate fatal
confrontation. In it, three excellent shooters—Tom Dunson, Matt Garth
his informally adopted son, and Cherry Valance who joins the cattle
drive because he admires the beauty of Matt's "gun," spend the film
challenging each other to draw and sizing each other up. However, an
ultimate deadly gunfight between any two of them never comes about.
Matt and Cherry enjoy showing off their shooting skills but not at each
other; both shoot Tom's gun away from him but do not shoot at him
when he threatens to hang two deserters; Cherry and Tom injure each

other to stop the gunfight between Tom and Matt, but that battle never takes place. Tom certainly threatens to kill Matt—but all they end up doing is throwing a few punches. We know all three are skillful enough to kill each other, and all three are "decent" enough according to the film's manly codes of honor—so actually seeing them destroy each other would be both superfluous and morally disturbing.

After learning from these films, we might wonder whether the truth-revealing death in our earlier examples was really necessary. Rommel's strategy would or would not work whether it killed people or not. The uniform would not be bulletproof even if Hynkel shot a dummy instead of its living inventor. Tom Dunson was an excellent sharpshooter before he fired the first shot in the film. Classical Westerns managed to be racist in their attitude toward Native Americans regardless of battles in which Indians were slaughtered wholesale by European Americans. James was already young and naïve, and Kay was already the neglected daughter even before their death. Hatfield could have admitted that he was Judge Greenfield's son on other dramatic occasions. The secret of the unknown woman's desire would remain the same even if it had been kept a secret and if she had remained alive. These deaths are meaningful in relation to the past precisely because they merely bring to light a truth, or a potential ability, which were already there. In principle, the deaths could have been avoided without denying the truths that they revealed. It cannot be ruled out that other ways to discover this truth can be found. Limited to this meaning, the death is actually superfluous—it "does" nothing, only exposes a truth that was already there.

The Misery of Truth

A second way to problematize the meaningfulness of death as revealing a preexisting truth is to wonder whether truth is really the best choice. As already noted, in some films, mortality seems to purify the falsehoods of the past in an almost magical and irrational way. It is as if the arrival of death somehow puts an end to games, inauthenticity, illusions, and lies. Yet although frequently valorized, it is far from obvious that truth and authenticity are always the best choice for everyone. Let us look at two examples—a black woman trying to "pass" as white in a society that discriminates against blacks and a possibly gay teenager trying to find his place in society.

In *Imitation of Life* (John Stahl, 1934) the truth that comes forth with death is that race and motherhood are natural and unquestioned ways of being that have nothing to do with choice or appearances to the contrary. One of the characters, Peola Johnson, so everybody in the film seems to agree, has the burden of being black while looking white. Her subservient black mother, Delilah, keeps interfering with Peola's attempts at "passing" for white. According to Delilah, this is sinful and false. If it is God's will that they be black, it is not for them to question it. When Peola grows older, she leaves the black college her mother sent her to and disowns Delilah. She asks her mother to ignore her even if she happens to see her, and let her live as white. Delilah says she does not have the strength to unborn her own daughter, and when she realizes she has lost Peola she becomes seriously ill and dies while calling out for her daughter.

It is only at her mother's funeral that Peola, standing within a small group of white people at the church, suddenly admits it is her mother. She runs to Delilah's casket and asks for her forgiveness, saying that her mother slaved for her and that she killed her own mother. Typically for melodrama, Peola's disillusionment comes "too late,"[35] when her mother is already dead, when, in the words of Thomas Elsaesser, "it is most wounding and contradictory."[36] But is also comes too late, on the deathbed or over a coffin, in agreement with the Western tradition of associating death with truth. Within this tradition of using death as truth-revealing, it is not that Peola happened to realize that she is black and has a mother only when her mother died, but rather that her mother's death enabled the painful truth to break free. The death of Delilah has the magical effect of bringing Peola back to what the film takes as the truth—her belonging to the black race and her having a mother even if it might appear otherwise. Peola's decision, of which we learn in a subsequent scene, to go back to the black college in the south just as her dead mother would have wanted, must come too late. The result, however, is not victory of the most decent, but just misery. Delilah is dead and for her it is indeed too late. As for Peola, her life—now as an openly black woman in a racist society—might take a turn to the worse. While death does function here to reveal a secret and allow the truth to come out, this truth was perhaps hidden for a good reason. There is no assurance that this revelation will be a happy one.

In *Rebel without a Cause* (Nicholas Ray, 1955), two of the adolescent protagonists, Jim and Judy, are constantly occupied with truth, clarity, and consistency. Judy complains that her father's attitude toward her has changed now that she is grown up and that nobody is sincere in the juvenile gang. Jim shouts at his grandmother for never telling the truth and vividly displays his annoyance at his father's inability to give him a clear and definite answer and his parents' tendency to always move and run away from problems. Instead of confronting reality, grown-ups in the film deny or belittle it; claim it is not serious or that the kids will grow out of it. When Jim is trying to decide whether to risk his life so as not to appear "chicken" in front of the other kids, and asks his father "What can you do when you have to be a man?" the reply he gets is not to make a decision, to consider the pros and cons, make a list, and get advice. All his father offers him is a perspective from which his problems are not serious: "Listen, Jimbo, I'm just trying to show you how, how foolish you are. Why, when you're older you'll look back at this and you'll, well, you'll, you'll laugh at yourself for, for thinking that this is so important."[37]

Death plays a key role in the transformation from denial and belittlement to seriousness and facing up to the truth, to putting an end to pretense and lies. Moreover, death itself undergoes such a transformation during the film. Death in the film's first scenes is systematically reduced like all other aspects of the teenagers' lives. In the scene at the police station, near the very beginning of the film, John Crawford, for example, is accused of shooting puppies—his victims, at this stage, are both non-human and small, and it is never clear whether by shooting he intended or managed to kill them. This will become more "serious" as the film progresses and John targets humans, other teenagers and policemen, and ends up dead.[38] At the planetarium, the adolescents see the destruction of the world, but only in a simulated light show. This is not very important since the moral of the fake destruction, so they are told, is that our world is insignificant. The teenagers set limits to their play so as to keep real death away. The knife-fight with Buzz has strict rules. It is not meant to kill anyone, and indeed does not result in death. Judy's little brother happily declares that it is the "atomic age" and starts shooting with his toy rifle. Presumably, it is an atomic one, but merely a make-believe, toy atomic rifle. Even the chickie race is not meant to be deadly, but mere mischief. The drivers are supposed to jump out before the stolen cars drive over the cliff, which Jim rather conveniently calls "the bluff." Death is present, but always as a joke, game, strictly limited make-believe, and meaningless simulation.

Having jumped out of his car, Jim walks to the edge of the bluff where the rest of the teenagers are. Laughing and apparently exhilarated, he asks the gang where the other driver, Buzz, is. They tell him he is "down there," in the abyss. After reaching his home, Jim wants to go and tell the police what happened, but his parents try to stop him, or at least his mother does ("I almost died giving birth to him!" she says trying to increase her importance in the argument by mentioning death—a technique Jim immediately uses as well). For Jim lies and deceptions are no longer possible. He cannot dissimulate his responsibility for what happened. "Mom, a boy, a kid, was killed tonight," he says, "I don't see how I could get out of that by pretending that it didn't happen."

Jim goes to the police but cannot find Ray, the friendly officer with whom he was hoping to talk. The members of Buzz's gang see Jim go inside and assume he is going to tell the police what happened. His falsely presumed truth telling makes him their target and they start chasing him through town. Jim and Judy run away from their homes and go to a secluded mansion, where they believe they can trust each other. There Judy not only tells Jim that she loves him, but also adds an assertion of truth: "I really mean it." Jim also means it. The truth seems to have won.

Rebel without a Cause is more complex however than this mere ascension of earnestness and truth in the wake of death. Its structure of games and falsehoods, which end with death and are exchanged for involvement, responsibility, and truth, is complicated by the presence of other characters who do not undergo the same process. Buzz's gang is still looking for Jim because they believe he is guilty of telling the truth. They are no longer mentioned at the end of the film with the issue never being resolved.

Another teenager, John Crawford, is however central to the film's story and its ending and his mode of behavior is completely tied to falsehoods. His nickname, Plato, is quite misleading, since he is a compulsive liar and his love for Jim and/or Jim's handsome Warnercolor red jacket does not quite seem Platonic. This Plato hides out in the cavernous shadow play of the planetarium, preferring its artificial heavens to the real night sky outside; shuts his eyes throughout the chickie race; and, at the end of the film, seems particularly afraid of the light. He tells Judy of his friendship with Jim, which to a large extent he makes up, and Jim stories about his father's fate (he is dead and was a hero in the China Sea; or maybe is alive and a "big wheel" in New York). Plato arrives at the house immediately after Jim and Judy break in and the three go back to pretending: Jim and Judy are newlyweds and are worried about those troublesome kids and Plato is selling them the house. Jim and Judy's declaration of truth only takes place after Plato falls asleep. For Plato, truth does not seem to be a preferable option. At the end of the film, he is shot dead by the police who are unable to see that he is merely a false threat since his gun is not loaded and it is Jim who has the bullets.[39] In addition, Jim's father initially thinks it is his son who was shot because Plato is wearing Jim's red jacket. With his death, these falsehoods and misunderstandings will be cleared up; Jim, Judy, and the truth shall prevail. But this is not a comforting ending. The shift to truth following Buzz's death did not leave room for the falsehoods with which Plato chose to live.

The narrative thrust in both *Imitation of Life* and *Rebel without a Cause* is from falsehoods to truth, but for it to take place, for death to be meaningful in this way, Peola and Plato both end up losing the lives they chose. Were the games and falsehoods necessarily bad for everyone? Is the truth necessarily pleasant or decent or worth preserving? For Peola and Plato, impersonations and playful takes on the white straight nuclear family are not an evil that needs to be eliminated. Falsehoods are a matter of survival and advancement; the truth brings with it only tragedy, or, at the very least, melodrama. It certainly does not justify death.

3
Embodying the Past

The Killability Test

A second way for death to be meaningful in relation to the past is by destroying someone who could not be stopped in any other way. It is a death that is meaningful, indeed, morally justified, by bringing an end to an evil that has been shown to be immutable so long as the perpetrator is alive. Those who die are bad guys who refuse to abandon their evil ways; they are, in Slavoj Žižek's terms, incarnated drives, creatures who persist in an unconditional demand with no trace of compromise or hesitation to the end.[1]

Bad guys in classical Hollywood and in later films in the classical tradition undergo unofficial tests throughout the film in order to show that they indeed cannot change or be stopped while alive and therefore must die; they prove their "killability." Again and again, heavy after heavy, they are given a chance not to die: to repent and to change, to settle for what they have, to split the money with the others, to give up, to turn themselves in, and to let the police arrest them when they really stand no chance. But they prove their killability; they refuse to alter their ways, they cannot help themselves, they act against their own survival, and perish. Their death, then, is meaningful in relation to the past: the killability tests that they have already undergone have proven that they are incapable of changing. There is no need for this death also to be meaningful in relation to the future, and, indeed, such a death can end the entire film; no ensuing events are necessary in order to make it meaningful.

In many cases, the inability to change causally leads, in a linear storyline, to death and demonstrates the logic by which these deaths are meaningful in relation to the past. They are meaningful by bringing to an end someone who could not otherwise be stopped. In *The Naked Spur* (Anthony Mann, 1952), only two of the films' five main characters remain alive in the end: Howard Kemp, the protagonist who is looking for a wanted murderer, and Lina, the woman who was riding with the murderer. The other three men: Ben the murderer and the two men who joined Howard to look for him, die. The reason is that each one of them is incapable of altering his behavior; they prove their killability by being unable or unwilling to change in a way that causally leads to their demise.

One of Howard's partners is a gold miner named Jesse. He is so obsessed with gold that he cannot resist the offer made by Ben, the murderer, for a trade: Jesse will help Ben escape and Ben will show him the place where, so he says, he discovered gold. On the way, Ben tricks Jesse, grabs his rifle, and kills Jesse who still wants to know where the mine is despite now being a prisoner. Had Jesse been able to change, had he not have remained so obsessed with gold, he would not have been killable and could have lived.

Ben the murderer also dies because he cannot change his ways. After shooting Jesse, he decides not to ride away and escape. Being a cold-blooded killer, he chooses to ambush Howard and his partner. Ben repeatedly shoots his rifle so they could know where he is and waits for them, perched on an overlooking ridge. In the gun battle that ensues, Howard climbs the ridge and throws his spur at Ben's face who gets up and becomes an easy target. He is shot dead by Howard's partner. Had he chosen to flee instead of trying to kill his pursuers, he could have survived.

Now, it is Howard's partner, Roy, who has a chance to change and survive, or to prove his killability, die like the other two men who could not alter their ways. Roy, a cavalry lieutenant who quit after getting "in trouble" with an Indian chief's daughter (it is implied that he raped her), is unable to change either. He is incapable of curbing his desire and tends to take whatever he wants regardless of any physical or social limitations. After he shoots Ben, the wanted murderer, the body falls into the turbulent river below. Since there is a reward on the corpse, Roy insists on crossing the rough water and is unwilling to let go of the lucrative body. He is hit by a log and carried off to his demise downstream. Here it is nature itself which kills the avaricious rapist who will not let go of that which he cannot have and therefore dies.

Finally, the protagonist, Howard, and Lina, the woman who rode with Ben, are tested for their killability. Howard manages to drag Ben's body on to the riverbank. Will he follow through with his plan to collect the reward for bringing in Ben dead or alive? Lina begs him to forget about it. He refuses and says he is only interested in the money but when she promises to follow him and marry him no matter what, even if he does bring in the corpse, he strangely gives up, starts crying, and buries the body instead. The film ends with its only two survivors riding away to California. Both are incoherent: he completely abandoned the goal that has driven him repeatedly to risk his life and she has switched her loyalty from one man to another particularly when the latter was willing to sell the former for money. Both lack "integrity." I am using the term in the purely formal sense of the word, that is, as an integration of a person's "values, his or her words, and his or her deeds,"[2] so that "integrity" can also be applied to those who "steadfastly pursue obviously wicked courses of action to which they are deeply committed."[3]

In Hollywood, it is the villains who have "integrity" in the formal sense of the word. It is they who are committed to courses of action that do not change. They can pass the killability test, be unable to alter their evil ways, and therefore their death is justified and meaningful. The good guys, in contrast, lack integrity, they do change, and so fail the killability tests. Their death would not have been meaningful in relation to the past by bringing to an end behavior which could not have been otherwise stopped. They *can* alter their ways and their death would not have been meaningful in this way. They often remain alive, or, if they die, their death is rendered meaningful in a different way.

The Naked Spur is useful because it in fact explains this logic. After killing Jesse, the gold miner, Ben, the wanted murderer, tries to calm Lina down by grinning and telling her that Jesse is not as worried as she is. He is lying peacefully in the sun, "ain't never gonna be hungry again, never want anything he can't have." The only way to stop Jesse's ridiculous and futile search for gold was to kill him, or else he would have just gone on searching for what he could never have, even if it would have meant remaining poor and starving. Likewise, killing Ben was the only way to stop the grinning and ruthless murderer; and Roy would have gone on taking whatever he liked had the river not ended his life.

In a way, their death is no different from their decision, much earlier in the film, to kill Lina's sick horse because it was suffering and had no chance of recovery: it puts an end to that which has no chance of recuperation, that which can never change. We need not see how the death leads to something good in the future—for example, that the characters could now eat the cadaver or that the horse's soul could now go to heaven. The very termination of its miserable life is a meaningful act in itself. It is meaningful in relation to the past, to what happened before it was killed, to its inability to change, to its suffering, and to the life that now ends.

So it is with the villains in countless films who die because of their past. Those who have integrity and act in a coherent fashion; those who know who they are, what they want, and adopt a consistent mode of behavior accordingly; those whose goals are clear and stable; and those who are what they do and cannot stop doing it, face a very real threat of dying in this way in classical Hollywood. Those who lack integrity, coherence, and loyalty, and those who change and violate their own convictions and ways, are spared such a fate—they either go on living or undergo a death that is meaningful in a different way.[4]

A Logic of Singular Evil

The Hollywood killability tests can be problematized if we follow films that ask what such immutable behavior consists in. What makes people evil in a way they cannot change? And if, in some cases, finding the cause is a crucial step on the way to finding a cure, would not finding out why people behave in such a way suggest that their behavior can be changed, thus taking away the justification for this type of death and making it less meaningful?

The classical Hollywood gangster films from the 1930s are a good example. At first blush, they seem to offer clear and unproblematic killability tests. The gangster protagonist, as Robert Warshow writes, "is *bound* to go on until he is killed."[5] The classical gangster's death is clearly meaningful in relation to the past. It can even be the last event in the film and stylistically it is often quite impressive. We can look at the triumvirate of films frequently taken as defining the cycle in the early 1930s: *Little Caesar* (Mervyn LeRoy, 1930), *The Public Enemy* (William Wellman, 1931), and *Scarface, the Shame of the Nation* (Howard Hawks, 1932).[6] All three end with the deaths of their protagonists. Rico's death in *Little Caesar*, as Stephen Prince writes, "is a legendary scene mainly because of his great exit line, 'Mother of Mercy, is this the end of Rico?' "[7] *The Public Enemy* shows the gangster's corpse trussed up on a stretcher and left outside his mother's door. "A low-angle camera frames the action, and Tom's corpse falls into the face of the camera," explains Prince. The result is a "sudden, jarring end to the film."[8] *Scarface*, the most notorious gangster picture at the time, has Tony machine-gunned by the police:

> A cross-cut series of four shots extends the moment and keeps him on his feet. [...] The film cuts to the police, who stop firing, watching Tony offscreen, and then blast him again. The film cuts back to Tony, still doing his puppet's dance of death, and he then begins to pitch forward, at which points the film cuts to a new set-up showing him hit the ground.[9]

One of the most extraordinary deaths of a gangster in classical Hollywood is that of Cody at the end of *White Heat* (Raoul Walsh, 1949), two decades after *Little Caesar*. Caught while attempting to rob a chemical plant, he is surrounded by the police climbing a giant storage tank. Not able to shoot his way out and having no intention of giving up, Cody shoots the tanks, setting off a series of explosions. The mushroom clouds of smoke and fire in this post–World War II film were understood by many commentators to be reminiscent of Hiroshima and Nagasaki.[10] Even taking into account Hollywood's penchant for spectacle this is something of an overkill and a showstopper. But even in less extreme examples, the gangster's story-terminating death seems to be meaningful enough to conclude the entire film. Nothing need follow it and, in many cases, nothing does. Its meaningfulness in relation to the past is sufficient.

Yet there is a potential difficulty. In many of these films from the 1930s, the question of whether or not the gangsters could change their evil ways was related to debates on the causes of crime, on why certain people act this way and are unwilling to change. Hollywood addressed this issue, but made its gangsters killable by never giving a single and coherent answer to this question. If it had found one clear cause, there is a chance it would also have been able to suggest a way to prevent or stop crime, to eliminate that cause. The gangster was killable exactly because he managed to elude any such easy explanation.

To be sure, by the 1930s there was no shortage of theories about the causes of criminality. However, the public and scientific discourse on the matter was confusing and shifting. During the nineteenth century, no one school in criminology and penology grew up to be strong in the United States.[11] The American Institute of Criminal Law and Criminology was founded only in 1909,[12] and the field saw changing trends in its first decades. According to Carl N. Degler, the 1920s and 1930s were a period of transition from biological theories of behavior to environmental ones both for parts of the lay public and among professionals. The shift was from nature, an account that relied on innate "instincts," inborn and inherited tendencies to understandings that had to do with "culture" in Franz Boas's sense and offered sometimes extreme cultural determinism, such as in the radical environmentalism of Watson's behaviorism or Mead's malleable human nature in her earlier anthropological works.[13]

The shift, Degler writes, was not related to any newly discovered scientific data. The reasons seem to have more to do with social changes, such as the stock market crash and the Great Depression during which "it was not difficult to look to the social environment as the cause of poverty rather than to innate deficiencies within the group or individual."[14] It was also related to more people who were not white protestant American-born men joining the field and their frequently avowed political beliefs.[15] They thought of environmental explanations as less fatalistic and more accommodating to quicker change toward equality, or at the very least to opportunity.[16] In addition, the Nazi adoption and practice of racism and eugenics was publicly opposed by scientists including the rather unusual resolution at the 1938 meeting of the American Anthropological Association denouncing racism. The impact of Nazi practices "can hardly be overestimated," writes Degler, "in explaining why during the 1930s and 1940s concepts and terms like 'heredity,' 'biological influences,' and 'instinct' dropped below the horizon in social science."[17] The shift from nature to environment, then, had historical and political reasons, but was not related to any scientific discoveries; it was "essentially the substitution of one unproved (though strongly held) assumption by another."[18] Small wonder that anyone trying to figure out how and why scientists were explaining criminality was bound to end up confused. The United States National Commission on Law Observance and Enforcement directed by Attorney General George W. Wickersham reported in 1931 that they "found it impossible comprehensively to discuss the causes of crime." Criminology, they explained, "is remaking, the social sciences are in transition, and the foundations of behavior are in dispute."[19] Furthermore, most mass-media accounts, according to David E. Ruth, rejected these sorts of scientific explanations altogether and more conservatively "contended that criminals possessed free choice and the responsibility that accompanied it."[20]

What side did Hollywood take on the issue? Apparently all of them. A "stock question gangster films raise" according to Thomas Leitch is "why people become criminals."[21] But the cause of criminality, perhaps like any theoretical question and certainly one that caused such confusion among professionals and the lay public, is never given a single and coherent answer within classical Hollywood films, or even merely within the gangster genre.[22]

In fact, some films seem amused by the widely divergent and contradictory causes of criminality offered to the public. The 1935 film *"G" Men* (William Keighley), for example, presents but mocks the idea that criminals have predetermined facial types, which would imply that criminality is inborn an immutable. Significantly, it stars James Cagney who at the time was famous for a previous role as the lead gangster in *The Public Enemy*,[23] only now acting tough on the right side of the law, without, however, changing his face. During his FBI training, Cagney's character, James Davis, exchanges bantering with Kay, a young woman he has just literally bumped into and who, he will soon discover, is the sister of the man training him. He apologizes for staring at her and explains that he is studying character and faces and finds hers most interesting. Consulting the book he is holding, he begins to diagnose her hostility toward him: "chin type number two—does not make friends easily, resents strangers. Yes, that's right. Eyes far apart indicates cruelty to animals." Finally, she asks him what the book says about rifles and ammunitions, noting that that is the wording on the cover. They go on to pun about weapons. The butt of the joke in this meet-cute dialogue seems to be both "Bertillonage"-like systems which attempted to translate bodies into a closed finite set of types ("chin type number two") and Lombroso-like theories which attempted to detect criminal tendencies by bodily types ("indicates cruelty to animals"); I will return to both below.

A similarly amused attitude to the question of why people become criminals can be found in the 1936 film *The Petrified Forest* (Archie Mayo), which takes place in a secluded desert service station run by three generations of the Maple family. The grandfather shows Alan, a world-weary English intellectual who wanders into the service station, a picture of gangster Duke Mantee in the newspaper. They then discuss whether or not gangsters could be distinguished by their looks. "He doesn't look very vicious" claims Alan, to which the grandfather responds that "you can't tell a killer except by his chin [...] A killer always holds his chin in." When halfway through the film the flesh-and-blood Duke Mantee also finds himself at the service station, the discussion on criminality resumes. The grandfather tells them to "look at that chin. He's a killer alright." Boze, an employee, states an alternative explanation: that Duke's entire gang is "a bunch of yellow dogs. That's what made 'em turn crooked in the first place." They are "too yellow to face the major problems of life," he explains. "They gotta fight their way through with guns instead of with principles." Alan intervenes during Boze's clarification of this theory and mockingly suggests that cowardice is not a cause of crime; he then offers a third account: "it has something to do with the glands."[24]

While indeed raising the stock question of why people become criminals, the films made a point of not answering it. Various theories about the causes of crime are addressed, but apparently only in order to be refuted and mocked. In the two examples above this is done explicitly as part of the dialogue. However, raising the question, at least implicitly, and not offering a clear answer is in fact quite common in many other films.

One possible cause of crime is the environment, the option of nurture. Jack Shadoian characterizes the opening sequence of *The Public Enemy*, which depicts the background and the trajectory from child to hood of its protagonist, as an exact exploration "with sociological awareness" of the social conditions from which disrespect for authority, and the "hardness and invulnerability" of the gangster originate.[25] "Here, indeed," he writes, "is an environment in which crime can 'breed.' "[26] The film does show how two boys, Tom Powers and his friend Matt Doyle, graduate from mischief and theft in 1909 to armed robbery with fatal results in 1915. In addition, they themselves blame Putty Nose, who runs a local "social club," for being a bad influence on them and initiating them into the world of crime. He taught them how to "cheat, steal, and kill" according to Tom. "If it hadn't been for you," accuses him Matt when they are older and stop him on the street, "we might have been on the level." They then go inside with Putty Nose and Tom shoots him off screen, the first of many acts of revenge of which the narrative is composed.

But the film frustrates such an easy understanding of the causes of crime. The exact reason for Tom's revenge upon Putty Nose is not that clear. He also accuses him of choosing to "lam out" on them, presumably when they needed to hide out after the armed burglary they committed according to his plans. Tom is also warned by his current gang leaders that Putty Nose thinks he and Matt are "soft" and is going to "get" them again. When Matt says they could have been on the level if Putty Nose had not corrupted them, Tom adds that they "might have been ding dings on a streetcar." This reminds us that Tom's brother does have a job on a streetcar and that Tom constantly mocks him for it and has done so since they were young.

In the film, each one of the hoodlums has a sibling who grew up in the exact same environment without ever turning to crime. Tom's straight-arrow brother, Mike, does work for a living, goes to night school to improve his position in life, and marries Matt's sister who has also grown up honest. Nothing in their environment forced Matt and Tom to become gangsters.[27] We see that Tom's mother loved him as a child and that his father tried to discipline him, even by beating him, a harsh punishment which we never see him administer to his more honest brother.[28] The scenes showing Tom's and Matt's path to becoming full-fledged gangsters, then, might not be a sociological exploration at all. They merely demonstrate how the children in both families split equally: half became honest citizens and stayed alive; half chose to join the gang at Putty Nose's club, became gangsters, and were dead by the end of the film. If anything, this seems to indicate that the environment is impartial as to the path the children growing up in it will take. The film, as many Hollywood films do, goes back to the characters' childhoods not to show us why they became that way but to demonstrate their consistency—that they already were like that. A character in a classical Hollywood film, as Bordwell shows, "is made a consistent bundle of a few salient traits." Sometimes, he writes, the film employs the device "of introducing us to the characters in childhood; the already-formed principal traits we observe will carry over into the adult lives."[29] In *Public Enemy*, Tom is already a charismatic crook stealing watches as well as a misogynist sadist who pulls a mean trick on Matt's sister as a child, long before he becomes a gangster who famously thrusts a grapefruit in his girlfriend's face. In fact, it was he and Matt who approached Putty Nose with watches they stole on their own initiative when they were children. If it is not quite definite that he was born bad, he was certainly quick at achieving badness and pulled it off before the film began. As far as we can see in the film, he did not have badness thrust upon him by any external influence.

Gangster films frequently show us that the environment determines nothing; that other people in the same situation, friends or family members, did not become or remain gangsters. In *Little Caesar*, Rico's friend who is with him from the beginning of the film, Joe, does manage to leave the gang. He becomes a successful dancer and remains alive at the end of the film. Rico's environment and influence are not enough to determine for others their course. Perhaps the cruelest of all is the social experiment executed upon the two children at the beginning of *Manhattan Melodrama* (W. S. Van Dyke II, 1934), in which the two boys lose their parents when a steamboat they are on sinks in a fire. Both are adopted by the same man, who then also dies in a violent communist rally. Despite growing up in the exact same environment due to their childhood tragedies, one of the boys ends up becoming a law-abiding district attorney, whereas the other is a criminal who is executed at the end of the film. Education and environment do not determine who becomes a criminal.

Were the films then advocating the opposite idea, that the cause of crime is inborn, nature not nurture? It would then mean that a gangster was born bad and could not change. All that was left to do was to kill him, destroy his evil body, which was the source of his immutable criminal tendencies. After all, worldwide, the end of the nineteenth century and the first decades of the twentieth century were a period preoccupied with the body, including the rebirth of the Olympic Games in 1896, modernist pantomime theater and dance, the physical culture movement with its celebrity gurus Bernarr Macfadden and Eugen Sandow, and the Boy Scout movement and its equivalents in assorted countries.[30] This was an era of rampant racism, with a psychiatry and sexology looking to the body for explanations.[31] Was this not also the case for crime? The body was certainly being used to *identify* criminals in order to discover recidivists and overcome imposters and mistaken identities. Since the nineteenth century "Bertillonage," a technique which converted the criminal body into a code, was used to file and quickly locate criminal records. It was, since the 1920s, gradually replaced by fingerprinting, yet another bodily technique for identifying criminals.[32]

But was the body also a *cause* of criminality? As Simon A. Cole shows, the history of criminal identification constantly reveals the intertwining of the link between the criminal body and a file or crime scene with the attempt to diagnose it, "to prevent crimes before they occur by identifying and stigmatizing potentially criminal bodies."[33] So "Bertillonage" and fingerprinting were in fact already related to an attempt to discover the causes of crime in the body.

I would like to take a closer look at some of the other nature explanation of crime available at the time, particularly in some parts of the American eugenics movement, which flourished in the first four decades of the twentieth century, and in the work of Italian scholar Cesare Lombroso. Some gangsters do possess innate criminal traits, as identified by eugenicists or other nature theories. However, just like the environmental ideas, these are never clearly articulated. The films allude to them, but hesitate to embrace them unreservedly. Let us look at some of the aspects in which the films come close to nature theories of criminality, but also keep their distance.

Lombroso argued that criminals who are "born for evil" are evolutionarily degenerate reproductions of savage men and the fiercest animals.[34] Just as in Hollywood, in Lombroso's work too, born criminals are irremediable and will not change. They must be eliminated completely, he argues, "even by death."[35] But it is not only the logic of the killability of criminals that Hollywood and Lombroso share.

Lombroso's born criminals show numerous specific characteristics that "are almost always atavistic," that is, a degeneracy placing them at a more inferior stage in evolution with traits that are frequently "presented by savage races"[36] and which "may go back far beyond the savage, even to the brutes themselves" displaying for example the animal instincts and anatomy of "lemurs and rodents."[37] These aspects can also be found in the classical Hollywood gangster. Thomas Schatz writes that by the end of *Scarface*, Tony has devolved "into a virtual human ape."[38] He walks, or rather swings from leg to leg, with his arms drooping.[39] The end of *Little Caesar* shows Rico intoxicated for the first time in the movie. Disheveled, he does look like a non-human animal and especially sounds like one, emitting rather curious groans. It is at this animal-like stage that he recklessly taunts the police who machine-guns him down.

The supporting criminals in the gangs can also at times come quite close to the savage-looking brutes Lombroso imagines. Scabby, the sinister mastermind, and Otero, Rico's faithful and loving minion, in *Little Caesar* both clearly possess homicidal noses, which according to Lombroso are "often aquiline, or rather hooked like that of birds of prey, always bulky."[40] Repeated shots of both in profile accentuate their atavistic criminal features. The nickname of the crime mentor in *The Public Enemy*, "Putty Nose," also focuses attention on what might be an incriminating schnozzle.

But the exact and complete physical features of born criminals that Lombroso lists are not universally found in the protagonists of gangster films, some of whom even have movie-star good looks, such as Blackie in *Manhattan Melodrama* who is portrayed by Clark Gable.[41] Even if the gangster was not outstandingly handsome, overall by the mid-1920s, as David E. Ruth shows, "Hollywood rarely characterized him as the physical monster previously popular in the films of Lon Chaney and his imitators."[42]

It is not in their looks but in their behavior and conduct that gangsters seem to fit Lombroso's descriptions best. According to him, the born criminal has "great agility" as well as "relative insensibility to pain" and "ability to recover quickly from wounds."[43] This could explain gangsters' miraculous skill at dodging bullets, at least during most of the film, or, when hit, nevertheless survive. It takes what seems to be an entire army of law enforcers to shoot down Tony at the end of *Scarface*. In *The Public Enemy*, Tom single-handedly attacks a rival gang off screen and comes out badly wounded and bleeding. He crawls for a few seconds and then lands in the gutter while commenting "I ain't so tough." Astonishingly he is: in the next scene we find him alive in the hospital and in the scene after that his brother says he is doing better. When Rico in *Little Caesar* is gunned in the street by rivals, it barely scratches him. With a bullet in his arm, he stops to calmly exchange hostile words with a police officer who is trying to collect enough evidence to arrest him.

Born criminals, according to Lombroso, have "violent but fleeting passions" and practice certain crimes "such as the pederasty and infanticide" which are explained by atavism if we recall "the Romans, the Greeks, the Chinese, and the Tahitians, who not only did not regard them as crimes, but sometimes even practiced them as a national custom."[44] While infanticide is not apparent in these films, the gangsters certainly do seem to adopt some of the other characteristics. Thomas Doherty neatly sums up the "social pathology and sexual aberration" in the three classic gangster films: "homosexuality (*Little Caesar*), misogyny (*The Public Enemy*), and incest (*Scarface*)."[45]

Since classical Hollywood even in the pre-code era did not spell them out, they turn out to be interestingly messy. Tony's incestuous desire for his sister also includes substantial violence to her (he tears her dress) and to others (he shoots her husband dead). Tom's misogyny is unclear: he seems to express fondness by punching people playfully (including his mother: when she visits him in the hospital he affectionately hits her on the head with his fists) and particularly dislikes women who sexually abuse him when he is drunk. Then again, he is not very nice to men either, so maybe it is more a matter of being equally violent to all sexes than a specific misogynous streak. As for Rico in *Little Caesar*, he certainly exhibits no attraction to women, leads an alternative lifestyle with the admiring Otero (they are seen innocently in bed together, Otero dresses him fondly), and is captivated by his handsome friend, Joe. When he realizes Joe is a threat and can no longer be trusted, he is unable to shoot him and even prevents Otero from killing Joe, later admitting: "this is what I get for liking a guy too much." But, he also works out a rather complex theory of proper gender relations during the film. Criminals should not be with women. Love is "soft stuff" that will make a man into a "sissy." He thus might "spill" something to the police (which is in fact what more or less happens in the end with Joe after he leaves Rico for a woman). With the exception of one scene, in which he ambivalently admires his mirror image with Otero, this fear of being "soft" places Rico at a distance from Lombroso's usual pederasts who stand out by their "feminine elegance,"[46] an account which Lombroso perhaps derives from an inversion model for same-sex attraction, not the hyper-masculine one in *Little Caesar*.[47]

Lombroso's work had close ties and was highly compatible with the eugenics movement in the United States.[48] Eugenics was defined by Charles B. Davenport, its leading figure in the United States for almost 30 years,[49] as "the science of the improvement of the human race by better breeding."[50] It was committed to garnering the knowledge and promoting the action necessary for improving the germ plasm of future generations. This included countless aspects that had to do with health, sex, and reproduction, some more on the side of nurture than nature, but from our point of view most important was its relation to heredity.[51]

August Weismann's theory that the substance of heredity, the germ plasm, was impermeable to environment was advanced in the English-speaking world since the 1890s. It helped bolster a form of hereditarianism which held that nature defied nurture, "that environmental reforms, however well intended, could work little if any social improvement over the long run because people's germ plasm remained the same."[52] In addition, within the rising popularity since 1900 of Mendel's discrete genetic elements, inherited traits were no longer understood as continuous. Defective germ plasm was therefore not obliterated in a "melting pot" with healthy variety. Rather, characters were inherited as units, and, as Mendel was understood to have shown, persisted.[53] They might remain recessive, in the "genotype" without expression in the "phenotype"; that is, some people might carry bad germ plasm without themselves being sick. It was therefore not enough to ban reproduction of those who were clearly defective; family history needed to be consulted. In practice, at least for large enough families, absence of genetic disease for three generations back was felt to be "sufficiently stringent."[54]

The eugenics movement identified crime as well as insanity, pauperism, race, and mental ability as single, genetically determined, traits.[55] It argued that the nation's genetic inheritance was endangered by bad blood from immigrants as well as genetic defects from within. Eugenicists lobbied for the Immigration Restriction Act of 1924 by supporting the restriction of immigrants from South and Eastern European countries who were believed to be genetically inferior and a potential source of pollution to the American blood stream. Eugenicists were also heavily involved in compulsory sterilization state laws for genetically inferior individuals whose sterilization, it was claimed, "would save millions of dollars in the future." By 1935, over 30 states passed such laws and over 21,000 sterilizations had taken place; by the 1960s, well over 60,000 had been sterilized.[56]

Enjoying the support of many eminent scientists and the silence of those biologists who found its claims tenuous and exaggerated,[57] eugenics was highly popularized in the media between 1910 and 1930, as Garland E. Allen explains:

> There were popular articles written in all major magazines [... and] at least 20–30 popular books published on eugenics in this period, numerous exhibits that traveled around to state fairs, the American Museum of Natural History and even in the Capitol rotunda in Washington during the period of the immigration debates following World War I [...]. With all of this publicity, it would have been difficult for any moderately well-read person at the time not to have known about eugenics and not to have thought it represented a new and legitimate area of modern biology.[58]

There were also films for, against, or mocking eugenics, as well as related issues like heredity, birth control, and euthanasia.[59] One of these, *The Black Stork*, originally released in 1916, is analyzed in detail by Martin J. Pernick. One of its stories is about a couple in which the husband carries a "hereditary" disease and which marries despite a doctor's warnings. The couple has a baby, who, as predicted, is "defective" and bound to die if not operated upon. Following a vision from God depicting the miserable fate of her baby should he live, the mother agrees to withhold treatment and, as Pernick explains, "the infant's tiny soul leaps into the arms of a waiting Jesus."[60]

But to what degree were these ideas still present in the 1930s and in Hollywood? It would seem that considering criminality as a discrete and genetically determined trait is in harmony with Hollywood's killability tests, since it creates a villain whose criminal behavior is immutable and who therefore must be killed. But were the classical gangster films of the 1930s committed to eugenics? The movement as already noted feared the genetic inheritance introduced into America by recent immigrants, particularly those who were not Protestant. The white-native-born bias against immigration is quite clear in the films as Thomas Doherty notes:

> In the merging of actor and persona, the three classic gangster films calibrated a demographically precise balance in their ethnic bloodlines: Edward G. Robinson/"Rico" Bandello (Jewish/Italian) in *Little Caesar*, James Cagney/Thomas Powers (Irish/Irish) in *The Public Enemy*, and Paul Muni/Tony Comonte (Jewish/Italian) in *Scarface*, together adding up to equal portions of Irish, Jewish, and Italian, America's dominant immigrant groups.[61]

What needs to be noted, however, is that the gangsters' ethnic background is *not* what drives them to criminality according to the films.

In *Scarface*, Tony's Italian mother clearly does not approve of her boy's career in crime and tries to keep his sister away from him. In *The Public Enemy*, the Irish parents and brother all try to pull Tom away from the wayward path. In *Little Caesar*, the protagonist does not seem to have a mother but one gang member, Tony, does. She tells her little Antonio she has some spaghetti for him on the stove and reminds him that he used to be a good boy, wearing white and singing in the church choir with Father McNeil. Tony is touched, asks her to stay, and kisses her on the lips as good boys were prone to do at the time in Hollywood. Excited, with gushing Italian music on the soundtrack, he calls out Father McNeil's name and goes to see him. On the way, he meets Otero the faithful gang member and tells him he does not want his split in the revenues from their recent lethal heist and is going to the priest. Rico shoots him on the church steps. Disagreeing with the eugenics movement, if these men turn to crime, it is despite, not because, of their families and Catholic heritage.[62]

This role of the Hollywood gangster's ethnically marked family is starkly different from the degenerate families nature accounts frequently presented to their readers in order to explain hereditary criminality. Lombroso, for example, never seems to tire of giving yet another anecdote of a family rife with murderers, thieves, prisoners, prostitutes, alcoholics, adulterers, and the sick. He tells of one "whole family of criminals" whose fearful story I shall quote only in part, nevertheless hoping that some sense of the extent of its depravity be conveyed:

> In this family the paternal grandfather died of an affection of the heart. He was of weak character and completely dominated by his wife. She, nervous and eccentric, struck her husband on all

occasions, and was so irascible that she even took pleasure in striking her sister when she was sick. The father was very nervous and violent, but a coward [...] He died of aortic insufficiency. [...] A cousin [...] was addicted to pederasty. [...] The maternal grandfather was intelligent, but a drunkard, and served two years in prison for theft. [...] The maternal grandmother abandoned her children [...]. The mother, very vicious, idle, and violent [...] had two children by her marriage. [...] Abandoning her family and children without concern, she spent her time playing cards in dives and quarreling with drunkards. She tried several times, while in a state of drunkenness, to kill her husband. [...] At the age of 39 she became pregnant once more, and had her paramour produce an abortion. This woman had three sisters. The first was vicious from infancy and abandoned herself to a life of prostitution at the age of 16. So irascible was she that in a fit of jealousy she tore off another woman's ear. The second sister [...] threw [one of her children] out of the window for some trifling reason; and another time, without apparent cause, she threw it in front of the wheels of a carriage. It suffered from meningitis, but recovered.[63]

By the third generation, such degeneracy could not but lead to crime. For example, one girl gave herself up to a precocious debauch, another was drunk and stole, and a third is described as lazy, deceitful, thievish, coquettish, and lascivious. Of the boys, for example, one is of weak character like his father and another is very nervous, irascible, and despotic.[64] These degenerate families are absent in crime films.[65] Nowhere in the films I have studied is there a substantial family of genetically inferior criminals that matches Lombroso's misfits or other depraved lineages.[66] While in certain aspects—their looks, behavior, sexuality, and ethnicity—some of the Hollywood gangsters are to some extent similar to the criminals that appear in nature accounts, overall, this fit is always partial and ambivalent.

It is not difficult to understand why the extant nature or nurture explanations of criminality were not appealing to Hollywood. The nurture approaches were problematic because part of the environment in the United States included films and puritanical elitist reformers who were hostile to working-class amusements also targeted movie houses.[67] Admitting that the environment creates criminals would also make it possible to blame films, especially violent gangster films, for influencing children and driving them to crime.[68] Thus Henry James Forman's popular 1933 exposé *Our Movie Made Children* repeatedly asserts that certain high-rate delinquency areas create criminality. Delinquency, he writes, "is no new thing and some environments are too heavily weighted against their young denizens."[69] Accepting this nurture assumption, Forman can now underline the role films play in encouraging delinquency. Throughout the book he argues that many young people sympathize with and imitate criminals in motion pictures; that films create desire for riches, luxury, and easy money which are obtainable through criminal or illegitimate enterprise; and that they play a significant part in showing techniques, methods, and means of committing crimes. These ideas were popular in 1930s America and posed a real threat to Hollywood. As Gregory Black writes, the moral guardians who held that gangster films led to an increase in crime and juvenile delinquency were "joined by police, judges, lawyers, mayors, newspapers, and civic organizations."[70] Even Al Capone took part in the protest against the genre which was so harmful to young children.[71] A belief in an environmental cause of crime could justify the banning of films from the lucrative crime cycle by censorship boards.[72] Hollywood therefore had an obvious interest not to promote the idea that criminality was a clear result of the environment.

As for nature, American eugenicists assumed that white Protestants of Northern European decent were genetically different from and superior to blacks, Jews, and Catholic immigrants, who threatened them by having higher birthrates and by the possibility of mixing races or "mongrelization."[73] The American eugenicists even developed warm ties with their colleagues in Germany, who quickly exceeded them.[74] Their form of nature explanation would not be very appealing to the Jews or Irish Catholics who were powerful groups within the Hollywood studios, the Production Code Administration, and the influential Catholic Legion of Decency which rated Hollywood films.[75] In fact, some films vilify those who voice eugenicist ideas (which during and after World War II might also have been identified as similar to Nazism). In *The Spiral Staircase* (Robert Siodmak, 1945) and *Rope* (Alfred Hitchcock, 1948), it is the *criminals* who talk about killing "inferiors" and it is these criminals who must be stopped—apprehended or killed—at the end of the films.

Whatever the exact historical reasons, our interest is in the ramifications for making death meaningful. If criminality has no one determining cause, it cannot be easily altered. Had it been clearly genetic, it could have been prevented, for example, by sterilization, by illegalizing some marriages and encouraging others, or by restricting immigration of inferior and violent races. Had the cause of criminality clearly been environmental, it could have been altered by having the bad influences removed, for example, by shutting down movie houses. If there had been such a way to prevent crime, then the criminal could have been stopped. He might even never have been born or made a criminal. His death would not have been inevitable or justified; it would have been unnecessary and thus less meaningful.

Hollywood avoided this predicament. It created its very own unique and singular villain. Neither an inevitable result of environment nor one of heredity criminality, the Hollywood bad guy is bad to the bone but for no one clear reason. Perhaps the villain's badness is *congenital and inborn* but *not hereditary*; a one-of-a-kind freak that is not the result of anything running in the family. Perhaps it is the result of circumstance, but one which could be overcome by others, and seems to have taken its effect at an extremely young age and then apparently remains immutable. Whatever we might speculate, Hollywood gives us ambiguous and contradictory information. Only that some singular people are very bad to the core and cannot change. The only way to stop their evil deeds is by stopping their bodies; if possible by incarceration; if not—usually because they resist—then by death.[76]

This is what makes their death meaningful merely in relation to the past without the need to continue the causal narrative chain and show any beneficial results of this death. In some cases the film lingers on, but as far as the storyline is concerned this is pointless. The story in *Public Enemy* ends with a rival gang delivering the dead body of Tom, the protagonist gangster, to his family's home. The film however continues—it shows us his mother who still expects him to come home alive and his brother who barely manages to stand up and slowly walk away from the corpse. The film even seems to comment on its own inability to end although the story has: we cut to a phonograph record which has just finished playing. The stylus, however, remains on the record, oscillating back and forth at the end of the groove with the sound registering a surface noise that becomes particularly audible now that the music has stopped.[77] This is not unlike the film which lingers on although the plot has ended and no good could come out of the fresh corpse just delivered to the family.[78] Finally acknowledging that the story is over, the film abandons the diegetic world altogether. It dissolves to a title declaring that "THE END OF TOM POWERS IS THE END OF EVERY HOODLUM" and "THAT SOONER OR LATER WE THE PUBLIC" will have to solve the problem of "THE PUBLIC ENEMY." This claim completely contradicts the plot in which the gangs seem quite capable of destroying each other without OUR help. If the death of Tom is meaningful and justified, it has nothing to do with what happens afterward and certainly not with the odd conclusion that the film tries to persuade its viewers they should have reached.[79]

The very fact that the villains are no longer is good in itself. It can even be a story-terminating death that ends the movie—there is nothing that needs to come after it to make it meaningful. Nothing can be deduced from these singular criminals and their demise. The films make an effort not to prove that movie houses should be shut down or that Catholics and Jews should be shut out. They can offer us a way to make death meaningful merely in relation to a past that has already taken place. It is a way to make death meaningful that is difficult to instrumentalize since there are no lessons to be gleaned from it, no generalizations to be made, and no action that must follow it. It demands no further violence. It leaves only a surface noise of a phonograph record that has come to an end.

4
Melodrama and the Shaping of Desires to Come

Sublating Death

Initial and intermediary deaths serve as causes within a storyline and thus affect the future. Since the Hollywood film is based on causality through the actions of individuals, losing a character mid-story can put a terrible burden on the narrative and incur difficulties, challenges, and strains to the individual-driven causal storyline. In fact, the character most clearly affected by the death—the individual who dies—is also the one who, being dead, is no longer directly an active agent in the story. In this chapter, I focus on some of the changes a death can make so as to have an effect on the causal storylines despite, or rather exactly because of, the absence of one of the characters. In the next, fifth, chapter, I will show how death is or becomes an issue for other characters that remain alive and discuss the bonds that entangle living characters in the death of others and thus enable death to be meaningful in relation to the future.

Generally, for death to be meaningful in relation to the future in a classical Hollywood film, the event should not overwhelm the remaining individuals in the world of the film to the point of paralysis. It is not that the death needs to be undone and ignored—it does influence the causal storyline—but it also cannot be fatal to it. The film does not stop to mourn and work through the loss for several months or years, while the audience waits or also takes part in overcoming the terrible loss of one of the film's characters. Nonetheless, if the death is to be meaningful it cannot be completely forgotten to the point of not having any effect. Death must have its sting.

We are left then with sometimes-incongruous demands to remember the dead, but not too much; to have death influence the plot, but not shut it down; change things, but only in directions that help the plot progress. Death must be acknowledged—someone is no longer—but not to the point of completely taking over and halting the plot. Not unlike the double meaning of sublation, *Aufhebung*, which, as Hegel mentions, is "at once a *negating* and a *preserving*,"[1] Hollywood demands of its dead to leave the plot, yet leave something behind in a way that allows the film to continue its progress to the next stage.

One popular way to achieve this stylistically is for the film not to show the event in which the character dies, but rather tell us about it after it has already happened and is already affecting other characters. In *The Crowd* (King Vidor, 1928), Johnny learns of his father's death from a woman on the steps to his house who tells him he must be brave. Neither he nor the viewers actually see the father die. We are already dealing with its effect on Johnny. The death of the youngest brother, James, in *My Darling Clementine* (John Ford, 1946) is not shown. We follow his elder brothers into town, and only find out that James has already died when they discover his corpse in the rain and in the dark. His murder is omitted from the film entirely, directly skipping to its results, to its effect on the rest of the narrative, in which the brothers seek revenge. In *White Heat* (Raoul Walsh, 1949) the death of Cody's mother, with whom he is completely obsessed, is not seen. Rather, it is whispered from prisoner to prisoner during mealtime, until the word finally reaches Cody. We then get to see Cody go mad. In all of these cases, the deaths are reported; they are neither seen nor heard by the viewers.[2] This does not mean that the film ignores the death, but rather that we learn of the death once it has already become the concern of others, has already had an impact on their lives, in a way that can continue the individual-driven causal narrative.

Obstacles and Goals

How exactly can death affect the storyline in relation to the future? At times, the demand made by death on the future is given explicitly, verbally or in writing, for example in wills or in last words on the deathbed. The dying Melanie in *Gone with the Wind* (Victor Fleming, 1939), for example, asks Scarlett to take care of her son and Ashley and to be kind to Rhett. Gangsters, with their no-nonsense attitude, make sure death means something in relation to the future by appending a letter addressed to those who have remained alive. They deliver the other side's casualties with a note attached to the corpse: "KEEP OUT OF THE NORTH SIDE" in *Scarface, the Shame of the Nation* (Howard Hawks, 1932) and "LET ME ALONE AND MAYBE I'LL LET YOU ALONE" in *The Roaring Twenties* (Raoul Walsh, 1939).

Less impulsive and more law-abiding than the gangsters who send notes on cadavers are the white Bea and the black Delilah, two women who build a business by making pancakes and build families while making melodramatic mistakes in *Imitation of Life* (John Stahl, 1934). They too find a way to make sure that events that take place among the living are still related to those who have passed away. While perhaps making some poetic sense, the logic—true to melodrama—is far from causal or even reasonable.[3]

After the business success story about pancakes is concluded, the film turns to deal with the important business of emotions, which is its focus to the end. Bea falls in love with a dashing ichthyologist and her daughter also falls in love with the same man. In the meantime, Delilah's daughter, Peola, decides to pass as white and disown her dark-skinned mother. Consequently, Delilah dies.

Remarkably, it is after her death that Delilah seems most powerful. In the film, Delilah, in the words of E. Ann Kaplan, is "maternity personified,"[4] and represents the belief that being born black is God's will and should not be questioned or challenged as her daughter does. For Delilah motherhood is the be all and end all of a woman's existence and passing as white when one is "really" black is wrong. At her funeral, her daughter Peola finally acknowledges her relation to Delilah, starts weeping, and asks for forgiveness for having killed her own mother. In the scene that follows, Bea decides to give up the man she loves, at least for now, in order not to lose her daughter who loves him too. This sacrifice for the sake of motherhood is of course perfectly in accord with Delilah's ways. Next, Bea's daughter informs her mother (and the viewers) that Delilah's daughter has decided to go back to the black college to which her mother sent her. "That's good," says Bea, "that's what Delilah would've wanted for her."

While Delilah herself is now dead, she is not visually absent. From quite early on in the film, detached iconic signifiers of Delilah were created, which now enable her to "live on" after she passes away and to continue to influence the plot posthumously, making sure the living obey her ways. When opening their first seaside pancake restaurant, Bea sees Delilah and realizes her face would make a perfect sign. She commands her to smile ("a great big one"), which she does. Bea is delighted and orders a sign made with a great big picture of Delilah smiling and underneath "Aunt Delilah's Homemade Pancakes." But her sign-ification process has only just begun. A passing vagabond, who is given pancakes on the house, tells Bea how she can make millions of dollars: "box it." She immediately hires him and begins marketing Aunt Delilah's Pancake Flour in boxes, which does indeed make the two women rich. This is followed by the mass production of the (white) pancake flour in boxes with Delilah's image printed on it. Finally, Delilah is converted into a rooftop moving sign—her image in light is animated showing her flipping a pancake in the pan.

This animated sign in lights showing Delilah flipping a pancake has remained alive. It is shown several times after her death, as the late Delilah's views on motherhood and race finally prevail. The electric sign, in fact, is not as automatic and predictable as we might think. The first time we see it, when Delilah is still alive, the words on top "32 MILLION PACKAGES SOLD LAST YEAR" light up one by one, followed by the circle around her and the pan, then the painting of Delilah is lit, and the animation of her flipping the pancake is run through. After this, "AUNT DELILAH PANCAKE FLOUR" lights up at the bottom of the sign, which is then turned off completely, perhaps to begin another round of animation. The second time it appears, however, immediately following her funeral, the sign's routine has changed. This time the entire first line lights up all at once, not word by word. It then continues the same way as before, with the pancake flipping, the name of the company at the bottom lighting up, and then the whole sign going dark. This, however, is followed by the entire sign lighting up again almost immediately, which we did not see the previous time. Finally, after all of the characters in the film followed her ways: her daughter forfeited her rebellion against her mother's dark skin and admitted she was black and Bea sacrificed her happiness as a married woman for the sake of being with her daughter, Delilah's sign appears again. This time, it is filmed from a completely new angle, perhaps seen from behind the fence in the garden where Bea and her daughter are. The sign, which appears more distant, lights up entirely all at once and remains lit until we cut away. There is no pancake flipping animation. Does this sign have a will of its own? Is there a ghost in the machine?

In most films, of course, the dead do not haunt machines and corpses are not delivered with written instructions. Yet a demand is still made on the living, if not explicitly by those who die, then through the causal logic of the storylines in the character-centered classical Hollywood narrative. According to David Bordwell, one of the characteristics of this storyline is that it is based upon "the drive toward overcoming obstacles and achieving goals."[5] Accordingly, death can effect a change in this narrative drive, in the obstacles and in the desired goals.

Death can remove or set up an obstacle that prevents characters from attaining certain goals which they desire. If two (or more) characters have goals that contradict each other, then the very existence of one of the characters is an obstacle to the others. The death of this character can therefore remove the obstacle and enable the other characters to attain their goal.[6] The German military men and politicians who plot to kill Hitler in *The Desert Fox* (Henry Hathaway, 1951), for example, clearly envision his death as a way to get him out of the way, removing an obstacle, in order to enable them either to conduct the war more skillfully and honorably or work to reach a peace agreement. Their assassination attempt fails; but in other cases, the death does take place and does remove an obstacle. In *Fort Apache* (John Ford, 1948), for example, Lt. Col. Owen Thursday objects to his daughter's marriage to a second lieutenant at the fort because the latter is the son of a mere sergeant major.[7] This conflict between Owen Thursday's will and that of his daughter and her lower class but beloved second lieutenant is resolved by Thursday's dying in battle, after which the young couple does marry.

In *Johnny Guitar* (Nicholas Ray, 1954), the Dancing Kid and Johnny Logan (who now sometimes goes by the name of Guitar) vie for the same woman—Vienna. By the end of the film, the Kid is dead and it is Johnny who gets the woman.[8] The Kid's death, then, removed the obstacle that he posed to their romance. In many films, a woman who is already committed to another man shows some interest in the protagonist. Once the other man is dead, an obstacle is removed and she and the protagonist are free to begin or continue their romance. In *The Man from Laramie* (Anthony Mann, 1955), Will invites Barbara to look for him in Laramie after Vic's death; in *My Darling Clementine*, Wyatt Earp says he will probably come for Clementine after Doc Holliday's death; and in *The Naked Spur* (Anthony Mann, 1952), Howard and Lina can head for California together after Ben's death. In all of these cases, this becomes possible because the other man that the woman was associated with is now dead.

Deaths can also influence the storyline by setting up goals, that is altering, or helping the characters to discover what they desire. Death could trigger an immediate and obvious emotional effect which sets up a new desired goal for one of the characters. One common way to do this is revenge, a popular element in Westerns and war films, in which the killing of a character affects the future of the storyline by making a demand on the living to avenge the death of a friend, family member, or lover.[9] *My Darling Clementine* has a causal storyline spanning much of the film which is completely motivated by revenge. The Earp brothers are traveling with their cattle to California when they run into Old Man Clanton and his son, Ike. Wyatt Earp refuses to sell his family's cattle to the Clantons for a price that he considers too low, so the Clantons rustle the cattle and kill the youngest brother, James Earp. As an act of revenge, Wyatt agrees to become marshal of the local town, Tombstone, and searches for his brother's killers. Chihuahua, a saloon girl, is coerced by him into revealing that James's pendant was given to her by Billy Clanton, who immediately shoots her. This begins the final strand of cause and effect in the film.[10] As an act of revenge (or justice), Virgil Earp chases Billy Clanton and shoots him dead. As an act of revenge, Old Man Clanton shoots Virgil dead. Chihuahua dies, and, as an act of revenge, her man, Doc Holliday, joins the two remaining Earp brothers, who, as an act of revenge, head to the OK Corral, where the Clantons are waiting for them. Other townsfolk would like to help, but Wyatt makes it clear that "this is strictly a family affair," that is, in this case, an act of revenge.[11] Finally, the Earps with Doc Holiday and the Clantons shoot it out. The Earps kill all of the Clantons and can now leave Tombstone. Although the modes of behavior of the two groups do differ—the Earps try to bring justice and at least ostensibly would rather arrest than kill whereas Old Man Clanton seems to particularly enjoy shooting people in the back—the actions of all sides are the same: killing someone from the other camp in an act of revenge.

In other cases, revenge does not encompass the entire film but still creates goals for characters. In *The Big Parade* (King Vidor, 1925), three American men, Jim, Bull, and Slim become friends as they train for World War I and later find themselves in a French village waiting to be shipped to the front. When they do finally reach the battlefield, Jim and Bull wait in a shell hole while they hear Slim who is wounded outside shouting for help and being shot again. Disobeying orders, they leave their shelter and go to find Slim. When they discover his body, Jim appears to lose all control. "You got my buddy, you b———s!" he curses the Germans in an intertitle which spares us the expletive. "Now...COME ON!" Consequently, Jim and Bull seem to confront, single-handedly, a substantial portion of the German army. Even after Bull dies, even after Jim himself is wounded and his rifle jams, his rage is not quenched, and he pursues, crawling and armed with a bayonet, a wounded German soldier. Due to Slim's death, Jim has become angrier, violent, bloodthirsty, and suicidal.[12]

Not all soldiers, of course, seek revenge or their own death upon the death of a comrade and other goals can be set up or reinforced following death. In *All Quiet on the Western Front* (Lewis Milestone, 1930), for example, Paul visits his friend, Franz Kemmerich, who is wounded and had his leg amputated. After Franz's death, Paul returns to his living friends and says that he saw Franz die and that he never felt more alive; that suddenly he is hungry, thinking of girls, feels as if electricity is passing through his body. The death of another person—even, or particularly, a comrade—is in this case invigorating; it intensifies Paul's desire for girls and food.

Death can also affect the goals of characters without having taken place yet. The very threat of a future death might be enough. We have seen how a death that has taken place can take someone who does not want to fight anymore and make him go back to killing. In *My Darling Clementine*, Wyatt Earp left his job as marshal in Dodge City and started raising cattle with his brothers. The murder of his younger brother makes him take the job of marshal again, this time in Tombstone, and so go back to a life of violence. Death can have a similar effect even when it is only a threat, a possible future. In *Shane* (George Stevens, 1953), the titular protagonist used to be a gunfighter and now works on a farm. The homesteaders in the area are terrorized by the local cattleman Ryker who wants to take over their lands and even brings in a professional gunfighter, Jack Wilson. After Wilson kills one of the homesteaders, Torrey, the other homesteaders want to leave, but Shane's employer, Joe, convinces them to stay promising to take care of Ryker. Shane knows Wilson is no match for Joe, and so is forced to go back to a life of violence and to confront Wilson himself. Shane did not do this immediately following Torrey's death as an act of revenge. Rather, he only went to confront Wilson when Joe's life was at stake, that is, due to a possible future death. In a similar fashion, it is the threat of future violence that leads Will Kane back to the job of marshal after he left town to live peacefully with his new Quaker wife in *High Noon* (Fred Zinnemann, 1952). And it is the threat of death to the woman he loves that takes Johnny back to the role of "gun crazy" Johnny Logan in *Johnny Guitar*. Wyatt, Shane, Will, and Johnny all find that they now once again have goals which they thought they had abandoned. Due to a death that has taken place or the threat of future death, they are back in their element as fighters after an attempt to live a nonviolent existence.

These new (or renewed) goals are immediate and direct. The characters act in response to past or potential future deaths. The effects of death could, however, also change a situation and more indirectly lead to action. Death can make a demand on the living, create a new goal for them, by leaving behind it an absence which the characters in the film take to be a lack that needs to be filled. In Dominick LaCapra's words, this lack is "a felt need or deficiency"; it signals that something "ought to be there but is missing."[13] An object of desire thus becomes specified—it is "the lost or lacking object or some substitute for it."[14]

It is a truth universally acknowledged that a widow must be in need of a new husband in classical Hollywood films—Mrs. Teasdale in *Duck Soup* (Leo McCary, 1933), Bea Pullman in *Imitation of Life*, and Meg Rinehart in *The Cobweb* (Vincent Minnelli, 1955) all desire to fill in the lack created by the deaths of their husbands. Meg Rinehart, who lost her son and husband in *The Cobweb*, is "obviously" looking for replacements to fill in these roles, since, so the films' characters seem to assume, a woman is lacking without a male spouse and offspring. In *Imitation of Life*, Bea Pullman has lost her husband, and so needs both a source of income (which she finds by becoming a successful businesswoman) and a new husband (which she postpones beyond the period depicted in the film, sacrificing her own happiness for her daughter who also loves the same man). Similarly, a child whose parents die desires to find new ones. This can lead to convoluted chains of noble and tear-jerking replacements. In *Tomorrow Is Forever* (Irving Pichel, 1946), John is believed to have died in World War I. His "widow" marries another man who raises John's and her son as if he were his father, replacing John who is lacking in the child's life. Two decades later, John returns, posing as an Austrian chemist. He is accompanied by a young girl, Margaret, whose parents were killed by the Nazis. When John dies, Margaret is taken home by his "widow" and the man she married, replacing John who replaced Margaret's parents.

In comedies, an initial death seems particularly useful if it creates a vacant social position—a millionaire, a senator, a head of state, a husband—that needs to be filled in, preferably by a surprising candidate who at least at first blush seems outright inadequate, the wrong person in the wrong place. In the Marx brothers' war comedy, *Duck Soup*, Mr. Chester V. Teasdale's passing away creates two lacks: the head of Freedonia and Mrs. Teasdale's spouse. Groucho's character, Rufus T. Firefly, becomes the new incompetent head of state and, upon learning that her deceased husband left Mrs. Teasdale all of his fortune, also declares his love and proposes to her. Other cases in which the person who fills in a lack created by death does so in a surprising way include Longfellow Deeds who becomes a millionaire by inheritance in *Mr. Deeds Goes to Town* (Frank Capra, 1936) and the protagonist in *Mr. Smith Goes to Washington* (Frank Capra, 1939) who takes the place of a deceased US senator.[15]

In war films, it is frequently assumed by all of the characters that someone must be in charge. A dead officer or NCO could therefore create a professional lack which the men feel a need to occupy with a new figure so that there are no gaps in a clearly defined chain of command.[16] Steve Neale, for example, describes the plot of *A Walk in the Sun* (Lewis Milestone, 1945) as a chain of replacements of dead (or otherwise incapacitated) commanders:

> Having lost one officer (Lieutenant Rand), who is killed by a stray shell as the soldiers wait to disembark, and another (Sergeant Halverson) who disappears on landing, the platoon nevertheless makes its way towards what it understands to be the military target [...]. On the way, led firstly by Sergeant Porter (Herbert Rudley), who later breaks down, then by Sergeant Tyne (Dana Andrews), the soldiers learn that Halverson has been killed.[17]

In this case, the final leader of the platoon—Tyne—does in fact get the job done, so the dead Rand and Halverson and the shell-shocked Porter are successfully replaced. At the end of *Sands of Iwo Jima* (Allan Dwan, 1949), Sgt. Stryker, who managed to hold on to his position throughout most of the film, is shot dead. Surprisingly, he is replaced by the one man in his squad, Conway, who spent most of the film contrasting himself as an educated, Shakespeare-reading, and "soft" alternative to tough military men, like Sgt. Stryker or even Conway's own father, Colonel Sam Conway, who was Stryker's idolized commanding officer. By the end of the film, though, the men in the squad have bonded, Conway decided to name his own son Sam (as Stryker had done), and, when Stryker dies, complete Stryker's letter to his son for him. At least unofficially, he seems to take over commanding the squad. Conway looks up at the flag being raised on Mount Suribachi and then at Stryker's corpse. He uses Stryker's catchphrase—"Saddle up!"—and calls, in a suddenly coarse voice, "Let's get back to the war!" The men follow Conway into the smoke and battle. A new Marine commander, who never desired to be one, is born out of a need, a lack, which was formed with Sgt. Stryker's death.

Desiring Death

Hollywood also offers us ways to problematize this use of death, to question the instrumentalization of death in removing obstacles or in redefining desires so as to set up new goals. These ways of making death meaningful in relation to the future can be questioned when the goals and desires of the living are contradictory or not fully known to them and when the films break away from a causal chain of events.

We have seen examples in which death is meaningful by creating a lack that needs to be filled in. These provide situations in which obstacles and desired goals are clear. They continue what Deleuze and Guattari label as the "traditional logic of desire" which "causes us to look upon it as primarily a lack."[18] However, this is not always the case. Absence does not always determine desire, and desire is not always well defined or known. As Mary Ann Doane shows, in diverse textual systems like literature, law, psychoanalysis, and film, the woman's relation to desire is at best difficult, and, paradoxically, "her only access is to the desire to desire."[19] Western culture has even produced one man who, so we are told, was not able to figure out what a woman *wanted*, despite claiming to know what a woman *lacked*.[20]

Melodramas, which are not limited to female characters or viewers, but have been associated with the "woman's film," do seem particularly skillful at questioning and complicating this traditional logic of desire as lack. They construct, in Joan Copjec's terms, "an *indeterminate reality*, one about which nothing definite can be said."[21] Characters might not have a clear desire, might not know what they want, might harbor conflicting or impossible desires, or might shift their desire inexplicably. What are we to do with this logic of desire, in say, *Caught* (Max Ophuls, 1949), where Leonora's lines include convoluted statements such as "You don't want me. Not really. You just want me to want you" or "I'm glad to see you and I wish I weren't." When desire is muddled so are the goals and obstacles, and the role of death is difficult to define—it is not always obvious whether a particular death has removed an obstacle in order to attain a desired goal (which is never quite certain), created an obstacle, or both. In the film, Leonora's baby dies in premature birth. Did she want the baby or not? Does she love the baby's father, or has she only convinced herself she does because she really married him for his money? Does she love the poorer Dr. Quinada? He says to her "you can only live if you want to, and you must want to"; but must she want to? Has her desire truly changed, as Dr. Hoffman, Quinada's friend and colleague suggests, when talking about the mink coat associated with her millionaire husband: "if my diagnoses is correct, she won't want that anyway." Is his diagnosis correct? Does he know what she wants? Does she? Does the death of the baby, then, free her to start living and be happy as Dr. Quinada tries to convince her? Does she lack/desire a mink coat and a rich husband or a loving pediatrician who will help her grow up and realize money is not everything?

There is a feeling that the baby's death is connected to the removal or setting up of obstacles on the way to achieving her goals, but we cannot know which of her goals is really hers and the closure in *Caught* remains uncertain.[22]

With the shifting and unclear desires of melodrama there is even a danger that death itself might become a goal without the characters ever wanting it or being completely aware of this fact. The protagonist of the silent film *The Crowd*, Johnny Sims, appears to have but one goal: to be "somebody big," different from "the crowd." Unfortunately, as Christine Gledhill notes, he is an "ordinary, unexciting character" with no particular distinction, a "hero without an agenda."[23] He has no idea how to achieve his goal of becoming "somebody big." Deaths in his family seem to solve that problem.

Twice in the film, he does become extraordinary—through death. The first time is when he is 12 years old and his father dies. He and his friends are sitting on a fence thinking what each of them will be. One wants to be a preacher, another a cowboy, yet all Johnny can say—and it is quite a bit—is "My Dad says *I'm* goin' to be somebody big!" We then see a carriage driven by galloping horses which stops at Johnny's house. The children rush over, but it is Johnny who is singled out. Slowly he starts climbing up the stairs. He is visually torn out of the large crowd that has gathered there and has remained below. The stairway is seen fully in long shot—from top to bottom, using distorted perspective lines to mark the slanted ceiling. Johnny's climb seems particularly slow and torturous, perhaps giving us a child's point of view. Finally, he reaches the top; he literally is somebody big due to the perspective which makes the crowd below him appear smaller. He is standing alone, at the center and foreground of the frame, someone unique and separate from the crowd, the focus of our attention as he gesticulates to convey his anxiety. Soon a woman comes down and stops beside him. She tells him, in an intertitle, that he "must be brave now" like his father would want him to be. After the intertitle, both are seen in the frame from a different angle (she is in medium close-up and he is in a medium shot). Johnny is now closer to the camera and above the crowd, which remains out of focus in the background.

The second time death does him the service of making him special and different is when his little daughter is hit by a truck. Again, Johnny becomes the center of attention, this time shot from above, as the crowd surrounds him in a circle, and he carries his wounded daughter in his arms. Again, he climbs up the stairs to his home; again, the crowd is behind him and watching. In the next scene, he tries to keep everybody quiet because his daughter is ill. While the members of his wife's family who are at his home seem to comply, the people on the street do not agree to halt. A policeman even shouts at him to get back inside, the "world can't stop because your baby's sick!" But it does once he goes home and learns that his daughter has died. A policeman is shown in the next scene as well, this time stopping traffic to allow the funeral procession to pass through. Johnny is unable to return to being a part of the crowd after this second death. He is one clerk out of a crowd of hundreds who copy numbers and sit behind identical desks. Although he goes back to work, he is unable to keep his mind on the job. Animated figures start circling his head, images of the truck and his daughter are superimposed on his forehead, and he finally quits and is unable to hold any other job.

So far, as Gledhill explains, Johnny became special "through the extreme of death and grief."[24] He has been singled out "not through achievement but through misfortune,"[25] by deaths that he never caused or wished. Yet after the chronically unemployed Johnny is told by his wife she would almost rather see him dead, he finally takes the initiative, goes out with his son running after him, and heads for a railway bridge. He spots an oncoming train, crosses the railing, and appears determined to jump as the train passes below. His goal throughout the film—defined by his dead father—has been to become somebody "big," different from the crowd. True to melodrama, his desire is vague and he has been unable to find a specific way to realize it. While death has twice served as a temporary and unintended means of achieving his ultimate goal of becoming special, it has now become (thanks to his wife) a goal in itself, which he intends to bring about on his own. He has now finally discovered exactly what he wants—to die.

Apparently, this is only a momentary lapse. Looking too exhausted and defeated to do anything, Johnny crosses back onto the bridge and starts sobbing as his son asks him extremely painful questions: why he never plays with him no more and if momma doesn't like him. His son then adds that he likes him and "When I grow up I wanta be just like *you*." Ascertaining that his son still loves him and believes in him, he hugs Junior, and declares: "We can do it, boy! We'll show them!" He suddenly becomes energetic, increasing his pace so radically that his boy can hardly keep up and even the camera wobbles as it tries to dolly back at the same speed. It seems, as Gledhill writes, that "his unremitting sense of failure is turned around by his son," that it finally offers him the identity he has been unable to name which allows him—in the role of the father—to become one of the crowd.[26]

The transition, however, is ambiguous. A remnant of his passion for death is still visible even if not acknowledged in any way by the plot or intertitles. After his son tells him he believes in him on the bridge, Johnny goes to look for a job. Since he cannot go to work with his son, he leaves Junior on a nice looking bench and sets off to find employment. We might recall that earlier the boy announced to Johnny "When I grow up I wanta be just like *you.*" Johnny seems to set him on the right path. The bench he sits him on is located in a pastoral graveyard.

Alongside with the linear causal narrative, the classical film also offers other systems of order which have been described by several scholars. Linda Williams states that "melodrama," that is, the "sensational, affective, destabilizing, spectacular, haptic, exciting, and moralizing dimensions of cinema," is exactly "the dominant form of popular moving picture narrative." It is not subordinated, submerged, embedded, or a mere tendency or exceptional genre in a classical norm.[27] Rick Altman suggests that we might imagine the Hollywood form as generated by a maxim to "[d]ecide which spectacles are needed, then make it seem that they are there for internally motivated reasons."[28] Raymond Bellour has found what he calls "symbolic blockage," a system of similarities which does not seem to depend on narrative progress, but is rather an insistence of order working in the entire film from end to end, "through and through, at all micro- and macro-elementary levels of content and expression."[29] Different elements in classical films echo each other, display similarities and contradictions, repetitions, and equivalences. For example, typically, in the classical cinema, "the end must reply to the beginning; [...] the last scene frequently recalls the first and constitutes its resolution."[30] Bellour prefers the terms "rhyme" or symbolic "contagion" for this non-perfect duplication, repetition together with difference, symmetry and dissymmetry.[31] Daniel Dayan's reading of *Stagecoach* (John Ford, 1939) suggests that beyond the meaning offered by the film's story, against the reigning cinematic order, the images exist

in a sometimes subversive manner, whisper against the silence that is forced upon them, puncture the regular progression of the narrative with unruly zones, inscribe intrusive [*parasites*] discourses, graffiti straight on the screen.[32]

Dayan discovers recurring contents which are inverted and perverted like the Freudian instinct, a series of ambivalences, reversals of aims and of contents, which are the origin of the narrative and run throughout the story irrespective of diachronic progression. He offers a way to read through the organizing work which imposes a "fatal linearization" upon the film,[33] and to rediscover in "a series of graffiti" the hidden turmoil that generates it.[34]

While death might seem to be instrumentalized within the linear storyline in order to serve the removal (or setting up) of obstacles or the creation of new goals, a reading which gives heed to these other orders working in the classical film can reveal a different logic, one that might problematize the meaning of death in relation to the future and the sageness of making such use of death.

A change of goals following deaths is evident in David O. Selznick's production of *Gone with the Wind*, even if accounting for it does not promise to make sense of this film fully. The changes in goals is this film are quite complex, if only because the world that the film depicts falls apart half way through it due to the Civil War and because its excessive length allows numerous shifts in obstacles and goals. The desires of its protagonist, Scarlett O'Hara, are not very stable or clear; they are particularly a riddle to Scarlett herself. As Linda Williams writes, the work's phenomenal popularity, as both novel and film, results from Scarlett's amazing and near-pathological self-ignorance:

> Thinking she loves the traditional cavalier Ashley, she fails to see that she really loves the rogue and scalawag Rhett; thinking she will live out the high ideals and morality of her French-bred aristocratic mother, she actually embraces the scrappy survivalism of her Irish immigrant father.[35]

In Helen Taylor's words, Scarlett is "a spectacular emotional failure" and "fails to understand her need and desires."[36] Is there any logic to what she wants? To a certain extent, she does maintain the traditional lack-generates-desire logic: she wants what she does not have. Her interest in Ashley Wilkes throughout the film is perhaps motivated by the fact that he seems to be the only man in the Old South who has not proposed to her. Yet, oddly enough, his indifference to her at the end somehow makes her lose interest in him, although it does not really differ from his indifference to her throughout the film.

To make sense of what Scarlett wants, why she suddenly realizes it is Rhett she loves, death needs to be introduced into our account. There are three deaths that match Scarlett's first three desires—all related to Mr. Wilkerson, a nasty Yankee overseer at the O'Hara plantation, and to the woman who later becomes his wife, Emmy Slattery, who, Scarlett's Mammy says, is poor white trash. Finally, a fourth death, that of Ashley's truly good and innocent wife, Melanie, brings in a new logic of desire and helps Scarlett realize what she really wants. None of these shifts in desire follows a cause-and-effect logic. Rather, they create models which Scarlett adopts following a death. In Bellour's terms we might say that they are a recurring "rhyme," in which shifts in desire are associated with deaths. Moreover, it is Wilkerson, the Yankee overseer, and Slattery, the poor white trash, who play key roles in the goal-orienting deaths in Scarlett's life. What the rich and honorable belle of the Old South wants is the desire of a Yankee man and a poor white trash woman. In this sense, even before the Civil War, the Old South already wants to be what it is not; it already is or should be no longer; in its desire, it already is longing to be gone with the wind.

The first death in the film is merely reported. Scarlett's mother returns to Tara and tells Mr. Wilkerson, the overseer, that she is coming from Emmy Slattery's bedside where his child was just born and mercifully died. Wilkerson feigns surprise, as if he never knew a thing about it and has no idea how it might have happened. Scarlett seems to adopt the relationship between Wilkerson and Slattery as a model for her own desire; one where the couple is not married and remains apart and a love whose existence the man at least seems to deny. Throughout the film she desires Ashley, a man she cannot marry—because he is already engaged to his cousin, Melanie Hamilton. The fact that they cannot be together and that Ashley constantly tells her so has no effect on her. She does not believe in marriage, and Ashley's devotion to his wife, Melanie, is of no concern to her: she continues to pursue him and tell him that he could not possibly love Melanie since he loves her. Scarlett also systematically marries men she does not love and as a means to attain other goals (get back at Ashley [first husband], save Tara [second husband], and to become rich or even richer [third husband]).

Scarlett's desire, however, does not stop with the unattainable Ashley. During the war, she returns to Tara only to discover that her mother died the night before. Mrs. O'Hara was nursing that "white trash" Emmy Slattery, caught the typhoid, and passed away. Following this second death, Scarlett suddenly has a new desire: to take over her mother's role and run Tara. At the beginning of the film, she told her father she did not care about the land or Tara. Now, she slaps her sister for saying the same, and explains that hating Tara is like hating their parents. Where did this new desire come from? We soon learn that Emmy Slattery would like to live on the plantation. Following the death of her mother, which was a result of nursing Emmy Slattery, Scarlett has adopted a new desire, which is also that of Emmy Slattery. Unfortunately, the carpetbaggers demand a $300 tax on Tara, which the O'Haras have no way of paying.

Wilkerson and Emmy Slattery have finally married and they come and offer to buy Tara. The Yankees are now wealthy and in control. Scarlett refuses and her father chases them away on horseback. He falls off while jumping a fence and dies. After this third death, Scarlett's desire crystallizes: she not only wants to save Tara, but also wants to be rich at any cost, even if that means doing business with the Yankees. Thus, becoming a scalawag, she is truly following Mr. and Mrs. Wilkerson—she even gets married again, as they have.

It is finally another death, one that has nothing to do with the Wilkersons, that makes Scarlett's desire clear to herself. It is a death that is first and foremost meaningful in relation to the past, by exposing the truth which Scarlett was unable to understand up to this point. Melanie, Ashley's wife, dies after getting pregnant although she knew it would most likely kill her. Her last words to Scarlett are to take care of her son and Ashley, and, in addition, that Scarlett should be kind to Captain Butler who loves her so. After Melanie's death, Scarlett, finally and for the first time, believes Ashley when he tells her he really loved Melanie and does not love her. In addition, she believes that Rhett really does love her so and that she loves him too. Unfortunately, Rhett either does not love her, or is still communicating in the old logic of desire, whereby the best way to win her love is by telling her he does not love her anymore.[37] Claiming that he is leaving her and does not care where she goes, he also bothers to carefully explain exactly where he is going. This additional information, which enables Scarlett to go after him if she chooses, indicates that Rhett might still be playing the old game of desire. But is Scarlett?

Scarlett is at a crossroads. She could embrace the new logic of desire that comes with Melanie's death—tell the truth, love what she has; or, she could continue to wish for that which she does not have because she does not have it and desire that which others desire (particularly the Wilkersons). In one sense, she seems to have chosen the former option— she will go back to Tara, that which she does have, because that is the source of her strength. But this is only to find a way to get Rhett, who has left her, back—she still desires that which she does not have. Even the return to Tara is linked to the old logic of desire. While she does have Tara, it is not very clear if this is what *she* wants. She reaches the conclusion that she needs to return there after we hear the voices of her father, Ashley, and Rhett tell her of Tara's importance to her. Is it her desire at all? She then adds—and for no clear logical reason now that she knows what she needs to do—that she will think about it tomorrow. After all, tomorrow is another day. By returning to desiring that which is another and indicated by the voices of other people of another gender, she is also returning to her old logic of desire. The Old South is indeed gone because it wishes to be other than it is and always has. That, however, is not enough in *Gone with the Wind*. Death is the power present at every shift of desire in Scarlett's story.

Impossible Legacies

I have argued that death makes a demand on the living, sometimes explicitly, verbally or in writing, sometimes by creating situations which demand revenge or create a lack that needs to be filled in. Yet the demands of the dead, just like the desires of the living, can be vague, unknown, and contradictory. They are not always easy to understand, coherent, or feasible.

Some comedies, for instance, show that the desires of the dead are at times ridiculous. In Buster Keaton's *Seven Chances* (1925), the protagonist's grandfather bequeaths him the balance of his estate—7 million dollars—provided he is married by 7 o'clock on the evening of his 27th birthday. Although a wonderful set up for a comedy—by the time he discovers this he only has one day to get married and hundreds of single women are willing to help—the capricious demand offers little to suggest that the grandfather was entirely of sound mind when he devised his will.

Death and desire meet repeatedly in David O. Selznick's production of *Duel in the Sun* (King Vidor, 1946), most memorably perhaps in the lust-in-the-dust climax, where the half-breed Pearl Chavez and the man who pleasurably ravished her, the no-good serenading outlaw, Lewt McCanles, die embracing after passionately shooting each other. Death serves in this film to define for the heroine, Pearl, desires that are not her own and that intensely confuse her. In a film that is excessive in many different ways, Pearl attempts to balance no less than three very different desires: the desire which Pearl inherits from her dead mother (to fall in love with a wild, exciting man); the desire which Pearl inherits from her dead father (to form a white aristocratic couple); and a melodramatic hysterical desire which is hers from the start and allows her to reconcile the conflicting demands made by those who have died (to protect a couple which excludes herself).

At the beginning, the half-breed Pearl is seen dancing outside the Presidio, a saloon and palace of chance, in front of children, while her Indian mother is dancing inside in front of adult men, raising her skirt and ecstatically shooting off a pistol.[38] This suggests an analogy between the two energetic, non-white women, indeed, as Robin Wood writes, an "unbreakable bond between mother and daughter."[39] The mother's lover, a melodramatic cad with a moustache and a sly smile, asks Pearl where her mother is and tries to grab her. He notes the similarity between the two dancing women and says he is commencing to like the daughter better. Pearl tells him to leave her alone and he goes inside, kisses her mother, and leaves with her. Pearl sees the two leave and go home. She looks very unpleased but only becomes truly alarmed when she notices her "fancy" father (white, prissy, and genteel), Scott Chavez, following them. Pearl runs to her father and asks him to take her inside, to the Presidio. He is shocked to see his little girl in such a wicked street at night and is sorry she has to pay for his sins and is not willing to take her there. Instead, he goes inside the house and shoots Pearl's mother and the lover. He then suggests that he should be hanged since he long ago killed someone far superior to those two who deserved to die—himself, when he gave that woman his family name. The death of Pearl's mother defines the first desire Pearl inherits—having a sexually fulfilling and wild lover as her mother did.

This is followed by a second desire-forming death, that of Scott Chavez, Pearl's father, which is made as an explicit demand. Minutes before his hanging, Scott tells Pearl of his second cousin, Laura Belle, whom he once loved and who loved him. He claims that Laura Belle chose security over love and gave herself in wedlock to a wealthy Yankee instead of him. Scott tells his daughter that it was his second cousin who could have and should have been her mother and that now she must go to her. Laura Belle will love Pearl and Pearl must give her all the love she had for him. Scott thus implants in Pearl his unfulfilled desire. It is her father's object of desire—the good white wife—that Pearl has now taken upon herself to love, identifying with her father.

Her father's desire not only conflicts with the desire Pearl has inherited from her dead mother, to have a wild lover, but is also contradictory in itself. If Pearl now has to carry out her father's desire, that would actually mean not being Laura Belle's daughter and learning to be a lady as he suggests, but rather, as the inheritor of her father's desire, being Laura Belle's husband, identifying with another generation, race, and gender. This could explain why, in Laura Mulvey's well-known analysis of the film, Pearl seems to oscillate between femininity and masculinity[40]— she is literally required to take the desiring role of a dead man, who, moreover, being "fancy," was not very manly by the standards of the community around him.

Pearl does go to Laura Belle, and the women do seem to care for each other dearly. However, an interracial, intergenerational, lesbian marriage does not seem to be an option in this film. Two alternatives seem to spring up. One option is to replace Laura Belle with her son Jesse, that is, someone similar to her in manner, but of a different generation and gender, which would be suitable for marrying Pearl. The second option is Sam, one of the employees on the ranch, who is not related to Laura Belle, but is old enough to be Pearl's father, that is, of the correct generation to fit Scott Chavez's desire. Both alternatives fail. Laura Belle's elder son, Jesse, is well educated and polite; he is truly his mother's son. He might seem to be the ideal husband to fulfill her father's desire, even if he is not his mother in gender and age. But Pearl could never be the perfect spouse for him. As she herself emphatically explains, she is "Trash; trash, trash, trash, trash, trash." Their relationship could never fulfill her father's desire, since Pearl herself is a "half breed," that is, she could never form the racially pure, if not incestuous,[41] relationship Chavez wanted with his second cousin. As to Sam, while being of the right age—that is closer to her father's and Laura Belle's generation—he just makes things worse, since marrying him could never lead to the union of aristocratic Southerners Pearl's father desired.

Laura Belle complicates things further when she tells Pearl a different story which she later confirms to her husband as she is about to die (endowing it with the aura of truth that death can endow in Hollywood, as we have already seen in Chapter 2). She did not marry for security. Rather, she found her new husband exciting, a wild man of the West. She did want to leave him at a certain stage, but not to go back to Scott Chavez. That is why Laura Belle never encourages Pearl, who wants to be like her, to marry Jesse, but rather brings up her other, wild and attractive, son, Lewt, who is more his father's boy than hers. If Pearl is to be an attractive husband to Laura Belle she must be wild, not lady-like and refined as her father thinks she ought to be and Laura Belle is. Then, however, she could not form the aristocratic couple her father desired. Learning from Laura Belle as her father wanted only leads Pearl to the desire she inherited from her murdered mother with whom she identified in energetic dancing—to find a cad who will sexually attract her. Her attempt to deal with the contradictory desires she inherited from her dead mother and dead father by following only the father's demand and going to Laura Belle has in fact ended up contradicting her father's desire.

The film offers a way out of this predicament. Pearl harbors yet a third desire, which can be noted from the start. Robin Wood comments that Pearl is a hysterical protagonist, and, moreover, that the film itself, "by virtue of its melodramatic excess [...] must be considered one of Hollywood's hysterical texts."[42] The meaning of "hysteria" in relation to melodrama has been illuminatingly dealt with in Joan Copjec's reading of *Stella Dallas* (King Vidor, 1937) which I would like to use here.[43] Taking Lacan's reading of Dora as an example, she claims that the hysteric's pleasure "is connected to her position outside the scene, not in it." She "eroticizes her solitude while acting as puppeteer of an erotic coupling elsewhere."[44] Stella, for example, aims at "the forming of a couple from which she would be excluded."[45] The melodramatic heroine uses her exile from society to "give mute testimony to all of society's failures" and thus to justify her exclusion from this society which does not write her into its contract.[46]

As we noted, the beginning of the film presents a similarity between Pearl, who is dancing outside the Presidio, and her mother, who is dancing inside. Her mother's lover comes up to her, but Pearl tells him to leave her alone and threatens to call her father. She does not want to be with her mother's lover. Despite the analogy in their simultaneous dancing, her strongest desire is not to take the place of her mother. She does not want a wild lover, as her mother, and, we later learn, Laura Belle, do. Rather, hers is a hysterical desire—to protect a couple from which she would be excluded. She herself remains outside the Presidio and stands outside the house that the couple entered. She becomes alarmed when she notices that Scott her father is following them. Pearl decides to expose herself in order to save her mother and the lover and runs to her father. Although as energetic and as sensual as her mother, Pearl's desire at this point is not, or not primarily, to have her mother's lover but rather to stop her father and save her mother's illicit romance. For that, she is willing to reveal her presence there, let her father know what a disrespectful place she frequents.[47]

At the beginning of the film, she fails, and the couple is shot dead. In the end of the film a couple is again shot dead—this time it is Pearl herself and Lewt, her outlaw lover, in their illicit affair (he refuses to marry her or let her marry anyone else) who shoot each other. But if we take her desire to be hysterical, this time she is successful in forming and protecting another couple and even manages to reconcile the two other, conflicting, desires which she has inherited from her father and from her mother (and Laura Belle).

Because he will let no one else have Pearl, the wild Lewt murders Sam (who intended to marry Pearl) and shoots his own brother, Jesse. He threatens to do so again until Jesse is dead, because Jesse and his fiancée, Helen, who is refined and white, have taken Pearl in and intend to educate her and make her into a lady. Pearl then leaves Jesse and his future wife, goes to Lewt, who, being wanted for the murder of Sam, is about to leave the country, and shoots him. He in return shoots her, and they die together. In this death, she has repeated the desire required in order to replace her dead mother (find a man she is sexually attracted to and be killed with him), but also the desire her about-to-die father dictated: By killing Lewt she has made Jesse's life safe and his marriage to Helen possible. A proper, noble, white, refined couple has been formed by Pearl, as her father desired. This relationship, however, meets Pearl's own melodramatic hysterical desire, since the refined couple excludes Pearl rather than involving her. In that, both desires that were dictated to her by the deaths at the beginning are echoed in the deaths in the end of the film and made to reconcile through the third, hysterical one.[48] She has found a wild man to love (her dead mother's and the dead Laura Belle's desire), formed a pure aristocratic white couple (her dead father's desire), and managed to exclude herself from this couple (her own hysterical desire, fulfilled when she dies). Identifying with the conflicting and self-contradictory desires of the dead, giving in to their explicit and implicit demands, can be ultimately resolved by Pearl in *Duel in the Sun*, but only by embracing the desire to exclude herself from love and life.

5
Cults of the Dead and Powers of the False

Retaining the Dead

Death, in order to be meaningful in relation to the future in a personal causal storyline, needs to be of interest not only to the dead persons but also to the living. The world of the living needs to enable the dead to exert some kind of influence, to alter in some way the goals and obstacles of those who remain behind. This chapter discusses the sorts of bonds that entangle living characters in the death of others.

In some cases, a type of social group related to the dead is necessary for death to be meaningful in relation to the future. Maurice Halbwachs's insight into real-life societies seems to apply to ones in certain fiction films as well, where remembering the dead is a collective issue:

> [T]o the extent that the dead retreat into the past, this is not because the material measure of time that separates them from us lengthens; it is because nothing remains of the group in which they passed their lives [...]. The only ancestors transmitted and retained are those whose memory has become the object of a cult by men who remain at least fictitiously in contact with them. The others become part of an anonymous mass.[1]

I will adopt the term "cult" to refer to this group that retains the memory of the deceased, that makes sure that the dead do not simply retreat into an anonymous mass. We might also, following an analysis by Jean-François Lyotard, compare this with a certain function of the Athenian "beautiful death," in which the dead escape their death and are perpetuated through a collective name (patronym, eponym, nationality). According to Lyotard, the collective name assures within itself the perenniality of individual proper names.[2] A cult, or a collectivity, is needed, according to both Halbwachs and Lyotard, for the dead to be retained, to escape their death.

Frequently, this cult already exists when the death takes place, and it often consists of family members. "Blood-relationship," writes Hegel, supplements "the abstract natural process by [...] interrupting the work of Nature and rescuing the blood-relation from destruction." The family "weds the blood-relation to the bosom of the earth" thereby making it "a member of a community" which prevails over the material forces and lower forms of life which seek to destroy the corpse and thus dishonor the dead.[3] Members of the family are similarly central when Hollywood attempts to offer a cult for retaining the dead and their obligation is self-evident according to the films. Even when, during the horrors of the Great Depression in *The Grapes of Wrath* (John Ford, 1940), the family seems to be disintegrating and unable to serve its members, as do many other social institutions, they still stop to bury a dead grandfather and leave a note behind. Even in Westerns, in which social institutions are struggling to come into existence and survive, the family still stands by its dead. No additional explanation seems necessary when the protagonist in *The Man from Laramie* (Anthony Mann, 1955), who happens to be a mysterious man from Laramie, has come to kill the man responsible for his brother's death. Did he like his brother? Was the brother justly killed? Should he not have assumed that someone serving in the cavalry might be killed while on patrol in Apache territory? The film does not dwell on such nonsense. The man from Laramie thinks someone (he assumes it is a single person and a man) sold repeating rifles to the Indians and he has come to kill him. This is so obvious that it requires no justification. When, in Westerns, a woman questions the need for such retaliatory violence, men do not reply. They "shift awkwardly through the speeches," as Scott Simmon explains, then dismiss the women's ideas with a terse phrase about "things a man just can't run away from," as the Ringo Kid, who is avenging the murder of his father and brother, does in *Stagecoach* (John Ford, 1939).[4] There is not much that can be argued against "things" like that.

At times, "escaping" death by being remembered by a collective can be a conscious decision made by the characters. Rommel in *The Desert Fox* (Henry Hathaway, 1951) knows he must die after being involved in the failed assassination attempt against the Führer. He is offered a chance to be remembered as a great general and hero as well as to ensure the safety of his widow and son if he commits suicide and does not stand trial. He makes the choice to kill himself and parts from his family.

The film, incidentally, seems to think he made a good choice and goes out of its way to ensure we understand that he has indeed become a myth. The whole story is told in flashbacks, beginning with Rommel the legend—an immortal superman who cannot be killed but also a modest, sandwich-eating human, who respects the laws regulating war, and is fair and decent. After we are told of Rommel's death, we see him in the desert again. His glory, as the Führer promised, has indeed lived on. The film ends with no less than Churchill's words honoring the memory of the great Rommel.

In other cases, while the cult which retains their memories and allows them to escape death is just as active, the characters who are about to die do not quite seem to realize how they and those around them are preparing for their posthumous fate. One of the clichés of the war and action film is that while it is dangerous to face the enemy, it is downright lethal to talk about your plans for after the war or about your fiancée or brother back home.[5] The logic is: tell us about your future or your mother/sister/girlfriend/children/wife/brother/father before you die, so that your death could be rescued from destruction, so that we know someone will interrupt "the work of Nature" and give meaning to the death; that there is a cult to retain your memory and a collective who will make this a "beautiful death." In pseudo-Hegelian terms, we know the person who remembers too much or has too many plans for the future is about to die because it bears witness to the cunning of screen-writerly Spirit. It might appear to be the individual character's desire to suddenly talk about things back home, but we, the Hollywood-savvy film viewers, know better. "For us," this is the film's design actualizing itself through the words and desire of its unaware characters: it is making sure that we know that a cult that will remember exists before the character dies. It is preparing the way to make death meaningful in relation to the future.[6]

In *My Darling Clementine* (John Ford, 1946), before James dies, the men with him bother to tell us that he is engaged to Corey-Sue; he refers to one of them as "brother Wyatt"; and parts, personally and by name, from each one of his brothers: "So long, Wyatt, Morgan; so long, Virgil." With this network of brothers and fiancée to remember him, he is clearly doomed. In *Red River*, Dan Latimer, one of the men on the drive, makes the grave mistake of explaining what he intends to do with the money he will receive, including his plans to buy his wife red shoes. Sure enough, within minutes he is crushed to death by stampeding cattle. It is decided that his widow will be given full pay as if he had completed the drive as well as red shoes.

When the cult preserving the dead does not yet exist, the film can show us how it is formed. One obvious way is by creating a family, for example, by getting married, or having children. The first death in *Jesse James* (Henry King, 1939) is of Jesse and Frank James's mother. Here the collective which is to revenge her death already exists—it is her two sons who love and protect her and each other from the first moment we see them. The last death in the film, that of Jesse himself, is also remembered by a cult in the following and last scene. This time however the very formation and binding of the cult was depicted in the film: Jesse marries his childhood sweetheart, Zee; they have a son (he is also named Jesse, and although he does not yet know who his father is, he enjoys playing "Jesse James" including being play shot down and play dead). In addition, since Jesse and his gang attack the hated railroad company whose agents swindled farmers out of their land, he literally has a cult following of the railroad company's many victims.[7] By the last scene— the unveiling of his tombstone—a large and loving crowd has assembled to remember him. His memory will be retained; his will be a beautiful death.

The cult of the dead that is formed during the film is not limited to blood relatives. In *Since You Went Away* (John Cromwell, 1944), Bill, whose parents are dead, is informally "adopted" by a family whose father went off to the war: one of the daughters becomes engaged to him, the mother sees him off at the train station, and even his estranged grandfather becomes a lodger in their house. The telegram informing of his death in battle is delivered to their house. They have become his cult of the dead.

In other cases, substantial effort is required to create the cult and become memorable to it. In *The Petrified Forest* (Archie Mayo, 1936), Alan, an extremely loquacious Englishman, spends almost the entire film first bemoaning the lack of meaning in his existence and then explaining how he has found it in a waitress he has fallen in love with at a desert service station in the United States. In order to allow her to go to France and become, perhaps, a painter, he changes his life insurance so that she is the beneficiary. He signs two honorable witnesses, begs and provokes a gangster to shoot him dead, and declares that he belongs with outmoded ideas, dead stumps, and that he should be exterminated by the law of nature—survival of the fittest. She, in contrast, is the future, the renewal of vitality, courage, and aspiration, and it is to her that he transfers the "major artist" that may have been hiding in him as a failed writer. While not actually marrying and having a child with her, he does manage to settle things legally and in writing in his insurance and has more than enough lines of dialogue to elaborate his *raison de ne pas être* and to form the cult that will remember him. In Hollywood war films, where words are scarce, the relationship of "brothers in arms" can function in a similar way to families. In addition to the combat sequences preceding the death, the long and grueling training sequences can contribute to the creation of the family-like bond between the warriors, who will remember, and sometimes revenge, the death of their comrades.

The necessity of a cult that retains the memory of the dead for some of the ways in which death can be meaningful in relation to the future can also indicate three ways in which it might be problematized: by questioning the veracity of the memory that is retained; by questioning the collective that performs this remembering and its connection to the deceased; and by questioning the function the death really serves for the collective. I will devote the next three sections to elaborating each.

Westerns and Falsehoods

It is the living who are entrusted with retaining the dead and it is they who can manipulate this memory. As Adi Ophir shows in his phenomenology of evils, a disappearance—and death is "disappearance with a capital D"[8]— becomes a loss if it is perceived as irreplaceable from the viewpoint of an interested person.[9] This can put the focus on the interested person, the living. The reality of the object that has disappeared, the dead, can remain secondary in Ophir's account.[10] It might never have existed or it could be remembered in an instrumentally distorted fashion. Films can show, implicitly or explicitly, how death is manipulated and how aspects of its meaning are fabricated in the service of the living. We can begin with two examples from Westerns, *Shane* (George Stevens, 1953) and *Fort Apache* (John Ford, 1948), which will be useful throughout this chapter.

In *Shane*, a rancher named Ryker wants to drive the homesteaders out of the valley and hires Jack Wilson, an experienced, deadly gunfighter who is fast on the draw. When Stonewall Torrey, one of the homesteaders, is shot by Wilson, it is his very death which seems to unite the community. One of the homesteaders, Joe Starrett, who is also Shane's employer, convinces the others to stay until Torrey is given a Christian burial. It is at the funeral that the community is formed. Joe and Shane promise the homesteaders that they can have a town, churches, and a school; a place where their families can live and children grow up. This works out rather well: the local farmers stay, Joe prepares to confront

Ryker, and, finally, Shane shoots down Ryker, his brother, and Wilson, their hired gun who had shot Torrey.

But why is it Stonewall Torrey's death that motivates them to stay there and form a community? In fact, while Joe takes pride in his community spirit—he defines his marriage (on the Fourth of July!) as a happy loss of independence—Torrey is repeatedly equated with the Southern secession, called a "reb," and is resolved on going to town alone despite the homesteaders' decision to only go there together. It is on one of his visits there—he came with another homesteader, Axel the "Swede," instead of urging Axel to wait until everybody goes together—that Torrey gets himself killed. He assumed that because he was a soldier in the Confederate army who has done fighting in real battle (or so he claimed), he could also defeat a deadly gunfighter like Jack Wilson. Wilson provokes Torrey into drawing by deriding the South. ("I'm saying that Stonewall Jackson was trash himself. Him and Lee and the rest of the rebs. You too.") Torrey replies by calling Wilson a "low-down lying Yankee" followed by the latter urging him to "prove it." Torrey hesitantly begins raising his gun—not certain whether he should pull the trigger—while Wilson calmly shoots him down. He falls down dead in the mud having proven that his boastful claims about his experience as a soldier making him fit to challenge Wilson were unwarranted. His corpse in the mud joins a less-than-distinguished line of "inauthentic" men in Westerns who according to Scott Simmon "cling to an identification with the South [...] and almost inevitably die."[11] There is something specious, or at the very least not quite fair, in enlisting the dead Torrey, of all characters in this film, to become the object of the beautiful death which the community remembers and, more importantly, forms around.

At the funeral, Joe begins his speech by saying that "Torrey was a pretty brave man and I figure we'd be doing wrong if we wasn't the same." But Torrey was killed not only because he was a "brave" man but also because he was a "reb" who betrayed the collective decision. While he might, perhaps, be associated with bravery, more apparent qualities include ignorance of real danger,[12] inability to assess his own incompetence correctly, rashness, arrogance, and perhaps alcoholism. His death was hardly beautiful and ends with his corpse in the mud. While none of the characters in the film protests this distortion of Torrey's memory, the film does give a very strong feeling of uneasiness. The funeral scene in which Shane and Joe talk of a town, churches, a school, and a place where their families can live and children grow up is set upon a bleak bare hill, communicating, as Bob Baker writes, the

extraordinary "sense of the precariousness of life at this place and time."
It registers the "awkwardness of the farmers in this quasi-formal situation." The camera even pans away from the grave to reveal "the bored,
not quite comprehending children, the patient animals."[13] Something
is very wrong here.

A more famous example is John Ford's *Fort Apache*, which tells of the
arrival of Col. Thursday at the communal fort and the way he leads the
men under his command to disastrous defeat and the physical destruction of the fort when almost all of them are needlessly butchered by
Apaches. At the end of the film, however, we learn that his failure has
been distorted and that he has now become a legend. A myth has been
invented in which he led his men and died a glorious and honorable
death. Thursday is in a position similar to that of Torrey in *Shane*. He
is, as Steve Neale notes, distinguished from most of the other characters
in this film in being unable and unwilling to integrate himself into the
community and environment. It is only after his death that Thursday
is "integrated into the cavalry, via the legend that becomes part of the
cavalry's tradition."[14]

Unlike the case of Torrey, however, not even the slightest effort is
required to note the misrepresentation in making him, the man who
according to Richard Slotkin disrupted "the tribal utopia that is Fort
Apache,"[15] of all people, part of a tradition. The film itself includes a
coda in which the distortions of the past are bluntly asserted. The Commanding Officer at the fort who has replaced Thursday is now Colonel
York, who was previously associated with the Fort Apache community
and who opposed Thursday's military actions. He receives a group of
Eastern journalists in his office and endorses an extremely inaccurate
painting of Thursday's "glorious" defeat as "correct in every detail."
As Douglas Pye writes, the "rigidity and studied control of York as he
responds to the visitors suggests [...] a sense of knowledge suppressed
and sympathies stifled."[16] In other words, York is clearly lying through
his teeth. But in this scene York also mentions the effect of the legend
of Thursday's "glorious" death. Fort Apache's massacred community has
now been replaced by "better men than they used to be." The false myth
of Thursday's death, the myth that "no man died more gallantly nor
won more honor for his regiment," has made the disorganized and forgotten outpost legendary. As Slotkin writes, "the myth has been good for
the regiment."[17] The dead Thursday "made it a command to be proud
of," says York, and *this* is probably quite accurate.

These distortions of the dead in Westerns are not surprising. Despite
their reputation for simplicity and forthrightness, the heroes of the

Western are no friends of the truth. When these "tight-lipped strong, silent"[18] protagonists do bother to talk it is often to tell lies, dissimulate, go back on previous commitments, or brag how they have been untruthful up to now. Shane decides to face Ryker and Wilson after one of Ryker's men betrayed his employer and secretly told Shane that Joe was up against a "stacked deck." Shane, however, does not let Joe know this, but rather hits him on the head and goes to fight in his place. "I changed my mind," he declares, when Marian, Joe's wife, mentions that he was supposedly through with gun fighting. Why he does not tell her (or Joe) the truth—that he has recently learned that Joe was being set up—is unclear. In *Stagecoach*, Curly, the lawman, lets Ringo the fugitive go and confront Luke Plummer when they reach Lordsburg. Ringo proudly declares "I lied to you, Curly," referring to the bullets he hid in his hat when they thought they were out of ammunition. At the end, Curly and another character, Doc Boone, trick Ringo and Dallas, a woman with a past, into thinking they are taking him to jail, when they really send them off across the border, "safe from the blessings of civilization." Telling the truth is just not done amongst friends in this film. "I'll kill you, Matt" vows Tom Dunson in *Red River* (Howard Hawks, 1948). He does no such thing and in fact asks Matt to add his initial to their ranch's brand. In *High Noon* (Fred Zinnemann, 1952), Amy tells her husband, Will Kane, that if he does not go with her, "I'll be on that train when it leaves here." Not only does she stay with her husband in the end, the intractable Quaker even kills a man by shooting him in the back in order to support Will.

In *Johnny Guitar* (Nicholas Ray, 1954), agreement between words, deeds, and thoughts is rare. Perhaps the best-remembered case is the dialogue between Vienna and Johnny Logan/Guitar. They parted five years earlier and now Johnny wants her to tell him "something nice" and deny that she has been with all those other men in order to become the owner of a saloon. "Lie to me," he asks, "tell me all these years you've waited, tell me." She does, but in such a cold voice, that it is clearly a lie. In a mechanical tone, she recites what he tells her to say, that she has waited, that she would have died if he had not come back, and that she still loves him like he loves her. Her tone says, as V. F. Perkins writes, "I am doing what you asked, telling you a lie."[19] "Thanks, thanks a lot," he replies sarcastically without meaning it. By the end of the scene, however, the two have given up their performances. He tells her to forget all she had to do to get her saloon, that it is "not real"; and she admits that she does love him. Even if this does now reflect their true feelings, their truthfulness is based on the decision to "forget" parts of the past.

The Western's protagonists are not simple, fair, or naïve. It is not just that "words are weak and misleading," as Jane Tompkins remarks;[20] actions are misleading too. As Scott Simmon shows, it is incorrect to assume that classical Westerns ethically rely on the open walkdown, a fair fight, "where antagonists stride in the clear sun toward each other down a town's main street, armed equally and weapons plainly visible."[21] In the final showdown in *My Darling Clementine*, for example, Tombstone's mayor and church deacon offer to help, but Wyatt Earp tells them that this is "strictly a family affair." In fact, they are part of an intricate scheme in which they impersonate Wyatt's brother, Morgan, and Doc Holliday, while the latter two sneak around "to shoot from the side."[22] There is a clear disagreement between Wyatt's words and his deeds but also an attempt to mislead with the deeds themselves.

Why these blunt lies, inconsistencies, and dissimulations in Westerns? I would like to suggest, with the help of Jane Tompkins, Friedrich Nietzsche, and Gilles Deleuze, that it is not unrelated to the meaning of deaths in relation to the future. In explaining how "stories about men who shoot each other down in the dusty main streets of desert towns"[23] came into being, Tompkins claims that the Western signaled "a major shift in cultural orientation."[24] This "secular, materialist, and antifeminist" genre pervaded by death,[25] she writes, rises at the beginning of the twentieth century as a reaction and in stark contrast to the massively successful sentimental, domestic, and female religious novels of the mid- and late-nineteenth century.[26] The Western answers the feminine Christian novel point-for-point; it is "the antithesis of the cult of domesticity that dominated American Victorian culture,"[27] an attempt by men to reclaim the literary landscape and to react to the "violence of women toward men" in the public life during the post–Civil War era.[28] She suggests that "[e]xchanging the cross for the gun" is also "replayed countless times in Western films," that is, this drama exists *within* the text as well as suggested by Tompkins to explain its existence.[29]

But if indeed, as Tompkins claims, the Western created a new culture and prepared the way for Hemingway and Camus,[30] would there not be more to the story than just what it opposed, more than just a rejection of "two thousand years of custom and belief" as Christianity was "forcibly ejected"?[31] The Western's struggle was not only *against* the existing dogma, but also an attempt to create something new. The activity the genre executes in Tompkins's text is quite exhausting— it "deliberately rejects," "pointedly repudiates," jettisons, sweeps the board clean, suppresses, and marginalizes—all of these verbs just in one paragraph.[32] But these are activities done *against* the existing domestic novel and Christian set of beliefs. When it comes to creating a new culture, to forming men's mastery and identity, which "the Western tirelessly reinvents,"[33] it often seems that things just happen as a side effect, on their own, while the eradication of the existing order of women is taking place. The Western's new beliefs come about "in ridding itself" of the existing ones,[34] or as the elements of the Western "arrange themselves,"[35] and when "men gravitated in imagination"— and even in this imaginary gravitation, it is first toward "a woman *less* milieu" and only afterward toward their own "set of rituals."[36] From Tompkins's account we might end up wondering if there is no labor and effort in the setting up of new beliefs. Does it just happen on its own while destroying previous cultures? Is "tirelessly" reinventing not tiring at all? It seems that Tompkins's book opens up a space for another one to tell us how and what was created.[37]

What if the drama replayed countless times in the films is not only that of offering an "antithesis" to the domestic novel point-for-point, but that of having to invent a new set of beliefs and to fabricate a new culture? What would such an invention of a new culture entail and could that perhaps explain the tendency toward lying amongst the protagonists of Westerns? Let us consider this possibility using some ideas from Nietzsche and Deleuze.

At the same period as the "violence of women toward men" was establishing itself as the mainspring that would drive men to invent the Western in the United States, Nietzsche was describing the over-human effort required to overcome the womanly, sublate the Judeo-Christian tradition, critique extant moral values, and invent new ones.[38] He fixes his hope in new philosophers with minds strong and original enough to take on the task of a "transvaluation of values," of an opposition and inversion of "eternal valuations."[39] The task of real philosophers is not to fix and formalize what is and was but to *create* values; they are commanders and lawgivers; "they grasp at the future with a creative hand."[40] They question the present and the past. This includes a critique of the will to truth; a calling into question of the value of truth, of the metaphysical faith, "a faith millennia old, the Christian faith, which was also Plato's, that God is truth, that truth is *divine*."[41] The opposite of this faith is not science, which continues the Christian ascetic ideal's belief that truth is inestimable and cannot be criticized, but a value-creating power. Nietzsche, as Deleuze explains, "does not criticize false claims to truth but truth in itself and as an ideal."[42] Life aims to mislead, dissimilate, and dupe and the ideal of the will to truth makes of it and of this world an "error" and mere "appearance." The ideal of the will to truth wants to depreciate life, the "high power of the false."[43] The living world "is will to power, *will to falsehood*."[44] What, for Nietzsche, is "the highest power of falsehood,"[45] and is fundamentally opposed to the ascetic ideal is art, "in which precisely the *lie* is sanctified and the *will to deception* has a good conscience."[46] "For the world to be true, or to be subject to a truthful description," writes Rodowick, "it would have to be static and unchanging."[47] But active and creative thought, that of philosophers and artists, change, becoming, and differentiation, an affirmation of life, the will to power, requires "Nietzschean powers of the false."[48]

Deleuze develops Nietzsche's artistic and creative powers of the false in his second cinema book.[49] He identifies it with post-war, modernist cinema, in which "the forger becomes *the* character of the cinema: not the criminal, the cowboy, the psycho-social man, the historical hero, the holder of power, etc."[50] But are the characters of Orson Welles— "the first," according to Deleuze's typically unsubstantiated history, who "makes the image go over to the power of the false"[51]—such as Bannister, Quinlan, Arkadin, and Iago[52] really the first higher men in cinema history? Are these not the cowboy or gunfighter who already "claim to judge life by their own standards, by their own authority," without law, by nature and perversion?[53] When Tom Dunson in *Red River* declares: "I'm the law" and condemns two men to death by hanging—a penalty that everyone else on the drive thinks is illegal, unfair, and quite mad—is he really that different from Nietzsche's real philosophers as commanders and lawgivers who say: "Thus *shall* it be!"[54] In the cinema of the 1960s, Deleuze identifies another change that is an instance of powers of the false, which includes the "cinema of the lived" of Pierre Perrault and the "*cinéma vérité*" of Jean Rouch. Perrault's concern is to belong to his dominated people of Quebec which no longer or not yet exist, "to rediscover a lost and repressed collective identity" whereas for Rouch it is another identity that is still becoming, in Africa, which he attempts to reach while "getting out of his dominant civilization."[55] Both oppose to the apparent veracity of classical cinema a fabulating, story-telling, function "in so far as it gives the false the power which makes it into a memory, a legend, a monster." The real character becomes another, starts to make fiction, "and so contributes to the invention of his people."[56] The filmmaker joins the character and also becomes another, thus forming a cinema which creates and produces a new truth in the invention of a people.

The Western takes us back to a fictitious past,[57] following the Civil War, at a time when law and order did not yet reign and a place, the "frontier," where civilization was only beginning to expand into unsettled land as part of "Manifest Destiny."[58] It sets its tale at the outskirts of a country recovering from war, reuniting, and reforming itself, a people no longer and not yet.[59] Moreover, the genre, according to Tompkins, depicts an attempt by men, and is itself an attempt, to transform their culture, to create new values, a new set of rituals, while rejecting feminine domestic culture and the reigning Christian set of beliefs. The Western, in the creation of a new community on the rubbles of a post–Civil War fragmented nation, seeks recourse to powers of the false. It presents its own artists and philosophers, its own creative lawmakers, for whom the extant truth is of no use. In the West, when the legend becomes fact, print the legend.[60]

We can now explain why Westerns offer instances of death whose meaning in relation to the future entails a distortion. If the Western is itself, and tells about, the creation of a new culture as an antithesis to women's domestic Christian values, then it will not only offer us masculine violence, that is, as Tompkins writes, "stories about men who shoot each other down in the dusty main streets of desert towns," but will also be about, and an instance of, powers of the false, which are necessary for fabulating a new culture and the transvaluation of values and are themselves a negation of the Christian faith in truth. Westerns can thus be useful for problematizing the meaning of death in relation to the future by questioning the veracity of the memory that is retained by the community and showing how it is instrumentally distorted. Of course, merely exposing the truth will probably not have much effect in cases in which powers of the false hold sway. But powers of the false can be taken over. We can resist the meaning of death by inventing a better and different legend.

The Forming of a Cult

Westerns can further hone our skills of problematizing the ways in which death is rendered meaningful. The fabulation and creativity involved in making death meaningful in relation to the future is not only that of making the facts into a legend but also of the very community that forms the cult that remembers the dead. In Adi Ophir's analysis, a death (or any disappearance) becomes a loss if it is perceived as irreplaceable from the viewpoint of an interested person.[61] The interested persons can become so *after* the loss has taken place. "The new interested parties," he writes, "could 'acquire' in retrospect what was lost and join the circle of those who lose. A terrible loss could be produced by creating new interested parties."[62] If a "circle of those who lose" can be formed after the death has taken place, might death play a role in the very formation of the circle? Could it be instrumental in uniting a group and in strengthening social bonds? Can death create a "we"?

While with some deaths in classical Hollywood films the community that remembers the dead already exists (such as families), or is formed during the film before the death takes place (for example, by marriage and having children, or by showing the recruits training and forming the bonds of "brothers in arms"), at other times, it is created or significantly altered *following* the death. It seems that in some films death has the power to bond a group together or strengthen its ties.[63] In *Shane* the homesteaders were not united and did not form a community before Torrey's death. In *Fort Apache*, the collective that falsely glorifies Thursday's last stand is not the fort's original community, which was massacred in the defeat, but a new one, mostly consisting of the "better men" who have replaced them. This creation of a community to remember the dead after the fact can create a feeling of uneasiness and help us to question the way death is rendered meaningful in relation to the future.

One problem in using the dead to create or strengthen a collective, a social bond, is that the status of the dead in this new collective is not clear. Does it encompass both the dead and the living? Can it? Do the living have a right to share in the glory of the dead? Although it is not his emphasis, Lyotard relates the Athenian "beautiful death" to the creation of a collective, to a "formation of the we," and to that which "forms the bond of a we."[64] More importantly for our current discussion, he mentions it as an object of criticism by Socrates in *Menexenus*, where the funeral oration is lampooned and described as "a kind of epideictic genre" whose "effect on the addressee is a 'charm.' "[65] An orator addresses the Assembly of the citizens in order to praise the citizens who died in battle for the fatherland. This corresponds to a sequence of displacements, as Lyotard explains:

> [D]eath in combat is a "beautiful death"; a beautiful death implies a "fine" life; Athenian life is fine; the Athenian living this life is fine; you are fine. [...] I, the orator, am telling you (the Assembly) that those dead in the field of honor are fine. In the copresented (latent) universe, the situations are as follows: I am telling you that you are fine. Or even, by taking note of the final prosopopeia (where the dead heroes begin to speak) through his (the orator's) mediation, we (the dead heroes) are telling us (the living citizens) that we (the living and the dead) are fine.[66]

Socrates, claims Lyotard, says this discourse is unjust because it allows the living who listen to it to be assimilated with those who have already proven their merit by dying for their city. It is covered over by the use of the same pronoun, "we," which refers to the dead heroes, the orator, and the assembly—all Athenians, part of the same collective—although only the dead have justly acquired the right to be named Athenians. The virtue of dying well becomes a privilege of being born well, Athenian, and so "turns the moment of virtue around: it has already taken place."[67]

Let us go back to Torrey's funeral in *Shane*, which unites the community of homesteaders who wanted to leave the area. Joe begins his speech by saying that "Torrey was a pretty brave man and I figure we'd be doing wrong if we wasn't the same" and ultimately convinces the local farmers to stay. An "is" (the alleged fact that Torrey was a brave man) is turned into an "ought" ("we'd be doing wrong"), but the demands of each are different. This "ought," this not "doing wrong," is understood to mean staying there; it does not require actually fighting and certainly not proving their bravery by dying as Torrey did (according to Joe, at least). Moreover, it is not the homesteaders who end up proving their bravery, but Shane who goes out and fights for them while realizing that he can never be a part of them. None of them really are "the same" as Torrey, that is, "brave," dead, or both.

It is not only that the living do not really share the traits of the dead, but that they probably do not want to. In fact the death itself was necessary to form the community, and it is essential that the people who died are no longer a part of the new collective. Freud's idea of the ambivalence that the band of brothers feel after the murder of the primal father, and especially his account of Moses and the formation of the Jewish people, is particularly revealing. In these texts, he constructs a narrative in which death forms a community. In his 1912–1913 *Totem and Taboo*, Freud famously suggests that the source of religion, initially totemic, might have been in a primeval horde ruled by a tyrannical and literally castrating father. In order to keep all of the horde's females to himself he exiled his sons who later returned to kill and devour him. The sons experienced contradictory feelings toward their father, both hating the violent man who denied them pleasure and loving and admiring him. Hence, they felt both satisfaction over that triumph and a burning sense of guilt for their deed and in "deferred obedience" denied themselves the claim to his women as well as the right to normally kill a totemic animal which served as a substitute for the father (which was later substituted by God)—the two taboos of totemism. This criminal deed and the amplified power of the dead father "was the beginning of so many things," writes Freud, "of social organization, of moral restrictions and of religion."[68] It should, however be noted, that the 1912–1913 text already begins with a tightly bound group, the familial horde. While the organization of society might have begun with this murder of the primal father, the very unity of the community as a family (or "horde") had already existed.

It is in *Moses and Monotheism*, the sequel, published in the late 1930s and in full only after Freud's exile in England,[69] that he gives more space to the possibility of forming a community that did not preexist and more importantly by means of the death of a foreigner.[70] He does not abandon the murder of the primal father; he reiterates it as the founding repressed traumatic event. Moreover, he emphasizes its repetition and universality: "the events I am about to describe occurred to all primitive men [...The story] covered thousands of years and was repeated countless times."[71] This original traumatic group of murders was then repeated for the Jews—the focus of *Moses and Monotheism*—when they murdered their tyrannical father-figure lawgiver who had chosen them, Moses. There are, to be precise, two Moseses in Freud's tale—"Jewish history is familiar to us for its dualities"[72]—but only one of them was killed by his people. I would like to note the similarities to our case. The first is that now the father figure is *not* genetically the ancestor of his people. Moses, the tyrant who was killed, was an aristocratic Egyptian according to Freud (the other Moses was the son-in-law of the priest Jethro of Midian). His alien people killed him and later "began to regret the murder of Moses and to seek to forget it."[73] This is the second point—the need to forget, which was achieved by distorting the event in memory, or by a repression that left its symptoms. We are dealing with the attempt to misrepresent in future histories the murder of a foreigner who was sacrificed in the forming of a society. The third point is that indeed the society had to be formed. Freud is no longer talking about one horde that was already a family. The Egyptian Moses is now credited with being able to "form a people out of random individuals and families."[74] At the very least one group, the Levites, was the retinue that accompanied the great Egyptian lord and later "became fused with the people they lived among."[75] The people of Israel, then, were not one people at all until the foreign Moses began uniting them.

Let us now return to Hollywood and to our two examples: Torrey in *Shane* and Thursday in *Fort Apache*.[76] Like Freud's story, here too we are dealing with the forming of a group, either the homesteaders who unite after the death of Torrey or Fort Apache, which became a command to be proud of and attracted new and better men to it after the massacre of the cavalrymen that were once, with their families, its community. Here too, deaths were somehow distorted—Torrey's being a "reb" forgotten and Thursday's catastrophic blunder glorified. Also, like Moses, those who died—Torrey and Thursday—were not an integral part of the community, but somehow foreign. These were the points I emphasized in Freud's account. What I would like to take from him is the ambivalence—the murder was both a triumph that rid the people of a hated tyrant and the source of remorse and guilt; they were both celebrating and mourning the loss.

What Freud could indicate for us is that there is something strange and ambivalent about a union and integration that needs to kill along the way. It is not only the forming of a people but also an exclusion; the integration would not come about without first getting rid of the Thursdays and Torreys of the community, of those who refused to integrate, who were not willing to belong to a collective. The members of the new community did not model their behavior on that of the primal father, but denied themselves his prerogatives, made them their founding taboos. While Joe might claim that it is right to be "the same" as Torrey who was "a pretty brave man," in fact, the homesteaders must not be the same as Torrey the "reb" in order to belong to the collective they are forming, to any collective in fact. The better men of the new Fort Apache are also better than Thursday who was a military and social failure.

More generally, when the meaning of a death in relation to the future involves forming a society, creating a group, strengthening a social bond, it also, *eo ipso*, acknowledges that this integration was achieved over the dead bodies of others, that the inclusion was not total, that something and someone was excluded. While the cult that remembers the dead might insist that its members model themselves, or should model themselves, upon the dead (or even believe unfairly that they already have, as Lyotard claims), the very fact that the formation of the collective did involve a death might question the accuracy of this claim. It might indicate a fundamental contradiction in the formation of society by a beautiful death: that it was impossible to achieve the ideal of a community free from internal conflicts; that someone had to be excluded, had to die, before a new collective of "better men" could be forged.[77]

A Brand that Sticks

Films could offer yet another way of problematizing the meaningfulness of death in relation to the future. If the previous example showed how the integration of a community entails exclusion, now we will see how what appears to be mere exclusion is also part of what is integrated. In Chapter 3, we saw that the death of villains could be meaningful in relation to the past if they could or would not change and could only be stopped by death. In Chapter 4, we noted that death could be meaningful in relation to the future by being the removal of an obstacle that prevented characters from attaining certain goals. In *Fort Apache*, for example, Lt. Col. Owen Thursday is the obstacle that prevents his daughter and her beloved second lieutenant from marrying. His death is meaningful, inter alia, by excluding him from the world of the living and thus making sure that he is no longer an obstacle.

It is tempting to claim that one of the most frequent plots in Westerns is of such an exclusion. The "classical Western" plot according to Will Wright is of "the lone stranger who rides into a troubled town and cleans it up, winning the respect of the townsfolk and the love of the schoolmarm."[78] By expelling the anti-social elements, the progress of law and order is served. According to this formula, the Western is focused on exclusion. As Peter French suggests, in the conversion from desert to garden, from wilderness to community, the hero must weed out those "mean and ornery individuals taking too much advantage of the freedom the wilderness offers" so as "to make things safe for law, order, and civilization."[79]

This formula however is famously more complicated. As John Cawelti explains the good townspeople might be virtuous and honorable pioneers and decent folk, but they are unable to cope with the savages or outlaws who threaten them. The hero, who is bound up with the wilderness and perhaps initially in conflict with the pioneers, eventually becomes committed to their cause. He frequently uses his own savage skills to protect them against the wilderness.[80] He thus helps them to transform the wilderness into a new social order. The hero, however, is torn between civilization and wilderness. Sometimes he might change and become a part of the community, at other times the conflict cannot be overcome and the hero must die or go into voluntary exile.[81]

In fact, even this formula is too simple to account for what we can find in the films. In *Shane*, after the hero defeats Wilson and the Ryker brothers, he feels that he must leave, because a man has to be what he is and there's no going back from a killing. "Right or wrong, it's a brand. A brand that sticks. There's no going back," he tells little Joey, the boy who admires him. Despite Joey's cries for him to return, Shane rides off and does not come back. But does his explanation make any sense? He was a gunfighter in the past so if killing is a brand that sticks, he was branded long ago. The brand however does not stick and there is going back from a killing. His peaceful presence in the homesteaders' community and their gradual willingness to accept the stranger show that. Nor should it be a problem that he killed the Rykers and Wilson. The homesteaders more or less demanded that Joe, Shane's employer, do it, and Joe had no intention of leaving the valley. It was quite obvious that he could and would stay there following the killing.

The problem might be the assumption that violence is associated with wilderness and not with civilization. In Walter Benjamin's 1921 "Critique of Violence," the law itself is created and preserved by the use of violence or force. It does not expel violence, but has an interest in maintaining a monopoly on it. The very foundation of the law, Benjamin claims, is an act of violence. The deadly violence of lawmaking—capital punishment is the origin of the law—is required not to punish an infringement but rather to establish a new law.[82] For the state, violence in the hands of individuals is a danger that undermines the legal system.[83] It threatens the state because of its lawmaking character—it possesses the ability to declare a new law.[84] The very use of violence is *not* then obviously connected to savagery and the wilderness in contrast to civilization. According to Benjamin, the way the law is founded and preserved is by means of violence; it is part of the process of instating law and order. The threat of the savages and outlaws might not be to let wilderness take over where law and order are beginning to form, but rather that their violence might end up founding a new law or preserving an older one that dominated the region before the arrival of the settlers.

The "not-very-convincing explanation"[85] Shane gives for leaving at the end had something to do with a "brand" that taints him now that he has killed. But, as we already noted, he had been a gunfighter in the past and elsewhere, he had killed, and no brand tainted him when he tried to move to a new place, the valley, and refrain from killing. What changed now? The shootout between Shane and Wilson is a competition between two legal systems, the old system of the cattlemen (the Ryker brothers who hire Wilson) and the new one of the settler farmers (Joe, Shane's employer, and the other homesteaders). It ends with the law-founding violence of Shane on behalf of the settlers vanquishing the law-preserving violence of Wilson on behalf of the cattlemen. In a remarkable piece of counterfactual criticism, Will Wright wonders what would have happened if Shane had not gone away. He has acquired, according to Wright, the position of "the deadliest man in the valley" and with "no law around for a hundred miles," he could have stayed and maximized "the rewards of his power and the farmers' gratitude."[86] But according to Benjamin's critique, he would have thus become "the great criminal," the one whose violence "confronts the law with the threat of declaring a new law,"[87] whose figure horrifies the public,[88] yet also arouses its "secret admiration."[89] Shane founded a new law using violence once and he could do it again. Indeed, as Derrida claims the paradox of iterability is that the origin is required to repeat itself and conservation is inscribed in the essential structure of foundation. Fundamental violence, in its structure, "calls for the repetition of itself and founds what ought to be conserved" and conservation in its turn "refounds, so that it can conserve what it claims to found."[90] Had Shane remained in the valley, he would have undermined the very law that he had founded by his very presence and ability to found a new law, or if Derrida is right, necessity to found the law over and over again in order to conserve it.

A problem that follows Benjamin's account and is certainly an issue for Hollywood, is how individuals, or a small group, who actually use, or threaten to use, violence, can be the violence of the "state" or the "law" in general. If "law and order" do not mean peace, but rather a monopoly on violence, there is not much difference, if any, between the violent means used by an individual on behalf of the law and the violent means used by an individual who is not (or not yet, or no longer) believed to be serving the law.

The Western hero, as Peter French writes, is not "in the business of righting wrongs wherever he rides across them" and is interested only when harm is "suffered either by him directly or by someone with whom he has established a relationship."[91] In the classical Western, as Wright claims, "he only decides to join in when a friend of his is endangered."[92] Once, however, the hero is motivated to act, and in Westerns this will eventually mean violence, this same violence can also serve law and order in the community, indeed can serve in the creation of the community and the founding of law and order. If it is never quite clear whether Wyatt Earp in *My Darling Clementine* merely wants to avenge the death of his little brother, or is taking his job as marshal seriously, it is because the difference is not clear. The dissimulation during the shootout in which Tombstone's mayor and church deacon impersonate Morgan Earp and Doc Holliday is a wonderful expression of the way church and state "turn out to validate the gunman,"[93] and, we might now add following Benjamin, vice versa. There is an unacknowledged identity of violence used personally and violence used by individual persons in order to maintain the state monopoly on violence, which is the law. In *High Noon*, why does Will Kane, the ex-marshal insist on returning to a town that does not want him there in order to kill an outlaw who has been legally released? If he did not go back, no killing would have taken place. And why does his wife who is a Quaker and opposed to violence nevertheless end up shooting one of the outlaws? Are they serving their communities or their own personal worries and desires? When the people in the town mostly refuse to help Will are they not telling him his violence is not theirs, is he not, as Slotkin writes, "in effect, a vigilante"?[94] And if he is acting on behalf of the town, is there any difference? Tom Dunson's conduct in *Red River* also reveals this paradox of personal violence which makes law and order and forms the community. He kills claiming he is the law, but then feels a need to gather the men and "read over" those he has killed. Killing is not only a way of excluding, or removing "wilderness" so as to make room for the "garden," law and order. It is also an inclusion, the very uniting of the community and the founding of the law.

While perhaps not always interchangeable, killing an outlaw and building a community, excluding a rogue element and binding a collective together, and disrupting law and order and founding or protecting law and order are not mutually exclusive. One of the meanings of death in Hollywood is that of excluding a harmful person by killing them. Hollywood can teach us that this exclusion by means of violence also has lawmaking potential, also creates collectives and the law, is also an inclusion.

Rendering death meaningful in relation to the future can leave an aftertaste of dishonesty, ambiguity, or contradiction. A "beautiful death" is problematic if it tries to claim that the living share some quality of the dead which could only be proven by death. There is always a chance that the memory of the dead has been distorted. Integration through killing is always the uneasy pairing of exclusion and inclusion, of having to expel the "rebs" in order to create a collective allegedly modeled upon them, or of actually creating a bond or the law when ostensibly only "cleaning up" and rejecting wilderness. Something might always be a bit wrong, unfair, dishonest, or unjust.

6

A Perpetual Present: Death and the War Film

An Absurd Death

It is a remarkable achievement of the classical Hollywood system that it managed to deal with mass deaths in modern war.[1] The automatic, mechanistic, and indiscriminate wounding and killing of arrays of soldiers by bombings and machine guns is not easily depicted as meaningful. Is there an art of dying, which is useful in the twentieth century, asks Edith Wyschogrod, "when millions of lives have been extinguished and the possibility of annihilating human life altogether remains open?"[2] According to Peter Sloterdijk, the "incomprehensibility and technologized indignity of death in the modern war of artillery burst all categories of conventional meaning."[3]

To be sure, films can ignore the mass deaths of modern war. They can focus on personal adventure stories and create a "war romance" with purpose and agency,[4] offering themes like "nationalism, honor, duty, and heroism,"[5] which can perhaps make death meaningful. Even in war, some deaths can be meaningful within the personal cause-and-effect chain of events; there might be a past which that death discloses, or some future effect it enables no matter how dishonestly. I have in fact given such examples of individuals who die in wars throughout the book.[6] There can also be somewhat extrinsic and artificial attempts to make death in war meaningful, such as blatant "why we fight" propaganda dialogues,[7] or a printed/narrated statement "dedicating" the film to those who lost their lives for some important military cause.[8]

Yet many films also depict death in war as mass killing which is not clearly compatible with Hollywood's individual-driven linear causal storyline or the propaganda messages it allegedly supports. "The most obvious casualty in World War I," Anton Kaes notes following Ernst

Jünger, "was the concept of the autonomous subject."[9] Hollywood films about the Great War as Pierre Sorlin writes included an anti-war theme in which killing "appeared to be random, accidental, arbitrary and brutal."[10] As Richard Slotkin writes of the Hollywood films made about World War I up to the late 1930s, for them realism meant "the representation of war as cruel, dirty, and ultimately futile."[11] The central lesson of the World War II films is that "the war is dirty in its unfairness and cruelty and in its remorselessness." According to Slotkin, in these films "[g]ood men and bad are killed alike; sometimes the deaths seem useless or absurd."[12] Thomas Schatz argues that one of the aspects in which the World War II films were unique as Hollywood features was by changing Hollywood's "classical narrative" formulation.[13] In the films, the individual yielded to the will and activity of the collective (such as the combat unit or nation).[14]

Some Hollywood war films, then, at least at certain moments, did not attempt to make modern battles qualitatively less impersonal and horrific, or disguise the overwhelming price in human lives the war seemed to demand. If there was some sense or meaning in these films, it was safely quarantined in specific scenes and moments, never infecting the overwhelming sheer absurdity of battle and mass killings. There was no attempt to tie these battles with a future community or a past truth that is revealed.

Some war films managed to focus on the present activity of fighting and to create a context in which mass killings could make sense. This was not done by having these deaths become logical or romantic—the constant barrage, enemy bombardment, machine guns, and pointless fighting in the trenches are an outrage to our sensibility; they are absurd, monstrous signs of the madness of war; they are nonsensical. But if there is no way for us to think of these deaths as meaningful, in some cases Hollywood opted not to change the deaths it showed but to change the way we think. An illogical context was created, in which these deaths made just as much sense as all that surrounded them.

The world of war as depicted in Hollywood films is strange and perverted. It is the state of emergency where the army has sovereignty over the political, friend and enemy are indistinguishable, law and order are powerless, language and communications break down but make sense, and space loses distinction. It is a world where a war machine and a cinematic machine roll on, together, through the bombings and machine guns, regardless of aims, failures, or the lives that are lost. Death is no longer a finitude abiding to the laws of the Hollywood narrative and its causal storyline which defines the way it can be meaningful. Death is not meaningful because of what already happened or because of what it might offer to the future. The Hollywood war film takes no notice of past successes or failures and looks forward to no future change. It is entrenched in repetitive monotony, a perpetual present, flux, becoming, and movement.

Death is a component of the functioning of a war machine, which takes no heed of individuals, breaking them apart and bringing them together as it sees fit. Death does have meaning, from the point of view of the war machine. However, it is still absurd, useless, unfair, and unnecessary from the point of view of the individuals whose lives are lost.

The next section in this chapter will describe how death is a part of the war machine depicted in classical Hollywood films. The following, and last, section of the chapter, "The Exception of State," will offer ways to problematize this way of making death meaningful. This will not be done by showing tensions or difficulties in making death meaningful in this way (death *is* an integral part of war), but by questioning whether war itself, according to Hollywood, can serve any other purposes but the indefinite prolongation of war.

The Hollywood War Machine

The war machine depicted in Hollywood films operates by killing humans, regardless of the side on which they are fighting, if they are fighting at all. Civilians and soldiers are targeted. The pilots in *Thirty Seconds over Tokyo* (Mervyn LeRoy, 1944) are told that their bombings will kill civilians and no one objects.[15] During the assault on Tarawa in *Sands of Iwo Jima* (Allan Dwan, 1949), Sgt. Stryker's squad is ordered to destroy a bunker. Two men attack using flamethrowers, but are shot and killed. Another man then heads toward the bunker with explosives, but he is shot down. A fourth man manages to bring the explosives closer to their target before he is killed. Finally, a fifth one—it happens to be Stryker—manages to complete the job. There is no reason to assume Stryker would have succeeded had he gone first. The other soldiers were not lazy, incompetent, or badly trained. They were each part of getting the job done. Dying was the correct way to gradually get the explosive there and blow up the bunker. That is the way the war machine works.

When troops are sent charging forward in large numbers, it is expected that many will die by being blown up or shot by snipers and machine guns. No one stops marching or slows down when people start falling down dead in the attacks in *The Big Parade* (King Vidor, 1925),

All Quiet on the Western Front (Lewis Milestone, 1930), or the final battle on the farmhouse in *A Walk in the Sun* (Lewis Milestone, 1945). They do not die because the attack has been executed incorrectly, their weapons malfunctioned, or they were inferior warriors. This was not some exchange or payment for the success (or failure) of the fighting. Their death revealed no truth, it was not necessitated by their being evil, and it did not leave behind it a legend necessary for forming a collective. They died because that is what happens when charging forward in battle. Those who made it alive and took shelter in a foxhole or trench have an excellent chance of dying in the next attack or in the attack after that.

In the march through the woods in *The Big Parade*, a quick rhythm is maintained regardless of the deaths of the men. Michael Isenberg discusses King Vidor's directing technique and the music which accompanied the screening—all, according to Isenberg, meant to convey a rhythmic cadence spelling death:

> For the sequence of the doughboys advancing through the woods, filmed in Los Angeles's Griffith Park, Vidor used a metronome for pacing and had a bass drum keep the beat for the actors. In theaters, the orchestra stopped playing during this sequence and only a muffled bass drum kept cadence with the warily advancing soldier on the screen [...].[16]

The marching had its own, external, pace, which had nothing to do with the "success" of the battle, or the lives lost along the way. The Hollywood war machine does not alter its speed because of the deaths that are part of the way that it functions.

The movie-making machine is sutured into the war machine. A typical sequence, which Lewis Milestone repeats in both *All Quiet on the Western Front* about World War I and *A Walk in the Sun* about World War II, has the camera alternate in shot/reverse shot between a panning machine gun shooting rows of infantrymen and a shot by the panning camera of the victims as they are hit and begin to fall down, not only alternating between both sides, but also creating a fusion between film and war, which Paul Virilio comments upon at length in *War and Cinema*.[17] By giving the point of view of both machine guns and dying soldiers, shot/reverse-shot editing merges the human with the impersonal and non-human. Furthermore, as Robert Baird notes when writing about the chaotic and confused staging in *All Quiet on the Western Front*, Milestone uses the "machine-gun tracking shot" for both sides, visually and formally marking World War I ground combat as "a mechanized and impersonal mass murder."[18] The machine works smoothly, quickly, and efficiently; it involves all warring sides; and it includes flesh, living and dead organic material, and non-organic material such as guns.

Films that have to do with waiting and immobility—the besieged group—which Jeanine Basinger identifies as unofficial *The Lost Patrol* (John Ford, 1936) remakes—offer no better fates to their members—they all, or almost all, die one by one.[19] Here too, the movie-making machine and war machine work in unison. As Dana Polan notes, not only does the dying not disturb the films, it in fact could intensify the Hollywood dream machine, since "the whittling down of the squadron coincides with the whittling down of the actors until only stars remain."[20] Dying does not stop the Hollywood war machine because it is the way the machine works.

A particularly memorable image in *All Quiet on the Western Front* makes this graphically clear. A soldier was blown apart attempting to reach the enemy trenches. Yet his hands—now completely severed from this body—still grasp the barbwire. His will to attack, intentionality displayed by the adamant clinched hands, was in no way diminished by the incidental fact that he happened to die and the rest of his body was blown to pieces. The war machine rolls on. Dead bodies are a part of its mode of behavior, not a sign of malfunction. They can become a part of the terrain and weaponry. In *The Steel Helmet* (Samuel Fuller, 1951), a corpse of an American soldier is booby-trapped. When another soldier is sent to get the deceased man's dog tags he is blown up. The dead body served the Koreans as a weapon of war.

The war machine's fuel is cannon fodder, human bodies of all sides, which are often taken apart. In *The Story of G. I. Joe* (William A. Wellman, 1945), "Wingless" Murphy suggests—perhaps he is joking— that he should cut his legs off because he is too long to be in an airborne unit. The humans and human parts are almost always incorporated into the war machine—canceling individuality and forming a united group that works and thinks as one, "an efficient machine or organism."[21] As Thomas Doherty notes, combat films of World War II typically bear the names not of a mythic single hero, but "of battle sites, battle stations, and branches of the armed services, the very titles repudiate surnames."[22] The airborne genre uses strained metaphors for the combat team: blending together like a good jazz band, coordinated as a precision watch, and of course, working together like in team sports such as baseball and football, "one of the few cultural areas where American males willingly acknowledge the value of cooperative enterprise."[23]

In *Gung Ho!* (Ray Enright, 1943), the commanding officer even explains he learnt this method from the Chinese and suggests the second Marine Raider Battalion adopt as its motto what he claims is the Chinese term for "working together"—"gung ho." This is the unique narrative shift in the classical paradigm that Schatz mentions, in which individuals yield to the will and activity of the collective. It is the "melting pot" cliché of American war films, where the war is perceived as "an intrinsic leveler of class pretensions"[24] in which "all groups can find a welcome place,"[25] a harmonic blend of ethnicities, "American All,"[26] forming a coherent group,[27] if not a surrogate family.[28] Bodies are incorporated into the war machine and individuals and their backgrounds matter not at all.

Entering the war machine is not always simple. Many war films open with long training sequences in which the group is formed. A new man sent to join a coherent fighting group that has already been formed can find it difficult to enter the war machine. Layton is sent in as a replacement in *Battleground* (William A. Wellman, 1949), and initially finds that he is mostly ignored and unable to find a cot or a foxhole. He is only gradually inducted into the squad as he proves his worth, both in and out of battle. Some bodies however might never be incorporated into the war machine; they are spat out of the machine—Williams, the old reporter in *Objective, Burma!* (Raoul Walsh, 1945), for example, manages to latch onto the platoon throughout most of the movie, but he is more a burden than a helpful component of the unit. Near the end of the film, the soldiers suddenly notice he has disappeared. They find his body nearby but clearly outside the trenches they dug. He has been ejected out of the war machine, and he was never really a part of it.

By far more difficult than becoming part of the machine is getting out alive and complete in one piece. There is no simple way to disconnect an organic portion of the war machine so as to have a living single complete individual body. Some individual soldiers do manage to come out, although they might leave the machine an arm (Homer in *Best Years of Our Lives* [William Wyler, 1946]), a leg (Jim in *Big Parade* and Lawson in *Thirty Seconds over Tokyo*), the ability to have a good night's sleep (Fred who has nightmares in *Best Years of Our Lives*), or their sobriety (Al in *Best Years of Our Lives*). Those who have the misfortune of making it back home—in whatever mental and bodily condition—fall prey to "the sadistic imaginations of stables of screenwriters," that condemn them to hellish chain gangs, state penitentiaries, and an ungrateful nation that has forgotten them.[29] If lucky, they might merely lose their jobs (Eddie in *The Roaring Twenties* [Raoul Walsh, 1939]) and girlfriends back home (Jim in *Big Parade*, fortunately he has a new girl in France) or find themselves returning to a menial position in the same workplace they once had which pales in comparison to their feats during the war (Fred in *Best Years of Our Lives*).

Some realize that there is no way to go back. Paul in *All Quiet on the Western Front* shortens his leave to return to battle because no one can understand him at home. He tells his comrade, Kat, that they can no longer return to civilian life; that they have been in the trenches for too long. Momentarily, Kat is in danger: he is shot by a passing plane. Wounded, he might be sent home, leave the war machine. Luckily, the plane shoots at them again and Kat is killed, spared from returning to a world that cannot understand him. Paul stays alive a while longer. He too, however, is spared once thoughts of his previous life enter his mind. Earlier in the film, we saw that Paul was fond of his butterfly collection at home. Suddenly, on the front, he sees one, and raises his body over the parapet in order to catch it. A sniper immediately shoots him dead. The war machine takes care of its own. It does not abandon them; it will not forsake the flesh that makes it run as the risk of the battle coming to a halt becomes real.

The death of Sgt. Stryker in *Sands of Iwo Jima* is perhaps the clearest instance. It occurs after the fighting dies down, the soldiers relax, and Stryker says he never felt so good in his life and offers cigarettes to his men. He is then shot in the back and dies. A letter found in his pocket is addressed to his son. Earlier, we learned that his wife had left him with his son five years before because he had been unable to balance his commitment to the Marines with family life. During the film, much to his disappointment, he never received a letter from his son. In the letter his squad now finds, he writes that he decided to try to write to his son again because he guessed that none of his letters reached him, and he has a feeling this may be the last time he has a chance to write to him. Stryker tells his son to take care of his mother, make her happy, and never hurt her or anyone as he did. "When you grow older," says the letter, "and get to know more about me you'll see that I've been a failure in many ways. This isn't what I wanted, but things just turned out that way." Stryker cannot leave the war machine—he has no home to go back to; there is no option for him to leave a limb and get out. All he can do is relax, light a cigarette, and let the war machine carry out its work, killing him along the way, and having his men go on fighting. As one of them says, "if he had to get it, that's the way he'd want it." War films have a logic of their own, in which bodies of men are incorporated into a cinema-war machine and whose death is part of the way the machine runs.

The Exception of State

This operation of the war machine by means of death and without respecting individual lives might not make it a very attractive option for rendering death meaningful (although some might find it philosophically or otherwise exciting exactly because it does without the sovereign subject; indeed some might find war alluring in general). My concern however is that war might be viewed as an unavoidable evil. Of course war is hell, but it might be thought of as necessary to protect a nation, to prevent an imminent attack, and to attain certain goals. Of course war is bad, but the alternatives, or procrastinating, are, or will be, much worse. Better to get it over with. It is in these cases that Hollywood might help us to resist these meanings.

Hollywood can help us to problematize the meaningfulness of death in war not by showing that death does not make sense within the war machine—it does—but by showing the absurdity of the world in which the war machine makes sense. War, as Annette Insdorf writes, is "a topsy-turvy situation devoid of human guidance."[30] Hollywood agrees. In the films, death is meaningful within the war machine, and the war machine is meaningful within the world of war that Hollywood creates. But this world is quite unusual and, more importantly, not amenable to other meanings. In the films, war does not serve the state and its safety; it does not attain any goals; and it does not get anything over with. We could thus problematize the meaningfulness of death in the war film, but only in the third degree—by questioning the ability of the world in which the war machine functions to enable any other purpose but the continuation of war. In this world, the war machine has no ultimate goal or time limit; space is not well-differentiated and the war machine has no destination or direction; the war machine's aim is not to get to any point, or to make a point that could be put in words; the war machine does not serve the state and is not directed only against the enemy. Signs and language take on a life of their own; even the cinematic style seems to change.

The war itself does not end in many of these films: the enemy is neither ultimately defeated nor victorious. In the end of *Battleground*, which takes place in December 1944, the soldiers sing a humorous cadence call as they march (a "Jody"), complaining that they won't get out until the end of the war, "in nineteen hundred and seventy-four." *They Were Expandable* (John Ford, 1945) ends with its protagonists going back to the United States in order to prepare to return back to fight the Japanese after an initial defeat. In *Gung Ho!*, the Marine Raiders blow up facilities and kill the "Japs" on Makin Island, but then rush out as a new Japanese task force is about to land. The island will need to be captured once more. Some war films, as Dana Polan writes, " 'conclude' with the soldiers confidently on their way to another battle."[31] There are objectives and goals, but they are never the *ultimate* objective or the *final* goal; the war machine does not stop working just because a certain aim has or has not been reached—the only thing it can do is go on. Most of the action in *Objective, Burma!*, for example, takes place after they have completed their declared mission; and Stryker is shot dead in *Sands of Iwo Jima* after they have conquered the mount. In *Gone with the Wind* (Victor Fleming, 1939), the two most reliable men in the story—Captain Rhett Butler and Major Ashley Wilkes both agree that wars are bad and that they cannot win. This stops neither one of them from going out to fight for a lost cause they know is doomed. Rhett in particular only joins the battle when it is clearly and truly lost.[32] Failure or success is no reason to stop fighting. The deaths and the war do not end, just go on, apparently forever, in a perpetual present that takes no account of attainable future goals or of events in the past.

The strange and perverted world of war does not make sense by the standards of regular logic. Forms of communication that function in the non-war world can become meaningless in war, and the logic of war can appear nonsensical by regular standards. It thus becomes highly unlikely that war can be used to convey a logical message successfully (for example, about our sovereignty, borders, values, courage, who we are and who our enemy is, or what we are or are not willing to tolerate). The characters at war are constantly coping with difficulties in communication: a lack of linguistic code that is still meaningful, a language that made sense in the normal world but cannot describe the realm of war, scarcity of signifiers which nevertheless need to be deciphered, and the impossible meeting of too many languages. In the topsy-turvy world of war, communications that seem to work do not, and communications that would seem to be impossible strangely enough do function.

In *Fort Apache* (John Ford, 1948), it seems that the normal state is to have the telegraph wires cut, not working. In fact, the film begins with the new commander of the post, Lt. Col. Owen Thursday arriving and no one knowing about it because they were not notified. In *A Farewell to Arms* (Frank Borzage, 1932), the doomed lovers have their letters stopped by Capt. Rinaldi in his capacity as a military censor. He does this out of lack of communication—he does not know his friend is seriously in love and married to the woman who is about to have his baby, and so tries to stop the wartime romance because he does not like to see him "lose his head with a woman." How different things could have turned out if only he had been told, if only the letters had passed through!

In battle, there are a few, not very informative signals—the sergeant's whistle in *Walk in the Sun*, the grenade setting off or the mirror reflecting the sunlight in *Objective, Burma!*, the loop in the light bulb's chord in *Stalag 17* (Billy Wilder, 1953), it being "too quiet" in an alarming way in *The Story of G. I. Joe*. Their meaning is a matter of context and is not highly informative: the same whistle might indicate "Hit the dirt!" "Start shooting!" "Clear the road!" or, perhaps, "We just heard something!" which ends up being one of our own jeeps. A grenade trap exploding, if translated into words, means something like "We are perhaps being attacked by an unknown group of unknown people of unknown military ability, from an unknown direction with unknown weapons." The loop in the chord indicates the will to communicate, but never the actual content of the message, which was passed between the spy and the sergeant in written notes hidden in a chess piece.

New soldiers are gradually taught to distinguish the different sounds shells and bombs make (in *All Quiet on the Western Front* and *Sergeant York* [Howard Hawks, 1941]). Yet this distinction makes no difference: some shells just make a lot of noise and are mostly harmless, whereas others are *really* deadly and we have nothing to do against them and often do not hear them at all. The veteran soldiers make it a point to decipher the sounds, although it is of no practical use. In *The Steel Helmet*, the sound of shells even turns out to be one of the soldiers breathing heavily when he sleeps.

Speech might be given up altogether, like the silence imposed upon the soldiers who try not to be discovered at the last rendezvous point in *Objective, Burma!* or the literal obliteration of dialogue by the sound of shelling in *All Quiet on the Western Front*.[33] In *The Story of G. I. Joe*, when one of the men talks to Ernie Pyle, a reporter who "has been around," he asks him about a star in Hollywood, but many of his words are "censored" by the explosions outside: does Pyle know Carol (explosion) who has big (explosion) and are they really (explosion)?

In other cases, speech is used. It might even make perfect sense, linguistically, but still be completely "mad" and irrelevant. Mr. O'Hara, Scarlett's father in *Gone with the Wind*, loses his mind by talking rather sensibly, only as if the war never took place and as if his dead wife were still alive. *A Walk in the Sun* gives us, linguistically, perfectly valid sentences. These, however in no way correspond to the world they are presumably meant to describe, or do so only ironically. The soldiers are frequently occupied with idle chattering about insignificant details of civilian life such as moving pictures or music records. They talk endlessly but somehow seem to say nothing. The film, in Neale's terms, balances "a communicative omniscience of depth with a very circumscribed narrative range."[34] Although we learn through extensive conversation, monologues, and even Sgt. Tyne's internal thoughts "a great deal about what goes on in the minds of the men," they themselves, "as the film insists throughout, know very little."[35] Indeed, over-eagerness to speak might end up being harmful to communication. Attempts to translate or get any useful information from the two Italians the American platoon meets in *A Walk in the Sun* are quite comic since their debriefing is unprofessional and one of them is unstoppably loquacious.

In addition, when the words in *A Walk in the Sun* are somehow correlated to their situation, it is often not by corresponding to the state of things in the world, but by inverting it.[36] Windy, for example, claims to write letters to his sister, which he actually only recites orally, and which he is never seen writing down. In these "letters," he describes the artillery fired at them as the "natives" on shore giving them a reception of "fireworks, music, and that sort of stuff." At the end of the film, he sums up the long and bloody battle in a few sarcastic words: "we just blew a bridge and took a farmhouse. It was so easy, so terribly easy." The men in the platoon frequently repeat the phrase "nobody dies" before carnage breaks out, despite ample evidence to the contrary.[37] Even the connotation of the film's title—a pleasant and pastoral walk in the sun— while technically not false (they do walk in the sun, quite a bit)—is ironic.

It is when language appears impossible or breaks down that it does make sense. The nonverbal utterances of the shell-shocked soldiers appear to be meaningless, a loss of language. Joey in *Stalag 17* is said to be "krank," because he saw nine of his pals splattered over his plane and communicates only by playing the ocarina and occasionally smiling; A soldier in the hospital in *The Big Parade* is apparently (it is a silent film) rambling nonsense; Sgt. Potter in *A Walk in the Sun* cries unstoppably. When Sgt. Warnicki "cracks up" in *The Story of G. I. Joe*, he does not remain speechless, but rather begins to imitate the voices of his wife and son, which were on a phonograph record she sent him, repeatedly and obsessively. He is finally punched out by his friends and taken to the medic, never to be seen again in the film. These are meaningless, sometimes non-linguistic and inarticulate, utterances, which nevertheless make perfect sense in this world. In these examples, the meaningless utterances indicate insanity, which is a means to be sent away from the front—in itself a rather sane objective. This Catch-22 interchangeability of illogical madness and the perfectly sensible attempt to leave the war is rather frankly acknowledged in *A Farewell to Arms*, when Capt. Rinaldi suggests that his friend Lt. Henry return to the front which he deliberately left and they all claim he was shell-shocked and wandered off.

The English language becomes foreign, and foreign languages gain a certain familiarity in this topsy-turvy world of signs, which nevertheless enables communication. Germans typically speak English, sometimes even with an English accent (*The Desert Fox* [Henry Hathaway, 1951], which confusingly also has British characters in it, not only German ones). Some of the Japanese can also speak English, even with a perfect American accent with which they try to convince the troops that they are American (*Objective, Burma!*), as do the Germans in *Battleground* and, in the case of the spy, in *Stalag 17*. Americans might speak English very badly, and be a handful to understand even for other Americans, such as the protagonist of *Sergeant York*. His Tennessee backwoods English includes words like "heerd" which baffle his friends in the army. In the film, a German explains in English to one of the Americans, whose nickname is Pusher, that the Germans have 25 machine guns on the ridge and that he should tell York that attacking them is useless. Pusher replies: "You tell him. You talk better English than I do." He is right.

When languages are foreign they are still uncannily familiar. They somehow make sense and are never pure noise. Much of the German and French in *Hell's Angels* (Howard Hughes, 1930) is not translated, or only partially translated in intertitles, in the film. It is nevertheless not difficult to understand what is taking place and what the characters are communicating to each other. Chaplin's speech in pseudo-German in *The Great Dictator* (Charles Chaplin, 1941) truly requires no translation, particularly not the ludicrously wry and brief understatements given by the translator during his speech. The odd blend of German and English (in addition to occasional Russian and dog barks) in *Stalag 17* includes phrases like "droppen Sie dead" which do not quite belong to any language, and are used by both the Americans and the German sergeant Schulz. In *The Big Parade*, the American Jim is stationed in a French village where he meets Melisande, a typically "foreign" character who gets away with behavior that no American woman on screen would be allowed in Hollywood at the period.[38] He says: "Gee...aimy...vowse...boo...coop"; she answers: "I...am... verree...happee." They fall in love using a phrase book. The impossible, broken communication somehow makes sense in this world of the war machine.

The war film is a suspension of the state and the political, in which the war displays its sovereignty over the state. For Carl Schmitt, the political rests on the ultimate distinction between friend and enemy, with whom the possibility of combat always exists.[39] "War," writes Schmitt, "discloses the possibility which underlies every political idea, namely, the distinction of friend and enemy."[40] The state, as a political entity, has "the right to demand from its own members the readiness to die and unhesitatingly to kill enemies."[41] In this aspect, the Hollywood war film completely disagrees with Schmitt. In fact, it uses a possibility which Schmitt himself seems to introduce into his argument—if the state has the right to demand the death of its own members and of the enemies, might this not lead to a lack of distinction between the two? How do these two forms of deaths differ? Is there not, as Paul Virilio writes, an "antagonistic homogeneity of the death wish" at operation here, a right to die, which establishes "a corporeal identity in the clinch of allies and enemies, victims and executioners"?[42]

Hollywood war films repeatedly challenge the distinction between friend and enemy. The comedies are perhaps the most revealing. In *Duck Soup* (Leo McCary, 1933), Firefly inadvertently, yet keenly, shoots at his own people. He hires Chicolini, a spy for the enemy, as secretary of war, who later changes to the other side, and, when he does return, takes a vacation as Freedonia is facing defeat. The last sequence, in which the Marx brothers feverishly change uniforms belonging to different periods and nationalities, makes any attempt to distinguish friend and foe, loyal follower and spy, nationality at all, absolutely futile. In *The Great Dictator*, the Jewish barber gets lost in the smoke-filled battlefield and finds himself on the wrong side, marching in the wrong direction, with the enemy's men; he would later be mistaken for his people's enemy from within, the great dictator, Hynkel. *Stalag 17*, a story of the zany antics of American airmen sergeants as prisoners of war in a German *Stammlager*, has the German sergeant Schulz constantly claiming to be the Americans' friend (he used to be a wrestler in the United States), and the American POW in charge of security discovered to be a Nazi spy. One of the pranks the Americans pull against the German figures of authority is to pretend to be indoctrinated by a copy of *Mein Kampf* that they were given and to sport false Führer moustaches. Schulz comments that one Führer is enough.

The inability to define the enemy clearly and to differentiate friend and foe is hardly limited to comedies, no matter how bluntly they are willing to express what, from the political-state point of view, is an absurdity. In *The Steel Helmet*, there is no a priori way to distinguish between a North Korean and a South Korean (South Koreans run with you whereas North Koreans run after you, as the veteran grunt, Sgt. Zack explains). In *The Big Parade*, Jim is unable to stab a German soldier to death and ends up giving him a cigarette instead. Likewise, in *All Quiet on the Western Front*, the German soldiers are unable to figure out who profits from the war and why they are fighting against men like them from other countries.[43] One of them, Paul, finds himself in a shell hole with a French soldier whom he stabbed. He regrets what he did, tries to give him water, and is extremely upset when he sees that the soldier—a man like him, he says—is dead. He asks for the dead enemy's forgiveness and goes through his things. The French soldier has a name—Duval—and Paul promises to write and help his wife. In *East of Eden* (1955, Elia Kazan), the opposite transformation is suggested, when the town's people attack Gustav Albrecht, a German immigrant, after a telegram announces that one of the town's boys was killed in the war. The protagonist and his brother defend the "German" and find it extremely strange that someone everybody once loved is suddenly thought of as a hated enemy.

According to Thomas Doherty, in this aspect the Great War and the Good War differ. Depiction of World War II battles, even decades after, never quite "deconstructed" the enemy–friend distinction. Doherty suggests that "as long as historical memory can conjure the Army Signal Corps footage of the Holocaust," there will be no easy moral equivalence and fraternity in regular battle scenes.[44] Nevertheless, even in World War II, some sense of analogy between the sides is still possible in battle. In *The Story of G. I. Joe*, Capt. Walker and Sgt. Warnicki try to find German snipers in the remains of an abandoned Church in Italy. Walker shouts "Lousy kraut swine!" and hears his voice echoed in the wrecks of the cathedral. After a few seconds, a German voice is heard, crying "Lausiges amerikanisches Schwein!" The sounds of the German's call not only echo in the chapel, but also echo the American sentence, sounding similar and having a similar albeit reversed meaning. Ironically, these hateful remarks against the other side do form some type of symmetry and equivalence between them.

Although fraternity with the enemy was not as easy to imagine in World War II, demonizing the other side was carefully limited. In 1942, according to the Hollywood chief of the Office of War Information, hatred of the "militaristic *system* which governs the Axis countries and of those responsible for its furtherance" was to be promoted; however, hatred of the enemy was to be directed neither at the whole German, Japanese, or Italian people, nor merely at a small group of fascist leaders.[45] By 1943, writes Lawrence H. Suid, the War Department advised the Office of War Information to notify the studios to stop producing Japanese atrocity films and this was followed by a certain complexity awarded even to the Nazi villains who became more human. Suid interestingly suggests that this decision was taken when the military situation improved, and Roosevelt realized that Germany and Japan would need to be rehabilitated after the war in order to serve as buffers to Soviet expansion when the coalition with Stalin's regime would come to an end.[46] As Ilan Avisar comments regarding the military experience in 1950s Hollywood films, the most common message was that "war is hell" and that this situation is universal: "horror and suffering are shared by the two sides, while the few brave individuals can also be on either side."[47]

Even if there was a limit to the degree to which the enemy was portrayed as a friend, particularly in the World War II films, the friend could still be portrayed as an enemy. Officers and soldiers in Hollywood battles are required to send themselves and others to die, to act against their own and against themselves. As Steve Neale notes, in anti-war, or ideologically ambivalent films, it is the high-ranking military authority, not, or not only, the enemy, "which is marked as responsible for the suffering and death of the men."[48] In *Fort Apache*, Thursday sends himself and his men off to die in a senseless war he forces upon the Apaches, although he was told by Captain York, who had much more experience in that region, that the Indians are ready to talk peace and that his tactics are suicidal. In *Hell's Angels*, a German Zeppelin commander orders his men to jump out so as to decrease the airship's weight. In *Objective, Burma!*, the identity of the causal agent governing the fate of the American soldiers oscillates between (the American) command and the Japanese. Both seem arbitrary and impersonal; and both seem to endanger the lives of the men. There is thus a lack of distinction between friend and enemy, as "the agents themselves, initially distinct—initially, indeed, at war with one another—now seem to converge."[49] As Capt. Walker says in *The Story of G. I. Joe* when talking about the new replacements who arrive and die, "I know it ain't my fault that they get killed, but it makes me feel like a murderer." In *The Desert Fox*,[50] the German generals gradually come to understand that Hitler, both a political superior and a military inferior (in rank and ability), is driving them to sure and suicidal defeat. They therefore plot against their own Führer. The German Field Marshal von Rundstedt is wrong only in attributing *uniqueness* to this situation when he says:

> From the moment that Bohemian corporal promoted himself to the supreme commander of our forces, the German army has been the victim of a unique situation: not only too many of the enemy, but one too many Germans.

Acting against one's own side and self is not limited to officers sending soldiers off to die. In *Gung Ho!*, after learning that the Japanese are sending planes, the American Raiders paint a US flag on the rooftop of a building and lure the Japanese "monkeys" there. Assuming it has been taken over by the Americans, the Japanese fighter planes attack the building and soldiers around it, that is, their own forces. In an unlikely series of events in *Wings* (William A. Wellman, 1927), David, an American fighter pilot in World War I, crashes his plane behind German lines. He manages to escape, steal a German plane, and shoot at the Germans using their own plane before heading back toward the American forces. He is shot down by his good friend Jack, who mistakenly believes that David is dead and that he is shooting down another "Heine" to avenge his friend's death. In *Hell's Angels*, two English brothers are sent on a suicidal mission by their commanders. They use a German plane to bomb a German weapon depot; their German plane is then attacked by German fighter planes. After they are seized, one of the English brothers shoots the other in the back and kills him to make sure he does not reveal any information to the Germans. In *Gone with the Wind*, Big Sam marches proudly to dig ditches for the confederate soldiers and in effect contributes to prolong and protect his own slavery.[51] Scarlett in the same film is accused of being a scalawag—doing business with the Yankees. She does not seem to mind that her business partners also ruined her world and were or maybe still are her enemies. Earlier in the film, she kills a Yankee soldier, but he, so she speculates with Melanie, must have been a deserter. Did she, then, kill her enemy or her enemy's enemy? Would this make the Yankee soldier who came to attack her a friend? The convergence of friend and enemy can also come from an NCO against one of the enlisted men he is training, as in *Sands of Iwo Jima*, in which Sgt. Stryker hits and injures one of the men, Choynski, with a rifle butt, because he fails to fight with his bayonet correctly. This violence, directed at his own men, is hardly justified since it does not help Choynski improve his fighting skills. Stryker ends up teaching him proper bayonet fighting steps by having Choynski do the Mexican hat dance together with him.

Hollywood's disagreement with Schmitt is much more fundamental. He claims that the political entity, that which distinguishes friend and enemy, if it exists, must be the decisive, sovereign entity, which pushes aside and subordinates all other human endeavors.[52] Yet the world of war as depicted by Hollywood is the exception of the state and in a state of exception. It is the military personnel who decide whether to obey the norm or to ignore it, and it is therefore the military that fits Schmitt's definition of sovereign.[53] Hollywood thus seems to be more in agreement with Deleuze and Guattari's treatise on nomadology and the war machine. Their first axiom is that the war machine is exterior to the state.[54] It "seems to be irreducible to the State apparatus, to be outside its sovereignty and prior to its law: it comes from elsewhere."[55] Moreover, it is directed against the State and its formation. Discipline is required only if and when the State appropriates a war machine, a difficult appropriation, which raises many questions.[56] The war machine itself "answers to other rules" which "animate a fundamental indiscipline of the warrior, a questioning of hierarchy, perpetual blackmail by abandonment or betrayal, and a very volatile sense of honor."[57] The regime of violence of the war machine differs from the regime of the State and lawful violence or policing; and it is first directed against the State apparatus when linked with war.[58]

Sgt. Stryker in *Sands of Iwo Jima* seems to have a troublesome past with army regulations, and it is only thanks to his fellow marines that the military police do not catch him drunk and an officer does not court-martial him for hitting one of his men (they convince the officer he is teaching him judo!). The doughboys in *The Big Parade* are also considerably insubordinate. In one sequence, which takes place in the French village before they are sent to the front, Jim's two friends, Bull and Slim, steal wine from a French family. Jim tries to stop the two thieves he cannot yet identify, but they beat him up and trap him in wine barrels. By the time he gets free, two military policemen are there and he suspects that they were the ones who hit him and stole the wine while they suspect him. Bull and Slim realize they got him in trouble and should also get him out of it, so they call the rest of the unit and begin a fight, in which the real military policemen are knocked out, the wine thieves steal their armbands, and Jim gets away. When an officer arrives, Bull and Slim pose as military policemen and explain that they were not stealing wine, just doing their duty. The warriors, in this case, have suspended regular criminal law. They have also taken over the state's regime of violence, policing, despite their being themselves the criminals. Soldiers are exempt from the regular standards of private (or familial) property and the legal attempts to punish any infringements of this norm.

In *All Quiet on the Western Front*, the young recruits are trained by a sadistic reserve army sergeant named Himmelstoss, who had previously served the state by being their mailman. When he suddenly appears at the front, the soldiers mock him and show no sign of discipline. There is, they say, justice in the army after all. They refuse to salute or respect him, and threats of a court martial that would get them out of battle only appeal to them. Defiantly, Paul tells him to join them in battle that night, and promises they would ask permission to leave if any one of them stops a bullet with his body. In battle, as they charge, Himmelstoss panics, clings to the dirt, and refuses to go on. Paul stands above him and shouts at him to get out. He calls him a coward. Military ranks have been inverted, court martial mocked, and justice takes on a peculiar meaning. It is the soldiers who decide when to obey the law and when to declare a state of exception and ignore it; it is the war machine that has become sovereign against the state.

Hollywood's war films are similar to the war machine as described by Deleuze and Guattari in other aspects as well. Deleuze and Guattari's war machine is the invention of nomads who create a smooth space, which differs from a sedentary, overcoded one.[59] A sedentary space, they write, "is striated, by walls, enclosures, and roads between enclosures,"[60] which "parcel out a closed space to people, assigning each person a share and regulating the communication between shares."[61] It is one of the fundamental tasks of the State to regulate all the flows traversing it, to "striate the space over which it reigns."[62] The war machine is at odds with this form of State space. A smooth space is not divisible by boundaries; its essential features include variability and polyvocality of directions.[63] It is characterized not by the extensive movement of departing and arriving, but by intensive speed and patient immobility.[64]

In Hollywood the soldiers do not seem to know for certain where they are.[65] In *Gung Ho!*, the American Raiders train on a base in Honolulu, and only when on the submarines taking them to their real destination are given maps of the island they are meant to attack. However, they are only later told which island it is or where it is located. Moreover, it turns out that the base in which they trained was already modeled on the real island, so in a way they were already there. The men in *Battleground* wonder whether they are in Luxemburg or Belgium. It seems that while the German enemy and newspapers back home have precise and detailed information about the battle they are involved in and their location, the soldiers on the ground have no idea what is going on and where they have been taken.

Trying to figure out one's location is no easy task. Hollywood does not help since it has particularly been loyal to recurrent settings that make each war, or at least theater, seem identical—a combat zone created on a soundstage or "location" shooting in California. For World War I, for example, Sorlin points out three clichés: the wide trenches where soldiers lead a subterranean life; the barbed wire in which the night patrol is caught; the disfigured landscape with "broken trunks, ruins, shell-holes and craters filled with water."[66] No matter where the plot is located and to which side the soldiers might belong, they always seem to act in the same type of place.

If the soldiers are lucky enough to figure out where they are, that knowledge is only temporary. The landscape of modern war is constantly in motion and changing; as Paul Virilio writes, it has become "cinematic": the terrain is turned upside down by high explosives, landmarks vanish, and maps lose all accuracy.[67] "You know, when this war is over, I'm gonna buy me a map and find out where I've been," says one of the men in *The Story of G. I. Joe*, postponing spatial orientation to less warlike days when maps might again be useful.

Soldiers are constantly in motion; they cross borders between countries and do not always know what the difference is. It is in no way relevant to their functioning within the war machine to know to which state the ground they are passing through is supposed to belong. A dialogue in *The Story of G. I. Joe* emphasizes the undifferentiated space they traverse, where one place is as good as the next:

> Murphy: Hey Dondaro, what town did we take today?
> Dondaro: San Raviollio.
> Murphy: Didn't we take that yesterday?
> Dondaro: No, that was San Something-else-io.

Not only are they unable to *see* for themselves where they are, they are often not even *told* where they are going: a map with no names on it in *Objective, Burma!*, boarding a ship and not knowing where it is heading in *Sands of Iwo Jima*. The men in *Thirty Seconds over Tokyo* volunteer for a mission that is kept a secret from them and board an aircraft carrier whose destination they do not know. Even on board, they are lost in the bowels of the ship; one of them wakes up and is not certain whether the ship has already set sail; and when they finally reach the deck, they are surrounded by fog. The American patrol in *The Steel Helmet* is first seen in the film lost, walking in circles and spends a large portion of the film walking in the fog. In this sense, the oft-ridiculed ending of John Wayne's attempt to make a Vietnam film as if it were a World War II war film in *The Green Berets* (1968) might be better understood. The film, famously, ends with the sun setting in the South China Sea, that is, in the East.[68] It is certainly possible that Wayne and all those on the set were incapable of figuring out where the sun would set; but it is also possible that it never occurred to them that anyone would care, that the difference between East and West could in any way be relevant in a war film.

To be sure, there is movement. Soldiers are constantly shipped off, crammed and sent in boats, ships, submarines, planes, trucks, and trains. They walk, dig, march, and crawl; on sand, in mud, through forests, down foxholes, and in rivers. But they do not clearly move from and to places. The soldiers in war films frequently go nowhere, attack, and flee in a counter-attack, and then go back in a counter–counter-attack, as in the endless to-and-fro of the war in the trenches in *All Quiet on the Western Front*, which at best ends in the same place it started.[69] In *The Big Parade*, the men are brainwashed to enlist by a big recruiting parade at home, remain, endlessly, in a village in France doing nothing. They are then suddenly and swiftly mobilized in a big parade to the front and later brought back, in another big parade—this time of ambulances—away from the front.[70] After three days and nights of fighting, the leatherneck squad in *Sands of Iwo Jima* finds itself back at the foot of Mount Suribachi, exactly where it started. The platoon in *Objective, Burma!* is told to head north, in the opposite direction of their base, in order to return to the base! The secret logic of the plan is indeed kept a secret from them and the viewers. In *Duck Soup*, whenever Firefly needs to travel somewhere, he dashes to a motorcycle, gets in the sidecar, and tells the driver to hurry. The driver does speed off, but leaves the sidecar standing there, immobile. Finally, Firefly learns the trick, gets on the motorcycle itself, only to see the sidecar drive off and again leave him behind. The Hollywood war machine speeds and remains immobile, goes nowhere in a non-striated terrain that belongs to no one and remains unmarked except by recurring clichés.

Even the stylistic choices made by Hollywood underline the break with conventional meanings. In *A Farewell to Arms*, Hollywood linear narrative and narrative editing are almost abandoned in a battle sequence that follows (more or less) Frederick as he witnesses the horrors of war after he deserts the front. This scene was deliberately designed to obscure the original book's condemnation of the Italian army so the film would not be banned in that market. Instead of Hemingway's detailed description the film offers a "surrealistic montage" which was endorsed by the Italian consul as well as the prominent Italian American who was the president of the Bank of America.[71] Icons of war and suffering, abstracted from any concrete context, are combined and superimposed in powerful compositions and machine-gun rate editing. One image shows the shadows of marching soldiers next to an icon of a crucified injured soldier standing in a frame whose lintel and jambs are so tilted they look like they could easily have been borrowed from the set of a German expressionist film. Similarly, near the end of *Battleground*, after supplies are parachuted to the besieged troops, the ultimate confrontation with the Germans is shown as a quick and confusing montage sequence. War, the films seem to be telling us, needs a Sergei Eisenstein, a Robert Wiene, at the very least a Busby Berkeley or a Slavko Vorkapitch, to display its madness. It has nothing to do with linear narratives or causality and has its own logic.

Death can be meaningful in the war film, by being part of the way in which the war machine functions. This functioning, however, is possible in the world of war, which in itself does not enable many of the meanings that are sometimes attributed to war. There is no ultimate goal, no final conclusion in sight. There is no clear direction, or destination, or even simple spatial divisions, like borders. The war machine does not serve the state, but rather suspends it. Meaningful language and signs are useless, and sometimes communication seems possible only through nonsense or a foreign language. Even the usual style of depicting narrative in a classical Hollywood film can be abandoned. The war film creates a world in which the war machine's power cannot be easily harnessed to serve the state or any other meaning. Death is meaningful by being a part of the war machine, but the films also offer us ways to question whether war itself can be justified, whether it can serve any other end but the perpetuation of war.

7
Conclusions: The Ends of Classical Death

Throughout this book we have elaborated and challenged ways of rendering death meaningful in classical Hollywood films. Each chapter has been devoted to a certain way in which death can be meaningful within Hollywood's personal causal linear storyline, isolating specific cases and aspects of death from numerous classical Hollywood films spanning three decades and four genres. The historical contexts of the films have not been pursued as topics in themselves, and have been used selectively, only when they contributed to the creation of ways in which death can be rendered meaningful. In many cases, the sources used were clearly anachronistic.

The ways of thinking the meaningfulness of death, however, can be used within more historically oriented research. This concluding chapter demonstrates how the ideas elaborated in previous chapters can be used to analyze historical changes within classical Hollywood, to show the complexity of an individual film made at a certain historical junction, and to discuss specific historical challenges confronting filmmakers within classical Hollywood, or within the classical tradition in later decades, after the demise of the classical studio system. It deals with Hollywood's reluctance to depict the Holocaust, particularly in the 1940s and 1950s; with the vicissitudes of deaths in the gangster or crime film in the 1930s and after; and with death in films made at the turn of the millennium. All of these historical junctions offer difficult challenges to the classical Hollywood tradition of death, pushing it to the limit, and, at times, driving it to dead ends and incoherence or into a qualitatively different way of being meaningful. This chapter deals with "conclusions" not in the sense of a summary and result of the preceding chapters, but by looking at some of the limits of the meaningfulness of classical Hollywood death, the places where it concludes, comes to an end. It uses the concepts elaborated throughout the book and films to think up to the boundaries of classical death and perhaps beyond them.

Billy Wilder and Hollywood's "Auschwitz"

The Hollywood Silence

The Holocaust of the Jews in Europe and especially the Final Solution, the mass murders designated by the synecdoche "Auschwitz," is frequently taken as the paradigm of the unimaginable, of that which could not be represented and testified to.[1] The "insistence on the impossibility of adequately comprehending and describing the Final Solution," as Anton Kaes claims in his contribution to the aptly named collection edited by Saul Friedlander, *Probing the Limits of Representation*, has "become a *topos* of Holocaust research."[2] As Jean-François Lyotard explains, for Holocaust deniers, the only acceptable eyewitness for the existence of the gas chambers "would be a victim of the gas chamber."[3] That is, only someone who has seen the gas chamber with their own eyes and died from it. But this witness cannot exist for "if one is dead, one cannot testify that it is on account of the gas chamber."[4] More generally, as Miriam Hansen writes, critically summarizing the viewpoint whose most radical proponent is Claude Lanzmann, it has been argued that the Shoah is "an event that defies depiction, whose horror renders any attempt at direct representation obscene."[5]

According to some historians, however, and long before Lanzmann voiced His prohibition on committing such blasphemy, the classical Hollywood studio system was already refusing to handle the persecution of Jews in Europe in its theatrical films. Unlike American newsreels and newspapers (including photographic evidence), contemporary European cinema, and television, major narrative Hollywood theatrical films left the Holocaust unrepresented.[6] As Ilan Avisar notes after discussing European postwar films that were made about the Holocaust and Hollywood's films about anti-Semitism, "not until 1959, in filming *The Diary of Anne Frank* [George Stevens], did Hollywood address itself directly to the Nazis' genocidal treatment of the Jews in Europe."[7] Even then, and as late as the end of the 1970s, Annette Insdorf could still write that only a handful of postwar American films brought the Holocaust to the fore.[8]

Why this ongoing difficulty and what happened in the late 1950s? One possibility is that as they approached the 1960s, Hollywood filmmakers introduced modernist cinematic techniques and felt free to break the constraints of classical Hollywood death conventions, which finally enabled them to deal with the Holocaust. This certainly does not explain the cinematically conventional *Diary of Anne Frank*.[9] Another is that it took some time to come to terms with the Holocaust, or perhaps a necessary "belatedness," which is part of the structure of trauma. This, however, does not explain why television, European cinema, or newsreels could deal with the topic.

I would like to offer a different account. Omer Bartov argues that the "murder machine" that swallowed up the vast majority of victims in the Holocaust in a unique and unprecedented way is unrepresentable "as far as Hollywood conventions are concerned."[10] I would like to follow Bartov's claim, only focusing specifically on ways in which the Final Solution cannot be represented within the conventions of *meaningful death* in classical Hollywood. Furthermore, I will suggest two ways that Hollywood did find to deal with the Holocaust: by discussing its very inability to depict the Final Solution and by changing history instead of its own conventions.[11] True to my method throughout the book, this thinking will be conducted using films; in this case, the five films that Billy Wilder made immediately after the war.

Given our discussion in previous chapters, we are now in a position to see how the particular ways which we discovered to render death meaningful as part of the classical Hollywood storyline are incompatible with "Auschwitz."

In relation to the past, death can be meaningful by destroying evil individuals who could not be stopped otherwise. For "Auschwitz" to be meaningful in such a way would require that the Jews, or rather, each and every Jew who dies, pass the Hollywood killability tests, that he or she be irremediably evil in their bodily existence. Depicting all of the Jews who were murdered in this way would take Hollywood's born-bad villains deep into the realm of eugenics and racism, in effect supporting the Final Solution. Another option that we have looked at is death as revelation of truth. If "Auschwitz" were to be understood as similar to a Western showdown, which reveals who the superior shootist is, we would have to conclude that the Jews were inferior, as the defeated side is in a shootout. This too would entail an unbearable agreement with Nazi propaganda. It is therefore not an option Hollywood would have embraced.

In relation to the future, death can be meaningful by becoming an issue for the living who have remained behind; it needs a collective, a "cult," that will go on living and remember, that will be able to sublate the deaths. If the Nazis had been successful in eradicating the Jewish people and destroying any evidence of the deed there literally would have been no community to remember.[12] More generally, presenting the Final Solution as a death which is meaningful in relation to the future requires the integration of the Holocaust within history, denying the rupture of "Auschwitz," making it possible for it to be *aufgehoben* into something like the Hegelian progress of historical actuality which is adequate to reason. This is believed to be impossible by some thinkers like Lyotard.[13] As Edith Wyschogrod comments, the world of the camps and world wars "seems to have established once and for all the radical incommensurability of reason and history."[14]

An additional option to make death meaningful would be that of the war film, in which death takes place within the perpetual present of the "mad" world of combat. I will return to this later on, as part of how Hollywood paved the way to dealing, to some extent at least, with the Holocaust. In itself, however, it demands that the Holocaust and "Auschwitz" be depicted as one more occurrence during the war, perhaps even a minor one, since no major battles were involved. This would be unacceptable to many.

It seems then that the ways we have found to make death meaningful within the classical Hollywood repertoire are not reconcilable with "Auschwitz," at least if understood as a unique rupture with history. I have not claimed (and would not know how to prove) that my account is exhaustive and complete and that there were no other ways of making death meaningful within this establishment; Hollywood's output tends to be much more diverse than some theories claim. However, insofar as Hollywood invariably relies on linear causal narrative storylines and "Auschwitz" is thought of as another planet, a radical historical rupture, a break with history as adequate to reason, there is a fundamental incommensurability between Hollywood and the Holocaust. One cannot sublate the Final Solution and go on with the linear chain of events. If not representation as such or the "universe of the cinema" in general, at least Hollywood's linear storyline cannot be reconciled with the "concentrationary universe," the "universe of the Lager,"[15] if understood as such a rupture.

Nevertheless, people in Hollywood—many of whom were European and Jewish émigrés—certainly knew about the Holocaust and "Auschwitz," and they were making films about the war, Nazism, and anti-Semitism, even if not directly about the Holocaust and certainly not about the Final Solution. Moreover, since the late 1950s Hollywood has attempted to deal with the depiction of the persecution of Jews by the Nazis in Europe. What, then, happened during a decade and a half of silence and what suddenly changed?

I would like to elaborate two of the ways in which Hollywood did attempt to deal with the Holocaust. One option is not by adequately depicting the Holocaust, but rather by showing what it would take and why it was not desirable. These are films whose characters suffer from an unhappy proximity to the world of the dead. They can be seen as warnings against the dangers of coming too close to "Auschwitz." The second option is to subsume the Holocaust under the Hollywood tradition; select stories that can be compatible with the way American cinema tells its stories. This is a strategy that has been popular in Hollywood and exists to this day, although some would say it distorts history.

I will be focusing on several films that Billy Wilder directed and co-wrote immediately following the war in order to suggest the two ways of dealing with the Holocaust: *The Emperor Waltz* (1948), *A Foreign Affair* (1948), *Sunset Blvd.* (1950), *Ace in the Hole* (a.k.a. *The Big Carnival*, 1951), and *Stalag 17* (1953).

Wilder's films can certainly be read as reflecting the historical situation, or his own personal one, as a Jew who was forced to leave Germany and whose family was killed in the Holocaust. Many of the films, indeed much of Wilder's work if not film noir in general, offer an extremely bleak view on humanity. They include characters who are forced to flee and travel, who are confined and trapped, and who are fascinated by death, of others and themselves. *The Emperor Waltz* climaxes in a rather chilling sequence in which puppies are almost killed because they are not "pure enough" and it features a doctor with a heavy German accent explaining that "orders have been given."[16] *Stalag 17* can be read as exploring the scapegoating which occurred during the Holocaust.[17] Wilder himself made various statements that connected his films with the Holocaust. My aim, however, is not to suggest that Wilder is an auteur whose films reflect his life and unconscious torment, nor that films reflect the historical moment. Perhaps they do, but I would like to use them as *part* of a discussion of two of the ways in which Hollywood managed to deal with the Holocaust, to think about two of the possible ways in which Hollywood and "Auschwitz" can come closer together, without claiming that this was, consciously or not, somehow Wilder's own intention.

I would like to suggest that these five films by Wilder could be divided into two groups. One group of films can be used to elaborate ways of dealing with an impossibility of representation related to the testimony of the dead and the struggle, in vain, to relay this testimony. The second group of films can be used to imagine a world in which "Auschwitz" could become a "beautiful death" which can serve as an intermediary death that is meaningful in relation to the future in the Hollywood tradition. I will be looking more closely at one film from each group.

Testimony of the Dead

The first group of films deals with the danger and perhaps ultimate impossibility of getting too close to "Auschwitz." Lyotard as noted earlier claimed that for Holocaust deniers the only acceptable eyewitnesses for the existence of the gas chambers would be those who have seen the gas chamber with their own eyes and died from it. Being dead, of course, such eyewitnesses do not exist, or at least cannot give testimony. More generally, Primo Levi claimed that he and other survivors are "not the true witnesses."[18] The "submerged," the "complete witnesses," those who "saw the Gorgon," could not speak both because they were "snuffed out" and because their death had already begun weeks and months before, when they "already lost the ability to observe, to remember, compare and express themselves." "When the destruction was terminated," he writes, "the work accomplished was not told by anyone, just as no one ever returned to recount his own death." The survivors, those who are the exception, those who did not touch bottom, "speak in their stead, by proxy."[19]

While according to some historians, Hollywood remained silent about the Holocaust for a decade and a half, what cannot be denied is the presence of such an attempt to let the dead speak, directly or by proxy, in its films. Many of the films made during or after the war, which were retrospectively dubbed as "film noir," offer voiceovers by loquacious corpses or dying narrators. They literally give us the testimony of the dead.[20] *Laura* (Otto Preminger, 1944) is memorable for its opening sentence, "I shall never forget the weekend Laura died," a sentence, which as Jacques Rancière notes, "turns out to be spoken by a dead man about a living being."[21] Wilder's *Double Indemnity* (1944) is told in flashback, narrated into a Dictaphone by its dying protagonist, Walter Neff. Most of *The Postman Always Rings Twice* (Tay Garnett, 1946) is narrated in voiceover by Frank Chambers, as a last confession before he is executed. And *D.O.A.* (Rudolph Maté, 1950) follows Frank Bigelow, who has already been murdered, and who is now trying to discover by whom and why. None of these, of course, are directly about the Holocaust; I will not be arguing that they are indirectly or "symptomatically" or in some "deeper" sense really about it. They can, however, be useful in elaborating a way of thinking about the testimony of the dead, a precondition of one of the ways of dealing with the Holocaust.

Let us look more closely at Wilder's 1951 *Ace in the Hole*. The film is the story of Chuck Tatum, a tough cynical journalist who got in trouble in every big newspaper in the country and now finds himself stuck in Albuquerque, New Mexico working for a local paper and waiting for the big story that would get him back to New York City. He discovers Leo Minosa, a World War II veteran, who is caved in inside a holy Indian mountain he was raiding. The story of the trapped man is a spectacular journalistic success, and Tatum makes sure the rescue is unnecessarily prolonged so that it takes a week instead of 12 hours. Leo ends up dying of pneumonia before he could be taken out, and Tatum is stabbed in the belly by Leo's unloving wife after he attempts to strangle her. He bleeds without seeking medical care and dies.

The film does not directly have anything to do with the Holocaust. What it does, however, offer is an attempt to depict an impossibility to depict, to show a failure at reporting that has something to do with death. The death in the film is not "Auschwitz" and it is moreover a death that the film itself can show to its viewers and that therefore can obviously be represented (although American viewers largely chose to stay away from this film). But the characters within the film find that they are unable to report the experience of the dead (or near-dead) to other characters, and it is this inability in the world of the film which I find relevant. Tatum, the journalist, either reports falsely and incompletely what he knows, or, worse, changes the facts so that he could then report them—a strategy, which as we will see, was in fact repeated by Hollywood.

But is it at all possible to report the experience of the dead and dying and if so at what price? The first sign that the trapped Leo might not make it out alive and well is the loss of mental health. He tells Tatum that the constant and monotonous pounding of the giant drill that is meant to dig him out from the top of the mountain is "enough to wake up the dead." When Leo realizes that he is sick and about to die and even requests a priest, he claims that "they" will never let him go, probably refereeing to the Indians whose sacred mountain he was raiding. "They are getting even with me for robbing their tomb," he tells the journalist who is profiting from his death, just as Leo was profiting from the dead Indians. By dying, he feels that he now belongs to the dead—they will not let him go. Tatum, however, is still alive and well, and unable to understand the testimony of the near-dead Leo. He promises to Leo that they will get him out in time. On his next visit, in fact, he is unwilling to hear Leo's delirious testimony, urging him to put on his oxygen mask, telling him that he is "talking too much" and should rather "breathe that oxygen! Breathe!" The living cannot understand the dead and near-dead; they are unable or unwilling to hear their insane ramblings.

Tatum, probably out of guilt, gives Leo's wife the fur Leo bought her for their anniversary day. She thinks it is ugly and refuses to wear it and Tatum begins to strangle her with the fur. "Don't, Chuck, don't, I can't breathe," she says. "He can't breathe either," Tatum answers. He is thus creating a chance for the living (Leo's wife) to understand the near-dead (Leo), feel what it is like not to be able to breathe. Mrs. Minosa helps Tatum join this group also by stabbing him with scissors. She will not join the dead, but Tatum will. He too has now become near-dead—instead of seeking medical treatment he just slowly bleeds.

Tatum brings a priest to Leo, who dies, staring directly at the camera. Tatum now wants to tell the truth and confess his part in the death (or murder, he insists) of Leo. Now that he too is near-dead, he can tell the story. But it turns out to be impossible; the system is unable to accept it. He is fired from his New York City newspaper, and the editor, Nagel, refuses to listen to him and hangs up. He then goes to the local Albuquerque newspaper, but dies—falling down and looking straight into the low-angle camera—before he manages to report anything. The film thus maintains a strict separation between the living and those who are not—the dead, the dying, and the near-dead. The dead Indians are joined by those who are about to die, first Leo, and later Tatum, while the living are unwilling or unable to hear their story. The testimony of the dead, the only acceptable testimony for the existence of the gas chambers according to Lyotard, the "drowned" in whose stead Primo Levi feels the survivors should bear witness by proxy, remains impossible in this film. Death is related to a truth, but this truth must remain hidden; it is intransmissible to the living. It cannot be told, it is not revealed shortly before or after the characters' demise.

In a similar way, *Sunset Blvd.* (1950) famously includes a voiceover flashback by the corpse of a writer, truly the impossible testimony of the dead. It refers to the limitations of the medium in what is perhaps its most memorable line—Norma Desmond's "I am big, it's the pictures that got small"—a perhaps overdramatic way of saying that some things can no longer be contained by the Hollywood system. Or, rather, that a screenwriter/gigolo who did try to get too close to the "big" Norma ended up as dead as her career and sanity. In an interview in Volker Schlöndorff's and Gisela Grischow's 1992 television series *Billy, How Did You Do It?*, Wilder tells Schlöndorff apropos of his *A Foreign Affair* (1948), "in a feature film you cannot show concentration camps."[22] What is interesting is the way his other films explored a precondition of one option of doing so, the testimony of the dead. They show that practically nobody wants to listen to the dead, and that the few who do might end up dead themselves.[23]

Making Death Beautiful

The second group of films prepares the way to bringing the Holocaust to Hollywood by transforming the former. Wilder's *Stalag 17* (1953) takes place in the topsy-turvy world of war according to Hollywood, which we have already discussed in Chapter 6. I would now like to suggest that it also attempts to imagine a world where the Holocaust could become a part of a Hollywood narrative. Like Wilder's other feature films, there is no direct attempt to "show concentration camps," and certainly not death camps, not "Auschwitz." It is rather the story of a prison camp for airmen sergeants. Yet, according to Wilder in the interview with Schlöndorff, when he received a letter from a studio official telling him they would like to distribute *Stalag 17* in Germany, but change the identity of the spy posing as an American from German to Polish, he was outraged. "I couldn't believe what I read," he tells Schlöndorff, "and this from a man whose mother and stepfather had not been in Auschwitz" (Wilder is alluding to the murder of his own mother and her husband by the Nazis).[24] Wilder then states he severed his ties with the studio because they did not apologize. The conflation of Nazi camps—concentration, death, or prisoner of war (POW)— is not rare in our culture, and *Stalag 17* could certainly be read as somehow related to Auschwitz even without Wilder explicitly making the connection. But if the POW camp was, for him, an ersatz Auschwitz, why was he unwilling to show a Polish collaborator working with and for the Nazis?

Wilder's odd reaction might suggest an interesting way of thinking about his film. *Stalag 17* could be read as an attempt to begin to imagine the conditions for making a Hollywood film about "Auschwitz," specifically making these deaths meaningful in relation to the future. As already noted, this is not possible as long as the Holocaust is understood as a rupture in history that cannot undergo a Hegelian sublation, cannot be superseded, for us, by the next stage in Spirit's progress; it cannot be integrated into history or a logical, causal story. This would be possible if the Holocaust were to become a "beautiful death."

As Lyotard writes, through a "beautiful death," one's name can enter into the collective name, form the bond of a "we," by making one's death a choice to prefer to die, a "reason to die": "*Die rather than escape* (Socrates in prison), *Die rather than be enslaved* (the Paris Commune), *Die rather than be defeated* (Thermopyles, Stalingrad)."[25] It is a "we," public authority (family, state, military, partisan, and denominational), which orders its *own* addressees to die, an identification of the one who dies with the legislator who orders the death, or at least the choice to prefer to die. According to Lyotard, "Auschwitz" is "the forbiddance of the beautiful death."[26] No alternative is permitted to the deportee and there is no "we," no possibility of a substitution of "I" for "you" in the decree to die—"[t]hat which orders death is excepted from the obligation, and that which undergoes the obligation is excepted from the legitimation."[27] The authority of the SS, he writes, "comes out of a we from which the deportee is excepted once and for all: the race."[28] The deportee does not have the right to live. Sacrifice is therefore not possible to the deportee so that there is no "accession to an immortal, collective name."[29] The addressee of the SS norm—that the deportee die—is the SS. As for the deportee, s/he knows nothing of the addressor of the proscription that s/he die. There is no third party, witness, who could form a "we," an instance which could sublate the Nazi side and the deportee's side. "Auschwitz" cannot be *aufgehoben*. It is "the coexistence of two secrets, the Nazi's secret and the deportee's secret."[30]

No "we" is possible which would totalize all the elements in play under the name of "Auschwitz," at most a "we" might exist— like Lyotard and his readers—which is "the reflective movement of this impossibility," that "designates the impossibility of such a totalization."[31] I have already suggested that some postwar films, like *Ace in the Hole* and *Sunset Blvd.*, might help us to form the reflective movement of this impossibility. But what Lyotard now adds is what it would require for "Auschwitz" to be imagined as sublatable, to be a death which could be meaningful in relation to the future: a common "we" of the Nazis and deportees, a substitution which disregards race, Aryans which could be conflated with non-Aryans. This never happened, according to Lyotard. But can history be reimagined so that the radical rift between the SS and the deportee no longer exist?

This is the idea to which the second group of Wilder's films points. He does not offer a merry vision of Auschwitz, certainly not directly involving the Jews or deportees as such. He never reintegrates Auschwitz back into regular history.[32] Nevertheless, he does insist, repeatedly, on creating and depicting situations in which Germans (or Austrians in *The Emperor Waltz*) can have a "we" with their others and their enemies, namely Americans; an intermediary stage on the way to imagining Germans who could form a "we" with the deportee. *Stalag 17* tells the story of the zany antics of American airmen sergeants as POWs in a German *Stammlager*. It has many of the characteristics of the topsy-turvy world of war according to Hollywood, which we described in Chapter 6.[33] As we already discussed there, linguistically, the film features a German who speaks in a perfect American accent, and Americans and Germans who use mixed phrases like "droppen Sie dead." It is difficult clearly to differentiate friend and foe in this world. The German sergeant Schulz insists that he is the Americans' friend (he used to be a wrestler in the United States) and "Security," the American POW who screens all the other Americans, turns out to be a Nazi spy. In the film, the Germans, as Volker Schlöndorff mentions, are not shown as villains but portrayed as idiots. One of the pranks the Americans pull against the German figures of authority is to pretend to be indoctrinated by a copy of *Mein Kampf* that they were given and to sport false Führer moustaches.

This attempt to create a "we" involving Germans and non-Germans can also be discerned in *A Foreign Affair*, in which American servicemen intimately fraternize with the German population after the war, including an American officer who becomes a patron for a woman who was intimate with top Nazis and was kissed on the hand by Hitler. In one case, a German woman is seen walking with US flags mounted on her perambulator, implying that the father of her child is American. An American congresswoman is mistaken for a German "Fräulein," and offered a "wunderbar" candy-bar in return for spending time with two American soldiers. While *The Emperor Waltz* deals with Austrians before World War I, and certainly before the Anschluss, it too goes out of its way to suggest that Americans and a German-speaking people could be brought together, indeed marry, and that an American salesman could be mistaken even by the Countess von Stolzenberg-Stolzenberg for an indigenous yodeling Tyrolean.

Wilder has not undone "Auschwitz." The films do not specifically deal with Jewish deportees and the SS, and they do not take place in a concentration or death camp. The films do not tell us which, if any, of the American characters are Jewish. They do however attempt to show the Germans, or German-speaking peoples, and at times Nazis, are not an isolated race, one which would except the Jewish deportee and enable no "we" between the Germans and their victims. They offer a vantage point from which we could at least imagine a future in which "Auschwitz" could be *aufgehoben*. This could explain why Wilder was, at least in his description, so flabbergasted by the suggestion that the spy posing as an American in *Stalag 17* would not be a German. One of the film's functions, at least in retrospect, was to create a Nazi camp where the Germans (not the Poles or anyone else) and the prisoners do have a common "we."

I do not know whether Wilder did, consciously or not, really attempt to begin to create a vantage point from which "Auschwitz" could be sub-lated, in which a common "we" did exist, from which the Holocaust becomes deaths that are meaningful in relation to the future, can be depicted within classical Hollywood's tradition of death. But it can be used by us to think about such an option. The frequent reference to the Nazis within war films meant that many other films in Hollywood cre-ated this universe, in which communication, if not conflation, between them and their victims was thinkable.

Thomas Elsaesser notes "the cruel irony that obliged German Jewish actors"—note that the camp's commander in *Stalag 17* is portrayed by Otto Preminger—"to make their living in Hollywood by playing—and even becoming in the public mind identified with—the Nazi villains from whom they had to flee."[34] Ilan Avisar writes of the "new attitudes toward the German people" in the 1950s, particularly Hollywood's view of the war as universal predicament, in which "the Germans appeared as the defeated underdogs, deserving of equal compassion as the Nazi victims were in the wartime movies."[35] Elsaesser and Avisar discuss the causes and contingencies which enabled these depictions; regardless of these, their effect was to offer representations in which Hollywood reimagined the world of Nazism without the rupture of the Holocaust, as the mad world of war where friend and foe are indistinguishable and where the Nazis are also Jewish. It is by establishing this universe that Hollywood found one of the ways in which it could finally allow itself to approach the Holocaust. "Auschwitz" could now be integrated into history. It too had a "beautiful death," which according to Lyotard was forbidden. It too can now be sublated, have a meaning for a "cult" in relation to the future. If Hollywood finally depicted the Holocaust in the late 1950s, it was after a decade and a half in which it prepared the ground for creating a "we" between the Germans and their victims which would allow to depict the Holocaust, and eventually "Auschwitz," as the "beautiful death" which is within the boundaries of Hollywood's classical death conventions.

Hollywood's depiction of Nazism and the Holocaust frequently allows some form of communication between Germans and their victims (if not a close friendship or even romantic relationship), the demand for justice and the possibility of a trial, the choice to rebel, to defy, or to sacrifice oneself and become a martyr, in other words, the option of a "beautiful death." These have remained present in many Hollywood theatrical feature films to this day, whether the film focuses on the plight of the Jews or not.

The camps might be encountered within the "mad" world of war, such as at the end of *The Big Red One* (Samuel Fuller, 1980). In the aftermath of the war, it is nearly impossible to tell whether a child is German or Jewish and to which nation a refugee child belongs, as in *The Search* (Fred Zinnemann, 1948).

A "good German," if not a "good Nazi," might be the central character, as in *Schindler's List* (Steven Spielberg, 1993), emphasizing that some bridges could be built between the Jews and their perpetrators. If footage from the liberation of the camps is shown in the film, it might be within a trial, the very existence of which reveals a vantage point that can sublate both Jews and Nazis, and can even allow the Germans to underline their similarity to other nations, such as the Americans, as in the defense in *Judgment at Nuremberg* (Stanley Kramer, 1961). In addition, the proceedings in the film take place in the ruins of a postwar Germany, so the suffering of the victims of the Germans that are shown in the film might pale in comparison to the present suffering of the German people. The dilapidated rubble that once was a German city is visually overwhelming in films like *Judgment at Nuremberg*. It could overshadow the brief documentary footage and verbal testimony of the Holocaust. Similarly, the postwar ruins of Germany in *The Search* could certainly surpass the impact of the flashbacks from the camps in this film.

The footage from the camps also famously appears in *The Stranger* (Orson Welles, 1946). Significantly, it is a film in which the Nazi is also mostly a composed professor in a small American town, teaching history to the sons of America's elite, clearly indicating that some confusion is possible. Indeed, according to *The Boys from Brazil* (Franklin J. Schaffner, 1978), the United States offers a milieu in which a Hitler redux might grow up. When the film is set at another time and another place, it could underline how the Holocaust was not a complete break with all known experience, that even American urban decay might arouse Holocaust memories, as in *The Pawnbroker* (Sidney Lumet, 1964),[36] as could a policeman or an immigrants' camp in the new state of Israel in *The Juggler* (Edward Dmytryk, 1953). Some films offer characters who are literally interchangeably Jewish and Nazis, such as the protagonist of *The Man in the Glass Booth* (Arthur Hiller, 1975), who is probably a rich Jewish industrialist, impersonating a Nazi war criminal, impersonating the Jewish industrialist he really is—information that is only revealed at the end of the film.[37]

Avenues of resistance, even if through martyrdom, might be open for Jews who can choose to commit suicide or laugh in the face of their executioners, as in *Jakob the Liar* (Peter Kassovitz, 1999). The television mini-series *Holocaust* (first aired on NBC, 16–19 April 1978) offers a whole plethora of options: beginning with a marriage between Karl Weiss, a Jewish German man, and Inga Helms, a Christian German woman; and ending with the prospect of trials for the SS murderers and a new start for those who survived, including Inga and the son she had with Karl. All of the members of the family Weiss defy the Nazis, many paying for it with their lives: the grandparents choose to commit suicide in Berlin rather than be tormented by the Nazis; the uncle is a leader of the Warsaw Ghetto rebellion; one of the sons, Rudi, becomes a partisan, fights the Germans, escapes from Sobibor, lives through the war, and might join the Zionists; the daughter dies after she is attacked when she defiantly chooses to go outside in a hostile Berlin; the parents are deported and killed at Auschwitz after setting up a counterfeit hospital at the Warsaw Ghetto in order to save Jews from the transport to Treblinka. Karl is tortured after being caught painting the horrors of the Holocaust at Theresienstadt and dies in Auschwitz, sketching right up to the end. His work is preserved by Inga who was told by Karl to show it to their son when he is old enough to understand. His is a "beautiful death" in Auschwitz.[38] Even *The Grey Zone* (Tim Blake Nelson, 2001), while unflinchingly showing the day-to-day horrors of the gas chambers and crematoria at Auschwitz–Birkenau,[39] also chooses to focus on the exception, on the uprising by the twelfth Sonderkommando. It shows how bribing, commerce, speaking out, and threats by the Jews were possible; that one could defiantly kill oneself when tortured to reveal the truth; and that the camp prisoners could fight back, destroy parts of the death machine, shoot and kill SS men, and make their inevitable death meaningful. It is this very violation of the rupture of the Holocaust, "Auschwitz" as understood by Lyotard, that made it an event that Hollywood could depict.

The Vicissitudes of the Killability Test

While the Final Solution is often believed to be unrepresentable, especially within the conventions of Hollywood, the rise of Nazism in Europe during the 1930s incurred additional difficulties for classical Hollywood. As discussed in Chapter 3, death can be meaningful in relation to the past by destroying someone who could not be stopped in any other way. Even when given another chance and facing death, these evildoers will not alter their ways. Villains undergo killability tests throughout the film in order to clearly demonstrate that they are bad to the core, cannot change, and so must be killed in order to be stopped. This death is meaningful in relation to the past—to what the villain has already done and proven. The very fact that the villains are no longer is good in itself. It can be a story-terminating death, the end of a storyline—there is nothing that needs to come after it to make it meaningful. In fact, it can end all of the storylines and be the concluding event of the entire film. A good example is the classical gangster from the 1930s, in films such as *Little Caesar* (Mervyn LeRoy, 1930), *The Public Enemy* (William Wellman, 1931), and *Scarface, the Shame of the Nation* (Howard Hawks, 1932). He is coherent, he has integrity, he cannot change, he will not surrender, and he is therefore ritually slaughtered in these films. Overall, this formula has never left Hollywood and it is still a staple of action films. A very bad person passes killability tests, that is will not change and "must" be somehow killed by the good guys, by rivals, or even by nature.

As discussed in Chapter 3, in certain aspects, the justification for the gangster's immutability, his being born bad and unable or unwilling to change, came close to nature explanations of human behavior and particularly criminality, such as those offered by the eugenics movement in the United States.[40] Yet, the 1920s and 1930s were a period of transition from biological theories of behavior to environmental ones, from nature to nurture. Moreover, the Nazi adoption and practice of racism and eugenics had a lasting impact on the decline of concepts like "heredity," "biological influences," and "instinct." Bodies—living and dead ones—did not, of course, go unnoticed, but could be accounted for using the nurture tools of social science and the humanities. Even death could be seen as more a matter of sociology than biology. Thus, in 1959, Erving Goffman seems to have no difficulty in describing the showing of a body at a funeral home as a performance. The deceased is "the center of the show" or "the star of the show" who "must stay in character as someone who is in a deep sleep,"[41] and the undertaker's workroom is described as "backstage" where the corpses are prepared for "their final performance."[42]

Nurture was used to account for everything from criminality to differences among "races," and was certainly present in Hollywood films. Noteworthy, in Hollywood and out, is the rise of an American brand of psychoanalysis and psychodynamic accounts of human behavior and therapy. Conveniently, given the dominant tendencies in American social science, Freud's writings were interpreted in the United States as refuting biological determinants and heredity and as being primarily environmentalist.[43] Hollywood in particular seemed to offer a simple version of psychoanalysis. For it, treatment was terminable and resulted in a cure, or successful "adjustment" of the patient. The illness, according to Hollywood, is caused by a repressed trauma. The cure comes about when the analyst, playing detective or interrogator, makes the patient remember or "confess" the repressed event. With the memory revealed the patient is cured.[44] Death can easily be integrated into such a storyline and become a part of the trauma that needs to be unveiled. In *The Three Faces of Eve* (Nunnally Johnson, 1957), for example, the patient recalls her childhood trauma—her mother forced her to kiss her dead grandmother—and is miraculously cured of her multiple personality. Killers, or potential killers, can also be cured by recalling their childhood trauma. An escaped convict happens to undergo psychoanalysis in *The Dark Past* (Rudolph Maté, 1948) and is no longer able to kill. A gothic husband who wants to murder his wife is led by her to remember his childhood trauma and ends up not killing her and even saving her life in *Secret beyond the Door* (Fritz Lang, 1948).[45]

But not all criminals underwent successful psychoanalysis. There was significant variation in gangsters and other criminals, various options spanning the gamut between extreme nature (like *Scarface*) and extreme nurture (like *The Dark Past*). Some criminals were born not-so-bad, or became bad later in life; some criminal behavior was not immutable. While our discussion in Chapter 3 focused on cases in which the gangsters were evil and unable to change and had to be killed, many other variations existed, which allowed, or required, other options for making the death of these criminals meaningful. I would like to look at some of these options in this section.

Some criminals had very little to do with the born-bad irremediable urban gangster of the early thirties that we studied in Chapter 3. One variation was young lovers-on-the-run, such as the protagonists of *You Only Live Once* (Fritz Lang, 1937) and *They Live by Night* (Nicholas Ray, 1949). Another was the folk hero, non-urban criminals of *Jesse James* (Henry King, 1939) and *High Sierra* (Raoul Walsh, 1941),[46] who are closer to the image of John Dillinger than to that of Al Capone. Their deaths are complex, and it is no longer enough in the films to suggest that they are meaningful in relation to the past, by putting an end to an evil gangster. The protagonists of *You Only Live Once* and *They Live by Night* are still young; we are told about how they reached the "correctional" facilities of justice, where they were tutored into a life of crime at a tender age. They and the protagonist criminals in the other films all seem earnestly to want to start leading an honest life but are never given a chance. With this strong nurture belief, they are not killable like the Hollywood criminals we dealt with in Chapter 3. All have deaths that are also, or mainly, meaningful in relation to the future, to a cult of the dead that will remember them.

The deaths of Jo and Eddie Taylor, for example, the two protagonists in *You Only Live Once*, are complex. They are overdetermined and meaningful in various ways. Like all Hollywood events, their deaths take place within a linear narrative which follows a logic of cause and effect: unaware of his pardon, Eddie breaks out of jail hours before his execution for a crime he did not commit while killing a priest. He is joined by Jo, his wife. On the way to the border, the police hunt the two fugitives down and kill them.

Beyond the linear storyline, there are those "rhymes" and symmetries within the classical Hollywood text that, in this case, doom the characters, such as their own dialogue early on in the film, in which they compare themselves with Romeo and Juliet. In the same scene, they mention that frogs die when their mates do. Their images are then reflected in the pond where the frogs are. It thus makes Hollywood-sense that they too die in a tragedy of errors, like Romeo and Juliet, and that once one of them dies (Jo dies first), so does the other.

There is another factor that seals their fate: they have a baby. Once their heir has been formed and sure to remain alive, once they have a cult to keep them alive, their death can become meaningful in relation to the future and take place. We can look at this as a variation on the action and war film cliché which we encountered in Chapter 5, by which talking about one's family or plans for the future can be deadly, since it indicates that one has a "cult" and that one's death will be meaningful in relation to the future. The logic by which the baby is essential for making their death meaningful, or at least for Eddie who otherwise, as far as we know, has no additional blood relatives, in a way also becomes a part of the linear causal plot. Before Jo and Eddie attempt to cross the border, she meets her sister and Eddie's lawyer at a motel in order to hand over their baby boy. Both hold and feed the child and it is apparent that he will have a safe future with them. It is during this visit that Jo is spotted by a motel employee who recognizes her photograph on a wanted ad and calls the police. The logic by which having a blood relative to remember the dead enables the death within the film thus becomes part of the causal narrative: were it not for the baby, Jo would not have been spotted and she and Eddie might have not been shot down by the police. In addition, were it not for the baby, Eddie would not have a blood relative and Jo would only have her sister, and so their death would be meaningless (or less meaningful in her case) and less likely in the moral world of Hollywood films. Either way, once a cult has been created to remember them, they can safely die.[47] In *They Live by Night*, in a similar fashion, escaped convict, "Bowie the Kid," patiently awaits until his wife becomes pregnant, leaves her a letter, and only then pulls out a gun when ambushed by the police who are therefore forced to shoot him down. His wife comes out and then reads her deceased husband's touching letter, assuring her of her abilities as a mother.

In *High Sierra*, by contrast, the family includes no child, merely a dog who is said to bring bad luck—which indeed it does—and a young woman, Marie, who is in love with Roy Earle, the soon-to-be-dead gangster. Perched in the Sierras, he refuses to hand himself in to the police. He leaves them a note in his pocket clarifying that Marie was never involved in any holdup or shooting when he suddenly hears the dog, gets up exposing himself, and starts calling Marie. He is immediately shot down. Marie runs to his corpse and starts weeping as does the dog. A journalist comments that big-shot Earle "ain't much now." Marie, who up to this point was extremely intelligent and had no difficulties understanding the gangster argot Roy used, asks the reporter "mister, what does it mean when a man 'crashes out?'" He tells her it means he is free. She takes the dog, smiles, and walks toward the camera ecstatically reiterating the word "free." Unless her linguistic abilities have taken a drastic fall due to the altitude, we might suspect that she is manipulating the reporter to construct Roy's death not as a failure but as an act of liberty. She has definitely done so for herself and the viewers. As Jack Shadoian writes, "the final shots do not focus on the gangster's death but rather on Marie, the survivor, who has understood his qualities and whose life will be informed by them."[48] By continuing to deal with his death, she has also definitely made it into an intermediary one with her, and maybe also the reporter and his readers, as the remembering cult which makes the death meaningful in relation to the future.

Interestingly, there are still remnants of the grounding that justified the gangster's story-terminating death and made it meaningful in relation to the past. The entire tradition that determines criminality through an immutable body that can only be stopped by being destroyed seems to take on a life of its own. These tragic criminals who would change if they were just given half a chance are haunted by incriminating representations, damning them forever. *You Only*

Live Once challenges the viewer to decide whether or not its protagonist, Eddie Taylor, is still a crook, guilty of the death of innocent lives during a robbery. His attorney claims he should not be convicted purely based on his past record, while his wife's sister insists that he "has been pounding on the door of an execution chamber ever since he was born." The viewers see a theft take place, but the criminal is wearing a gas mask and has a hat with Eddie's initials on it. Is it him? The hat is one of many signifiers that seem to continue Eddie's career in crime despite his going straight. The very first time we see him, he is being released from prison and the warden is reviewing his prison record which includes his photographs and past convictions. The warden warns him that a fourth conviction according to the state laws will sentence him to jail for life. He goes out, marries Jo, and they reach the Valley Tavern motel where his name in the registry represents him. Soon this is joined by a sensational magazine article with Eddie's photograph and the title "PUBLIC! BEWARE: Desperados Soon To Be Pardoned." The motel owners ask them to leave because "convicts and their wives ain't welcome in this tavern." The newspapers continue to report of his criminal action during his trial for the robbery he did not commit and before his execution. Not trusting representations that have to do with him, it is no wonder Eddie does not believe the jail authorities when they show him a telegraph saying he has been pardoned. After he does commit a murder and escapes, his crimes continue to mount in representations—wanted posters and reports blaming them, as his attorney says, "for every crime committed in the country" while they can barely get enough food to survive. Similarly, in *They Live by Night*, fingerprints on a gun cause Bowie to be thought guilty for a shooting he did not commit, and in *High Sierra* newspaper and radio reports continue to haunt Earle Roy and Marie. Whatever they do or do not do, the criminal body, once marked and branded as guilty, seems to have a very difficult time proving its innocence, even if it attempts to go straight. While still haunted by the old immutable born-bad gangster, ultimately the films disprove the justification for a story-terminating death that is meaningful in relation to the past—the evil body that must be destroyed. The criminals cannot successfully exorcize their pasts, but their deaths are now meaningful in relation to the future.

This complexity is not exclusively the domain of rural folk heroes and young lovers on the run. Even films about urban gangsters in the 1930s, and certainly later ones, were giving more expression to environmental causes of crime and challenging the idea that criminality is inborn or immutable. The protagonists of these films were not as easily killable as the gangsters in the films that we discussed in Chapter 3 like *Little Caesar, The Public Enemy,* and *Scarface.* Moreover, whether born that way or not, and whether their criminal behavior was immutable or not, some gangsters were not exactly "bad." Some of them were honest about their being criminals and moreover followed certain moral principles, which were beyond formal definitions of legality. Whether they were willing to change or not, these were "decent" criminals, not unstoppable violent homicidal monsters. In both cases—when environmental causes were more dominant and when the gangster was not all bad—a story-terminating death which is meaningful in relation to the past and can even be the last plot event in the film was no longer enough to render their deaths meaningful.

One way of dealing with this complexity is by not ending the film with the gangster's death at all. *Little Caesar*'s Edward G. Robinson plays a criminal kingpin who manages to go straight (more or less) in a series of comedies, and manages to remain alive and well at the end of the films: he becomes a legitimate if not quite successful beer maker after prohibition ends in *A Slight Case of Murder* (Lloyd Bacon, 1938); joins a monastery and remains alive despite an attempted murder by a rival gangster in *Brother Orchid* (Lloyd Bacon, 1940); and opens a successful luggage shop in *Larceny, Inc.* (Lloyd Bacon, 1942).[49]

In other cases, the gangster does die, but while his death is a story-terminating event in one storyline, it is also meaningful by being an intermediary death which is meaningful in relation to the future in another. A rather simple case is William Wyler's 1937 *Dead End.* It is frequently understood as a nurture film exposing how tenement life breeds crime,[50] perhaps because many of the characters are given didactic lines of dialogue saying so. Yet its plot, in fact, seems to indicate otherwise. While in this milieu of poverty, one man, "Baby Face" Martin became a murderous gangster and one woman, his old girlfriend Francey, became "no good" to make a living and as a result "sick" (the film never quite says what her no-good profession is and which illness she contracted due to it), others do not. Two of the central characters in the film, Drina and Dave, do manage to make a living honestly, and Dave even worked his way through college to become an architect. So tenement life perhaps does breed crime, but not in an inevitable and universal way. The neighborhood is not quite the cradle of crime it is supposed to be, yet the dialogue frequently insists that it is. When "Baby Face" Martin returns back to the old neighborhood no one, including his mother who tells him to stay away and die, wants him there, and he ends up being shot dead by Dave after refusing to leave and planning to kidnap a rich child.

This double understanding of the causes of crime is complemented by a double role the death holds in two different storylines in the narrative. The death of the gangster is meaningful in relation to the past in terminating his own story: he would not change his behavior,[51] he would not leave, and he was therefore killable and had to be destroyed. However, the film then continues with its other storylines, in which Martin's death plays an intermediary role which is meaningful in relation to the future in a story that has to do with an environmental understanding of the causes of crime. Due to discovering him, Dave will be given reward money, which he plans to use in order to hire a lawyer to make sure Drina's brother is not sent to a juvenile delinquent institute which, everybody agrees, would nurture him to become a criminal. Offering two different approaches to the causes of crime, the film also offers two ways in which the death functions in its narrative. It is both a story-terminating and an intermediary one in different stories which adhere to two different accounts of the causes of crime; it is rendered meaningful in two different ways. While this does make extracting a single and simplistic understanding of what causes crime difficult, for viewers who do not expect the film to serve as a one-sided coherent essay on criminality, this is not particularly troubling. The two storylines coexist in harmony in the film—having two or more intertwining narrative threads is the norm in Hollywood and many would no doubt agree that crime is not universally determined by one single cause and can have more than one reason. The double role that death plays in the overall narrative is thus not particularly confusing or disturbing, even if it is more complex than the simple story-terminating death of earlier gangsters.

Other examples from the period are more ambivalent and make much more of an issue of what the meaning of the gangster's death should be once the problem of the causes of crime is brought to the fore. The 1938 film *Angels with Dirty Faces* (Michael Curtiz) follows two boys. One, Rocky Sullivan, becomes a gangster, the other Jerry Connelly, perhaps due to the son-of-God-like initials of his name, becomes a priest. The film does seem to offer a plausible nurture reason for the difference between the two. Both engage in petty theft as youngsters, but only Rocky is caught. He is sent to a "Society for Juvenile Delinquents" and becomes an example of the belief, also voiced in *Dead End*, that "reform" schools teach youngsters how to become criminals. So, while Jerry manages to change and go straight, a quick montage shows Rocky's passage through the rungs of crime: Warrington Reform School, State Reformatory, State Penitentiary, and finally newspaper headlines depicting how he escapes punishment for manslaughter but is later caught again as "TERROR SWEEPS CITY." When he is finally released from jail, a new generation of youngsters in their old neighborhood idolizes him and makes Jerry's attempts to set them on the righteous path—he is now Father Connelly—almost impossible. Jerry has no choice but to fight Rocky and all those who take part in his corrupt world of organized crime and he sets off on a media crusade to uncover the filth surrounding his childhood buddy. Some of Rocky's rival gangsters decide to murder Jerry, but Rocky kills them first. He is caught and sentenced to death. Ten minutes before his execution, Jerry comes to his cell and asks him to give up the one thing Hollywood gangsters cherish most in the 1930s: not being yellow. If he goes to his death a coward, the boys in the neighborhood will no longer consider him a hero and then Jerry has a chance of influencing them. Rocky refuses, Jerry prays, and we now hear (but we do not see) Rocky become a coward as he is about to be electrocuted. The newspaper screams that "ROCKY DIES YELLOW," the kids are crushed, and they then follow Jerry to pray for Rocky. This is an intermediary death which is meaningful in relation to the future: a cult is created throughout the film to remember Rocky (the juvenile delinquents who worship him); his death becomes an issue for them (they remember, read, talk, and follow it); it also influences their behavior after he dies (they go to pray instead of commit crimes). Yet there is still considerable ambivalence in the film. Oddly, this is an intermediary death that will encourage the cult of the dead to disband, not unite after the death. More importantly, we can never know with certainty whether Rocky indeed was "yellow" or only pretending to be in order to influence his young admirers not to follow his example. Such dishonesty about the deceased, as we saw in Chapter 5, is by no means unusual in the fabulations that follow deaths that are meaningful in relation to the future. However, the dishonesty goes beyond the possible intervention of Jerry in Rocky's death.

While Jerry insists that influence causes crime, the film seems to criticize him. For his ideas to make sense he must not let the facts bother him—not just stage Rocky's death but also rewrite history. After Rocky's execution, Jerry calls the kids to come and say a prayer "for a boy who couldn't run as fast as I could." He is alluding to their childhood—when he managed to outrun the police, but Rocky was caught and led into "reform" school which only teaches crime. But this is an extremely selective way to look at the events. What we actually saw in their childhood episode was that the two boys were never really the same. Rocky was from the start more energetic and more criminally inclined. He had to persuade Jerry to steal pens off a freight car. Discovered on the train, they tried to run away from the police. Jerry's leg was caught in a rail and Rocky went back to help him get out. Unfortunately, this slowed Rocky down and he was caught by the police while Jerry managed to escape. It is not that he couldn't run as fast, but rather that he was always willing to sacrifice himself for his friend. Awaiting trial, the young Rocky insisted that young Jerry not confess to being an accessory in the crime because no one should be a "sucker"—but Rocky was and would continue to be. He remains decent, loyal to Jerry, and a criminal throughout the film—as a child, later when murdering the rival gangsters who want to kill Jerry, and finally when faking his cowardice at his execution, if indeed he is faking it. Rocky was always willing to help others even if it meant paying a very heavy personal price—incarceration, death, and his reputation of not being "yellow."

Significantly, the differences between Rocky and Jerry preceded Rocky's being sent to reform school as a child, and have remained immutable throughout the film. "Influence" probably had little to do with it. In its conclusion, the film emphasizes—with choir music and stark bright lighting—Jerry's holiness as he descends the steps into the youngster's hideout and summons them to pray. The shameful death of the bad role model has been their salvation and in a way also Rocky's. But at the same time, Jerry's entire reasoning is questioned by the film's narrative, which in fact shows criminality is inborn and immutable.[52] Is influence as important as Jerry insists? The film makes an issue of Rocky's death and the distortions required to make it meaningful. While offering us Rocky's death as both a story-terminating death of a born criminal which is meaningful in relation to the past and as an intermediary death which is meaningful in relation to the future since it is intended to influence the juvenile delinquents in Rocky's old neighborhood not to follow his ways and become criminals as well, it makes sense only if we are willing to accept Jerry's distorted rewriting of the very film we have been watching.[53] The born-bad gangster who passes the killability tests could die a story-terminating death at the end of the film that was clearly meaningful in relation to the past. Removing the born-bad rational, or insisting that the cause of crime is the environment, complicates the meaningfulness of death and can result in incoherence.[54]

Like *Angels with Dirty Faces*, *The Roaring Twenties* (Raoul Walsh, 1939) abandons, at least as far as its protagonist is concerned, the logic of the story-terminating death that is meaningful in relation to the past, but still tries to maintain the rise-and-death scheme of the lone urban gangster. The result, like *Angels with Dirty Faces*, is more troubling than coherent. The story begins in World War I with three war buddies— Lloyd, George, and Eddie—meeting in a shell hole. They will continue to meet each other as the film advances through the 1920s. We meet them when they are already adults, without a childhood sequence and have no way of knowing which combination of nature and nurture caused them to be the way they already are at the beginning of the film: George is violent with a tendency toward criminality; Lloyd is honest and fears shooting; and Eddie is decent and hard working yet somehow finds himself becoming a gangster.

Lloyd is a law graduate who admits he is afraid of battle and not cut out for war. He is unable to shoot a German enemy soldier who is only 15 years old. During the film, he works for Eddie, but leaves the racketeering business and starts working for the district attorney once he realizes murder is involved and not just giving the public what it wants despite an unpopular law making alcohol illegal. He is alive, married, and on his way to success at the end of the film.

George, is a tough and unlikable man from the start. He seems to get annoyed easily and to thoroughly enjoy violence, as when he happily shoots "Heinies," including the 15-year-old Lloyd could not kill, happily explaining the German boy "won't be sixteen" and later joking about keeping his rifle when the war is over. He is set on being a criminal— intends to stay in the alcohol business even if prohibition does come into effect. We never see how he enters the world of crime after the war; only encounter him much later, as he already is involved in smuggling. At the end of the film, he refuses to quit his criminal career and insists on killing Lloyd and Eddie. He has to be killed in order to be stopped. He is moreover played by Humphrey Bogart, who in the 1930s was the irremediably evil rival gangster in both *Angels with Dirty Faces* and *Dead End* and had to be killed in these cases as well. His is a death that is clearly meaningful in relation to the past.

Eddie, the third soldier, is the protagonist of the film. He is played by Cagney, who also starred as the born-bad gangster in the earlier well-known *The Public Enemy* and as the sacrificial Rocky in *Angels with Dirty Faces*. Here, he says that after the war he intends to return to his old job in a garage and save money in the hopes of opening his own business. The film closely follows his return home and his inability to return to his old job, which has now been filled by the men who stayed home. He is also unable to find a new job. The people back home are cold and cruel to the men who returned from the front, mocking them and offering them no hope of employment. In addition, it seems that those who have seen the carnage in Europe cannot adapt to civilian life again. A suicidal man he meets in jail immediately spots his unrest which he says characterizes World War I veterans. Eddie is encouraged to become a gangster—distributing illegal alcohol—because no other avenue is open to him and the alternative to forgotten men in his condition is getting a gun again and using it on themselves. Moreover, he can change and leave his old ways. In love with Jean, a decent New Jersey girl, he promises to retire as soon as he has enough money so she need not be involved in a criminal life style. The fact that he invests his money in a fleet of taxicabs and stocks seems to indicate that he is serious. What ultimately condemns him is not the police but Jean who is not in love with him and leaves with Lloyd whom she will later marry. For the first time in the film, he starts drinking his own "stuff"—up to this point he tended to settle for milk. When he loses his money in the 1929 stock market crash, he returns to driving a cab and leaves crime altogether.

Eddie does not pass the killability tests. There is not much that would justify his death in relation to the past. The film is accompanied by narrated montage sequences which place the unfolding events in their wider historical context. His story is placed within larger historical processes, explaining how social and economic conditions could push a decent person into a life of crime. Moreover, the first montage sequence shows images of historical events, going from the future back to World War I, superimposed upon a shot of planet earth spinning, as the narrator excitingly warns us about the dire events that might await us and tells about our difficult-to-believe past. The year "1940" followed by a "?" fly down and shrink until they disappear into an image of the White House. This dissolves into a smiling FDR on the left and then into Hitler on the right giving a ferocious speech as a highlighted newspaper headline reading "CZECHOSLOVAKIA" flashes above his arm and the year "1938" flies down and into the background. The montage continues to go back into time, until it reaches 1918 and the plot begins, yet Hitler is clearly overshadowing this story. It is perhaps then no accident that the film tells of a gangster who is led to crime through circumstances and is not born bad. Nature would come too close to Nazism. With Hitler lurking in the immediate future, the idea that criminals are irremediably bad and must be exterminated is not one this film will follow. While Eddie does die, he also leaves behind a woman, Panama, who loves him. However, Eddie never seems to be in love with her, and Panama is alone in the world. This is not quite a community that would remember him.

Eddie's death comes after Lloyd, now working for the district attorney and married to Jean, decides to pursue George in court. George sends men to threaten Jean who turns to Eddie for help. Reluctant at first, he confronts George, but is unable to persuade him that their world is changing and he too should go straight. Eddie also learns that George intends to kill him as well because he believes Eddie will talk to the police out of love for Jean. Eddie shoots George assuring him that this is "one rap you won't beat." He and George's men shoot at each other, killing a few of them and being shot himself before running out of the house. In a way then, Jean and Lloyd will remember Eddie who saved their lives, but they no longer have anything in common; he is not part of their community and they are in no way like him. They are not even there to witness it. The film does find a way to make Eddie's death meaningful in relation to the future. As he staggers to his death, as countless gangsters have done before him, instead of landing in the gutter, he reaches steps and a sign reading "COMMUNITY CHURCH." This is a new community, one that could surely include the sacrificial Eddie as well. To drive the Christ-metaphor home, Panama rushes to him and holds his dead body on her lap forming a Pietà composition.[55] This is all rather unexpected since nothing previously indicated the possibility of any Christian symbolism in the film. Unlike Jerry Connelly in *Angels with Dirty Faces*, where lighting, music, his vocation, and Jesus Christ initials, seemed to demand such an ending, here it is perfectly alien to anything that preceded it. If not quite intrinsic to the film, it certainly shows its struggle to make sense of death. His death is clearly not meaningful in relation to the past—he is not evil and killable; yet making it meaningful in relation to the future already requires considerable effort and faith.

A different way to complicate the formula is not by turning the story-terminating death which is meaningful in relation to the past into one that is, or is also, meaningful in relation to the future, but by divorcing the meaningfulness of story-terminating deaths in relation to the past from the linear causal narrative. In film noir, as Dudley Andrew writes, there is an "absurd randomness of violence,"[56] and death is "treated as unpredictable and rash rather than philosophically necessary."[57] We are now in a better position to understand this feeling. It is not that death occurs outside linear causality is these films—it is not a miraculous event that defies the laws of physics or human behavior; nor is it unrelated to the various ways in which death can be meaningful in a Hollywood storyline that we discussed in previous chapters. Rather, death in film noir can be meaningful while, at the same time, working against, or independently of, the main narrative drive, resulting in an uneasy feeling.

For example, the death of Eddie Harwood, the (possible) death of his associate Leo, and the death one of their henchmen, in *The Blue Dahlia* (George Marshall, 1946), are all perhaps meaningful, insofar as all three are guilty, indecent, and maybe immutable criminals, who are killable by Hollywood standards. Yet their deaths take place in a plot that follows the murder of a woman they in fact are not guilty of; it is completely incidental to the story we have been following. In fact, Eddie's death is even accidental—he is shot when a gun goes off during a struggle between two other men, without either one of them even noticing where the gun is aimed.

In *The Asphalt Jungle* (John Huston, 1950), all those who die are habitual criminals and therefore killable. Yet they do not die *because* they will not change, but in rather arbitrary, sometimes inane, ways: A seedy private detective, Bob Brannom, tries to hold up tough and professional criminals, who simply shoot back and kill him. An expert at breaking safes, Louis, is shot by pure chance during the robbery when a watchman is hit and drops his gun which accidently goes off. Dix, a naïve Kentucky hoodlum, seems to die out of sheer neglect. Shot and superficially wounded, he refuses to accept medical care and slowly, during several days, continues to function as usual while quietly bleeding to death. Without in any way violating the formula, the film separates the moral justification from narrative causality. It manages to offer the deaths of killable villains, which are meaningful in relation to the past and also seem arbitrary.

An additional interesting variation has to do with the pervasiveness of killable criminals in the disillusioned world of film noir who indeed are killed, resulting in a depleted roster of characters by the time the film ends. When the film's protagonist is a man trying to clear his name, he might discover that with all the killable bad guys dead, no one is left alive to help him prove his innocence. While their deaths are perhaps meaningful in the sense that the criminals were unchangeable and evil, in other words, they were killable, they also work against the narrative drive to prove that the noir protagonist is not guilty. In *Out of the Past* (Jacques Tourneur, 1947), the wrongly accused protagonist, Jeff, realizes he stands no chance of clearing his name once almost everyone is dead and chooses to die with the femme fatale, the last person remaining alive in the gang that framed him[58]; in *Dark Passage* (Delmer Daves, 1947), after the real murderer commits suicide, the protagonist Vincent has no way of proving his innocence. Having undergone plastic surgery to alter his face, he assumes a false identity and leaves the country, with hardly anyone knowing that he is not guilty of the murders with which he has been wrongly accused.

The Virtual Frankenstein

Post-Photographic Ghosts

In this final section, I would like to look at American cinema's understanding of death at the turn of the millennium. To be sure, this is no longer classical Hollywood cinema.[59] Moreover, in a way, it is no longer death, at least not as we know it, since some of the films question our very assumptions about mortality, indeed, the very necessity or even possibility of dying and can help us to begin to imagine what would happen were death eliminated. My discussion focuses on two of the shifts that took place in the 1990s and that no longer accepted the inevitability and meaningfulness of death: the "return" to the body and the alleged irrelevancy of the body (or "meat") in certain cyberculture texts.[60] Two films written and directed by Andrew Niccol can be used to explore how American cinema approached each of these directly: *S1m0ne* (2002) and *Gattaca* (1997). Less directly, other films from the period—we will look at *Fight Club* (David Fincher, 1999) and *American Psycho* (Mary Harron, 2000)—can bring out some of the difficulties in thinking of death as meaningful in light of the changes that were taking place in the understanding of identity and the body.

One apparent change in the last decades of the millennium was the imminent loss of the body. In a world of proliferating communication technologies and increased mediation, user controlled, interactive computerized environments, "cyberspace" or "virtual realities," were imagined as sites where people could appear to themselves and to other users as "avatars" regardless of any limitations of their actual physical bodies.[61] The internet was frequently imagined as an "alternative space" transcending the physical body and offering a "bodiless, post-identity cyberspace."[62] Cyberpunk science-fiction works, such as novels by William Gibson, showed contempt for "flesh" or "meat." The Cartesian mind–body split seemed to culminate in cyberculture metaphors of the body as soft and weak and abandoning it was thought of as an ideal built into virtual reality.[63]

This unimportance of the body (or "meat") entailed that bodily death was no longer the complete annihilation of the self. Summing up millennia of Western belief, Jacques Choron explains that "if we 'feel' our bodily life as the only life," then in the physical death of our bodies "our personality will be completely destroyed."[64] If, however—and this would be the case for the Cartesian cyberspace ideal—"we experience the autonomy of our spiritual being,"[65] that is, of a non-bodily existence, then "its continuation after physical death will appear to be self-evident."[66] In William Gibson's 1984 *Neuromancer*, "cyberpunk's acknowledged ur-text,"[67] one of the computer cowboys who goes into The Matrix, McCoy Pauley, the Flatline, is dead. When alive he was "recorded" into a ROM personality, which is a black storage unit that resembles "the magazine of a large assault rifle."[68] Although he is dead, this hardwire ROM cassette or "construct" replicates his "skills, obsessions, knee-jerk responses."[69] In a world in which people can "flip" into cyberspace leaving their bodies behind, a "construct" of a personality, whose human body or "meat" has died, seems to make perfect sense. Bodily death is by no means the end of the self.

For Hollywood in the 1990s, this virtual world of potential immortality was not only a science-fiction possibility/fantasy, but also part of a technological change that was threatening to alter the industry. Digital technology promised a transformation of modes of distribution, exhibition, and reception.[70] In particular, the way motion pictures were produced—filmed, edited, and altered with visual effects—was changing in a fundamental way. As Warren Buckland writes, a transition was taking place in the film industry from "cinema's nineteenth century technologies (optics, mechanics, photochemistry)" to "post-photographic (that is, digital)" technology.[71]

A curious connection between death and the shift to digital filmmaking can be made if Alejandro Amenábar's 2001 *The Others* is read reflexively and allegorically. Although taking place shortly after World War II, as A. O. Scott notes, there is no telephone, no radio, and no electricity and "the house and its inhabitants [...] belong to the timeless, vaguely Victorian world of classic English fright fiction."[72] Amenábar has included reflexive references to the cinema in his previous feature films as well as in the next one,[73] and quite interestingly, two of the characters in this film are ludicrously similar to celluloid, the material basis for nineteenth-century photochemical cinema that was being phased out of the motion picture industry at the time *The Others* was made. As the mother in the film explains, her children have a "serious allergy" to light—they are "photosensitive"—and exposure to too much light could kill them. The entire Victorian house is carefully managed to give the photochemical-like children enough light to live without fatally overexposing them. This is no simple task: there are 50 doors and 15 keys.

The only thing that moves in the house, explains the mother, is the light. It is like a ship, she says, the light must be contained by opening and closing the doors. If this is read as a reflexive allusion to the cinematic apparatus, the film describes it as an exhausting and cumbersome Victorian practice. Moreover, this film, made as digital technology was replacing the nineteenth-century technologies, also suggests it is obsolete. The children, in fact, are no longer photosensitive. Not unlike the protagonist of *The Sixth Sense* (M. Night Shyamalan, 1999), they are actually ghosts who are denying the fact that they are dead, perhaps as the traditional cinematic techniques were still lingering on in the 1990s although technically they could have been superseded by digital alternatives.

One new digital effect was the ability to create "synthespians," "cyberstars," or "vactors"—virtual performers who could replace living actors.[74] Virtual actors were associated by many writers with loss of death. As Barbara Creed claims, "cyberstars" are not subject to the same experiences as living stars, such as "mothering, Oedipal anxiety, hunger, loss, ecstasy, desire, death."[75] Watching their potentially perfect beauty never entails the threat of its inevitable loss through aging and death.[76] Moreover, it was argued that "[l]ong-deceased movie stars could even be digitally resurrected,"[77] brought back "to play new roles in new projects with new co-stars."[78] Noël Burch dubbed the belief that technology will vanquish death, which can be discernable from the very beginning of cinema, the "great Frankensteinian dream of the nineteenth century."[79] Whether or not dead movie stars were digitally brought back, the great Frankensteinian dream of the nineteenth century certainly had been successfully resurrected in much of the discourse surrounding digitally simulated performers. As for the virtual characters—in practice, the various attempts were frequently less than perfect and did not quite result in the promised seamless on-screen interaction of computer-generated virtual and living carbon-based players.[80]

Hollywood displayed in its films an understandable interested in this change in its own industry and in the ways it might be related to death. In the satire *S1m0ne*, Viktor Taransky is a failed movie director whose star decides to leave the set of the film they are working on. Luckily, a dying software engineer thinks Viktor is talented and bequeaths to him a program which creates a perfect virtual actress, Simone. Viktor replaces the living star with the virtual one and she becomes an amazing success. Yet this Viktor soon learns that he has created a monster, the great Frankensteinian nightmare of the twenty-first century. The world thinks Simone is real, and, jealous of her, Viktor decides to destroy Simone by faking her death and infecting the program with a computer virus. He is subsequently arrested for murder—no one believes him she is not real— and later released when it is discovered that she is not dead after all. Her reincarnation was made possible by his daughter and ex-wife discovering his computer, removing the computer virus that "killed" Simone, and releasing a tape of her alive and well. By the end of the film, she has a virtual baby with Viktor and plans to go into politics. An actress who is merely computer data, a group of zeroes and ones, so the film seems to imply, can never be irreversibly killed. There is always a chance that the data, and with it the virtual person, could be restored. There is always something of the immortal in these virtual beings. If the film is not yet able to imagine where exactly this invention could go (or go beyond a Frankenstein story in which the creator loses control over the creature), it is at the very least acknowledging that the presence of this new technology, as the film imagines it, will have ramifications for death or lack thereof.

Genetically Engineered Immortality

At the same time that Western culture was imagining virtual actors with no profilmic bodies, it was also obsessing about the body and the various technological ways it can be altered. Both cyberspace and cyborgs thus offered an alternative to those whom David Lavery calls "Carbon Chauvinists" by searching for "potentially immortal cyber- or robotic selves."[81] Both thus ended up challenging some of the assumptions grounding mortality's meaningfulness, necessity, and its very existence.

In the previous section we discussed the rise of nurture ideas since the 1920s and 1930s. After World War II, however, the social sciences in the United States were having second thoughts. The banishing of biology and instinct and the assumption that behavior was only a matter of nurture were no longer convincing. The attention given to studies of animal behavior and the success of genetics with the discovery of the double helix of DNA as well as the severing of genetics's ties with eugenics and social Darwinism led to a reconsideration of the uses of biology. By the 1960s, a growing number of social scientists, as Carl N. Degler writes, were taking "a hard second look at earlier decisions to extirpate biology and heredity from explanations for human behavior."[82] By the 1980s, the evolutionary speculations of sociobiology and the interpretations of ethology were in fact questioning the very separation between biology and culture or nature and nurture, suggesting a co-evolution.

Non-human animals, assumed to be similar to our evolutionary ancestors, also have cultures and transmit knowledge, so the environment in which our bodies evolved included culture; our nurture thus took part in our nature. Conversely, our nature includes an innate capacity for nurture. So any attempt to give an evolutionary account of one without the other no longer seemed tenable.[83] While many scientists, even within sociobiology, were offering complex and nuanced accounts of bodies and cultures, other lay and professional utterances could certainly give a more one-sided impression, that of a return to the body. I would like to emphasize several aspects of this discourse on the return to the body, particularly how it was understood as unsettling previous conceptions of the self and how it was understood as a way to battle our being mortal.

In the last decades of the millennium, several new options that had to do with the body were discussed as if social, environmental, and psychodynamic accounts had become redundant, and the body could offer a new way in which one could understand oneself. Neuroscience and psychopharmacology were frequently interpreted as superseding psychoanalysis and received tremendous publicity. A four-page 1991 article by neuroscientist Simon LeVay in *Science* showed statistical differences in the size of one group of cells in the anterior hypothalamus that were correlated to presumed sexual orientation in men and aroused wide-ranging interpretations by "academic, scientific, political, legal and media commentators," including the prolific LeVay himself.[84] He understood his finding as suggesting "that sexual orientation has a biological substrate."[85] What is perhaps more interesting, he placed his own research in contradistinction with the traditional study of sexual orientation "at the level of psychology, anthropology, or ethics" citing, among others, the Vatican Council and Freud,[86] with whom he has continued to engage in a one-sided battle in later publications.[87] For LeVay, at least, biology was clearly meant to put an end to psychoanalysis, which, as already noted in the previous section, was often understood in the United States as being primarily environmentalist and as refuting biological determinants.

At the same period, new pharmacological options were understood within a context of a change in the way psychiatrists and the public were thinking about the self/brain/mind/soul. Particularly well-known to the public were Eli Lilly's Prozac (fluoxetine) introduced for clinical use in 1986 and Pfizer's Viagra (sildenafil) launched in 1998 and followed by intensive media coverage in print, radio, and television.[88] Frequently employing facile technological determinism, the very existence of these drugs was understood in the professional and lay public discourse as bringing about massive shifts in our perceptions about mind–body relations. Their highly publicized success was related to a revival of "biological psychiatry" and its search for causes of illnesses within the body. Unlike 1950s antidepressants, Prozac had less objectionable side effects and was much less toxic in large doses and therefore less likely to become a successful instrument for suicide. These traits were understood as encouraging prescription of the new antidepressant in the treatment of symptoms other than depression such as difficulties with self-esteem and with experiencing pleasure, and in coping with criticism and rejection.[89] This, it was claimed, led to questions about what constituted an "illness," about the possible preference of "pharmacologic to psychologic self-actualization," about the new possibility of what Peter D. Kramer called "cosmetic psychopharmacology," about the use of chemicals to modify personality, and about the very notion of the self.[90] It also became tempting to engage in "drug cartography," that is to conclude that all of the illnesses which could be treated by a certain drug had a common, primarily biological, cause.[91] In addition, many patients with behavioral disorders that were traditionally treated by psychotherapy (such as psychoanalysis, cognitive-behavioral therapy, and group therapy) were now responding to these new drugs.[92] Psychiatry, a field whose theoretical basis, it was claimed, derived from "the writings of Sigmund Freud and his successors," was undergoing a major attitudinal shift, with clinical psychiatrists, like Kramer, reevaluating their basic assumptions and exhibiting new openness to biological treatment.[93] Augmenting Levay's claims, these drugs were understood as supporting a corporeal cause for behavior and as taking the place of psychoanalysis.

The turn to the body was also related to the increased attention that research on genomics received, particularly following the Human Genome Project's mapping of "the" human DNA and the 1997 cloning of the sheep Dolly, who become famous worldwide as the first mammal to be successfully cloned using the DNA from an adult somatic cell. DNA was frequently presented as if it were the only and complete essence of the organism.[94] Following the "enormous excitement around the science of genetics," with the promise of new cures for diseases and the ability to reengineer the human body, Simon A. Cole wrote in 2001, we "have come to conceive ourselves as essentially genetic beings."[95]

One area in which the public interest in genetics has been apparent is DNA "typing" or "profiling" ("genetic fingerprinting") for forensic and criminal identification, put into use since the 1980s and sometimes attracting global attention, as in the 1994 O. J. Simpson trial.[96] Another is the Human Genome Project, scheduled for 15 years with an estimated budget of three billion dollars, which was launched in 1990 and would announce the completion of the mapping of the human genome in 2003. Regardless of its value or danger to life on earth or at least biologists, there is a good chance that in the future it will be deemed as one of humanity's greatest achievements in the field of public relations. The ability to garner support and funding for this massive and expensive endeavor should not be underestimated. Public discourse on the topic often took the shape of facile genetic determinism, and the media was quick to announce the discovery of various "genes for" certain politically sensitive traits like criminality, intelligence, violence, and homosexuality.[97] James Watson, Nobel Prize recipient and, at the time, director of the National Center for Human Genome Research at the National Institutes of Health, declared in a 1989 meeting that the objective of the Human Genome Project was nothing less than "to find out what being human is."[98] In a 1990 letter that he co-wrote to the editor of *The New York Times* with Norton Zinder, chairman of the N.I.H. Program Advisory Committee on the Human Genome, they defended the project against critical opinions. They suggested it would help scientists understand cancer and also "the molecular essence of other tragic and devastating illnesses like schizophrenia, Alzheimer's disease, alcoholism and manic depression" in addition to providing the "technological basis for a new era in drug development."[99]

Back in the late nineteenth and early decades of the twentieth century, the body was thought of as a source of immutable identity. Bodies could be changed, but only over long periods of time (although whether one was Lamarckian or not mattered) and for large groups (the nation, the race, mankind), for example, by positive and negative eugenics. By the end of the twentieth century, however, the focus shifted to individuals, not groups,[100] and the bodies of individuals were increasingly constituted as changeable. As Cole writes, molecular biology is not content with identifying; rather it is interventionist. Genetic engineering, and cloning threaten "our century-and-a-half bodily notion of identity."[101] It was expected that the full control and understanding of the DNA would follow its mapping immediately and automatically. Nature was perhaps becoming more central than nurture, but nature, at least for individuals who have access to these technologies, was now believed to be, or soon to become, malleable. An inborn genetic hereditary trait could still be viewed as impervious to environmental influences; it was not however immutable. Rather it was given to genetic alterations and screening.

Who we were was increasingly a matter of our bodies, and these were increasingly being constructed as alterable by technology, such as new drugs and genetic engineering, making Donna Haraway's famous claim in her 1985 "Manifesto for Cyborgs" that "we are cyborgs" and that the "cyborg is our ontology"[102] more clearly true. This shaping of the body and therefore of the self by technology questioned the past assumption that a stable individual identity could be found in the body.

This, it was implied or imagined, could "cure" humans of mortality. In many ways the public discourse on the Human Genome Project and cloning continued what Evelyn Fox Keller identifies as "the perennial motif that underlines much of scientific creativity—namely the urge to fathom the secrets of nature," in the hope that in doing so we will fathom and gain control "of our own mortality."[103] One scholarly article by two geneticists from 2000 begins by simply asserting that genes "determine all human traits." Among the benefits that "may, or can, be expected as the genome yields its secrets" are "medical treatments that alleviate or avoid the ravages of genes that cause morbidity, disease, and death."[104] Presumably, then, once the three billion bases of the human genome are sequenced, that pesky death gene will be unveiled and it "may, or can, be expected" that the realm of medicine will find a way to "alleviate or avoid" its "ravages."

It might seem to be a mere coincidence that under the rubric of "return to the body," we can find both a challenge to previous understandings of the self (such as through psychoanalysis) and to a stable identity (because the body was now understood as malleable and the singular self could be cloned), and an endeavor to control mortality and cure death. In fact, the writings of earlier twentieth-century thinkers can already be understood as making or enabling such a connection between identity and death.

Jean Baudrillard announced that "[t]he question concerning cloning is the question of immortality."[105] He suggested that it was possible "to imagine entirely new functions for clones," such as vicarious suicide: "Kill your clone, destroy yourself with no risk of actually dying."[106] Actually, this was hardly a new function and Baudrillard was cloning an idea that can already be found in Otto Rank's 1925 study of the motif of the double in myth, folklore, and more recent arts (including the cinema). With primitives, writes Rank, the double (in the form of a shadow, a reflection, or a soul, for example) is related to a fear of death as annihilation of the self. Primitives can deny the idea of death "by a duplication of the self,"[107] something like a soul that allows a possible survival of the self after death. More complicatedly, their modern equivalents who suffer from "thanatophobia," an acute fear of death, which is a narcis-sist fear of change and aging, would like to commit suicide so as to put an end to their intolerable expectation of death. But, being narcissists who love their ego too much to destroy it, cannot directly kill them-selves. Rather, at least in fiction, they can create a double, whom they then slay, in what is really a suicidal act that leaves them intact.[108] For Rank too, then, a loss of singular identity, the existence of a double, is related to a loss of death, a suicide without dying, or a soul that is not annihilated with the body. He did not wait for genetic cloning to come up with this idea.

A different connection between loss of death and loss of identity can be suggested if we take into account attempts to define human exis-tence and singularity as essentially tied with mortality. "Death," Martin Heidegger writes in his 1927 *Being and Time*, "is a way to be, which Dasein takes over as soon as it is."[109] We humans, or "Dasein," are ready to die the moment we are born. Dasein cannot lose this possi-bility of death. If Dasein exists "it has already been *thrown* into this possibility." [110] For Heidegger, not only is this possibility, our being-towards-death, always already our way of being, but it is also tied to our singularity. Death, he claims, "reveals itself as that *possibility which is one's ownmost, which is non-relational, and which is not to be outstripped* [*unüberholbare*]."[111] Unlike any other activity, death does not enable "representation." In Dasein's everyday concern, one is what one does and in this everyday manner can be represented by someone else.[112] However, this possibility of representing breaks down in the case of death which is one's ownmost. No one can "die for" someone else. Such "dying for," he writes, "can never signify that the Other has thus had his death taken away in even the slightest degree." Death, by its very essence, "is in every case mine."[113] Of course, there are many actions that cannot be done for me. No one can eat for me, take a shower for me, or defecate for me. Yet anything else but death can be *taken away* from me. Someone can prevent me from defecating or taking a shower. Someone can take my food from me, eat it, and leave me with no food. I might starve to death, but that is exactly his point. No one can take my death away from me, no one can, in that sense, die in my place, spare me from dying, and "represent" me in death. Death, in this sense, grounds individual identity. What would it then mean if one could have death taken away? Would one still have a sense of being singular and different from others? What would be our way of being?

At the turn of the millennium, humans were not yet massively cloned (as far as I know), we did not fiddle with our DNA for recreation, and there was still no pill that could cure us of death-causing genes. Despite the considerable hype, and more like the US Space Program than the Manhattan Project, the Human Genome Project ended with a sense of anticlimax and with no obvious immediate applications for its findings.[114]

But, here too, as with virtual actors, Hollywood was certainly eager to explore such new worlds. It too chose to couple loss of mortality with loss of a stable and singular identity.

Andrew Niccol's *Gattaca* is set, according to a title at the beginning, in a "not too distant future," in a world in which DNA is used to engineer, identify, and select individuals. It focuses on Vincent, a "de-gene-erate," who was tragically "conceived in love," instead of by means of genetic selection; and on Jerome, who was genetically designed to be perfect. Yet Jerome (whose middle name is appropriately "Eugene") never managed to live up to his genetic potential. He became crippled after he tried to commit suicide by walking in front of a car. It turns out that a person's actual achievements cannot be reduced to her or his genetic potential. Vincent, on the contrary, despite his inferior genetic profile, dreams of becoming a space navigator at Gattaca, where only the genetically fittest—in mental and physical skills—that fulfill their potential are accepted. He does this by impersonating Jerome through low-tech cyborg corporeal redesigning. He dyes his hair, wears contact lenses, and exercises relentlessly ("the future still believes in Rocky," J. Hoberman quipped).[115] He undergoes what we are told is an excruciating process that makes him taller so as to match Jerome's height. Furthermore, he impersonates him genetically, by leaving behind bits of Jerome's hair and fingernails, and taking Jerome's blood samples and urine samples in order to outsmart the genetic surveillance in the film.

It is in this world of high-tech gene manipulation and Rocky-style low-tech deception that the end of death could be envisioned. A person like Jerome does not need to die. Bodily, he is perfect. Being perfect and surrounded by genetically perfect, non-violent, companions, there is also no need for genetically engineered people like Jerome to ever die as a result of an accident or murder. As the black-market gene dealer explains to Vincent, he has an expiration date "you wouldn't believe" and he is "practically gonna live forever."

Yet his perfect immortal existence also denies him the will to hope for future achievements. Jerome was genetically designed to be perfect and yet never managed to become the best in what he tried (he has *silver* medals in swimming). Even Jerome's attempt to walk in front of a car ended up merely crippling him. Only at the very end of the film does he successfully manage to commit suicide. The problem is not that he was badly designed, but that he is perfect, and therefore seems to be bored with life (he actually shouts during an infuriating phone call about a perfect hair dye color that he is bored). What he receives from Vincent, as he explains to him, is a "dream." This is completely in line with the Western tradition that views desire as a result of lack, which we encountered in Chapter 4. Accordingly, Jerome, who does not lack anything, also has no clear desires (except perhaps a desire to die—the one thing in a perfect life he cannot have). In contradistinction, Vincent's diligent and painful reshaping of his body has allowed him to achieve his dream to fly into space and even to exceed his expiration date (his brother tells him their parents passed away thinking he had already died).

In addition to raising the question of what a perfect immortal might desire, in the film's exploration of a world that challenges the necessity of death, that is, in which there are immortals who are practically going to live forever and mortals who have already exceeded their expiration date, personal identity is also questioned. As Jackie Stacey claims, the impersonation of "Jerome" is the result of both Vincent's and the "real" Jerome's labor. It is not just Vincent impersonating Jerome, but a creation of a new bond, a new kinship, a new joint identity, a new division of labor within and outside the home they share, indeed, a "reconceptualization of identity beyond traditional definitions of genealogy, gender, and heterosexuality."[116] There is a "criminal intimacy of genetic deception in this film,"[117] intimate exchanges "of fluids, of knowledge, of dreams, of identities," which "expose the limits of their individual autonomy and push to the surface the mutuality of their improvised embodiment."[118] Identity is in the body in this film—whether in the DNA, in the athletically trained and redesigned body of the young white man faking another person's DNA, or in the crippled body which by the film's logic incapacitates its DNA potential. And because this body can be altered, mutilated, forged, and cloned, stable identity is brought to crisis in the film. Unlike death for Heidegger, which grounds personal identity because no one can die for another, the "Jerome" that becomes an immaculate space navigator at Gattaca is a joint project of a queer intimacy. He could continue to exist in new impersonators should Vincent die as well as after the source of its DNA, the "original" Jerome, commits suicide. "Jerome" 's death could be split between different people and his individual identity as we might therefore expect, greatly problematized.

The film ultimately recuperates and returns to our familiar world. The technology the film dealt with turned out to be more a matter of rhetoric than actual capabilities and is completely undermined by the end of the film: genetic profiles predict nothing, DNA identification can be easily overcome, even the low-tech impersonation technology failed as we gradually learn that many people were in no way fooled by Vincent's masquerade, including his brother, the doctor at Gattaca, a co-worker who has fallen in love with him, and the head janitor. This is perhaps a successful representation of the film's historical context, in which extant DNA technology in no way matched many of the promises and "discoveries" announced in the media. In the end, Vincent is launched into space, and Jerome enters the bio-waste incinerator at their home and kills himself.[119] Death is clearly back in the game, even for the genetically perfect specimen of the master race, and identity is also much clearer now that there are no longer two living people co-queerly inhabiting a third identity. For several scenes, however, the film allowed us to imagine a different way of being, in which both identity and mortality were altered.

Body–Mind Game Films

While suggesting that the return to the body and the virtual body can have ramifications for our understanding of death and related phenomena, such as personal identity, *Gattaca* and *S1m0ne* remain relatively coherent and ultimately return to familiar territory.

Other films, however, while not explicitly about virtual actors or the future of genetic cloning and engineering, do go farther. On the one hand, these films are obsessed with the body and with the various ways in which it can be altered: perfected, repaired, and/or mutilated. On the other hand, they also, in a certain sense, deal with the virtual: they belong to what has been variously labeled as "mindfuck films," "mind game films," or "puzzle films."[120] For many scenes, perhaps the entire film, we are misled or unsure about the ontological status of what we are seeing, which might be a dream, a hallucination, or the world from the point of view of characters who suffer from acute misunderstandings about themselves and the worlds they live in.

In some cases, this misunderstood non-reality is, or might be, a computer-generated virtual environment, and is also directly related to attempts to control death and the body, such as *Vanilla Sky* (Cameron Crowe, 2001), whose protagonist discovers that he has been resurrected after committing suicide and living in a computer simulation, while concerned with repairing his injured body.[121] I would like to look more closely at two turn-of-the-millennium examples which are less explicit about the two themes I have discussed in this section, and certainly more difficult to make sense of or contextualize than *Gattaca* and *S1m0ne*.

One of the strangest moments in films from the period is the denouement of *Fight Club*, which offers an intersection of the virtual, return to the body, cloning, and lack of death. In the film, on the one hand, the unnamed protagonist (his voiceover accompanies the film and I will call him "the narrator") sees and sometimes is his imaginary friend/alternate personality, Tyler Durden, who has no independent bodily existence of his own and looks a lot like Brad Pitt. He walks inside virtual space that merges his own material apartment with an Ikea catalogue. His narration is sometimes accompanied by what is clearly computer-generated animation of impossible camera shots (inside a wastebasket, down a building and into the parking garage, a speculation on how his condominium blew up).[122] On the other hand, the narrator heads and participates in "fight club," in which men beat up other men resulting in considerable bodily injury. There are many other alterations of the body in *Fight Club*, such as fantasies about plane accidents, reconstructions of car accidents, men growing breasts, human fat stolen from a liposuction clinic and made into soap, and the charring of men's hands with acid.[123]

At the end of the film, the narrator cures himself of his multiple personality. In the age of neuroscience and psychopharmacology and in a film whose opening (computer-generated, virtual) shot starts at the center of emotion (the amygdala) in the brain of the narrator,[124] there is no need for psychoanalysis or recollection of a repressed childhood trauma to solve his psychological malady. He shoves a pistol up his mouth and pulls the trigger. The virtual product of his imagination, Tyler, is shot in the back of the head, falls down dead, and disappears. The narrator's other personality, however, is only injured, and although bleeding, manages to get up and seems relatively intact. Why did the same bullet have such disparate effects on the two personalities inhabiting the same body? Has he just conducted some kind of brain surgery with a gun, thus healing himself? Do he and his double have a different body image of the body they share?[125] We have no idea and no time to find out: soon explosives go off and the buildings outside start imploding. They are buildings of credit-card companies, literally embodying virtual money. The buildings are really there, but also virtual. We expect such large-scale explosions in a 1999 film to be computer-generated effects.[126] We are also told that no one will be hurt since they were evacuated. Like the narrator who committed suicide but only killed his double while remaining alive, it is destruction with no death, and moreover the destruction of the virtual (credit) by means of the destruction of physical reality (the buildings), which, as viewers, we know is virtual—no actors or characters were killed and the explosions are simulated by CGI.[127] The film gives us no information about what will happen now and what comes after the fall of the symbols of virtual capitalism and all the credit records that are stored inside (or the simulation thereof). The film, indeed, "the cultural work of the period," as John McCullough writes, is "incoherent, multivalent, incomplete, and tentative" which is "entirely consistent with what we know about this historical conjuncture."[128] We cannot quite figure out what happened and what will follow. At the intersection of the return to the body (the brain "surgery") and the loss of the material body (the virtual Tyler and CGI explosions), the film suggests, death becomes less real—one can survive a bullet through the head and no one needs to die as massive buildings are destroyed.

American Psycho is another case where loss of death, loss of clear identity, and loss of coherence come together. Set in the 1980s, the 2000 film, like the book by Bret Easton Ellis, can be seen as exposing the vacuity of commodity worship by Reagan-era yuppies.[129] Nevertheless, as some commentators noted, the film's critique transcends the historical period in which its plot takes place and it is also relevant for its own present, the dot-com era of conspicuous consumption.[130] While its plot does not directly address turn-of-the-millennium post-photographic digital technology, the film's protagonist, Patrick Bateman, is immersed in a media-generated environment, which he does not distinguish from other registers of reality. He is frequently seen with headphones, shutting himself off from others and escaping to pop music. Many of his lines are a hodgepodge of incoherent political media sound bites, such as First Lady Nancy Reagan's "just say no," and an entire monologue of problems that "affect us" and are more important than "the Sikhs killing like tons of Israelis" in Sri Lanka, which consists of slogans ranging from stopping terrorism to stopping world hunger, from promoting equality for women to encouraging a return to traditional moral values. He is clearly influenced by the media and interacting with it. He watches *The Texas Chain Saw Massacre* (Tobe Hooper, 1974) and later chases a woman and kills her with a chainsaw. He claims he is supposed to have lunch with "Cliff Huxtable," the name of the character played by Bill Cosby on the popular sitcom *The Cosby Show* (NBC, 1984–1992). An ATM machine asks him to feed it a stray cat, after which he finds himself in an action-film-like shootout with the police, which involves a generous body count and even an exploding car.

While Patrick inhabits a virtual, media world, the film also gives attention to the return to the body. It is populated by lookalike clones who are all vice presidents at Pierce & Peirce Mergers and Acquisitions. Patrick, the well-groomed yuppie serial killer (or perhaps he only imagines he is), is portrayed in the film "as an 'object-to-be-looked-at' with his perfectly sculpted body."[131] The film gives attention to his "morning ablutions, during which he applies a dizzying array of creams, gels, and facial masks,"[132] and to his diet and exercise regime resulting in a body "that's at once hypermasculine and feminized."[133] The woman he is having an affair with uses psychiatric drugs which clearly affect her behavior. The violence he inflicts on his victims' bodies is bloody and graphic.

His voiceovers in the first few sequences of the film still follow a Cartesian search for a deeper internal self within the body. As we see him peeling off a facial mask, his voiceover explains that Patrick Bateman is an idea, an abstraction, a body ("you can shake my hand and feel flesh gripping yours"). This, to him at this stage, is still insufficient. "I simply am not there," he says. He later complains that while his body is human, something horrible is happening "inside" him and that his "mask of sanity" is about to slip.

But these concerns are no longer present by the end of the film. While at the beginning he still argues that he is "not there," during the film, he comes to realize that he has a self, an "I" that is there, but that it is in no way beyond, beneath, or within his body. He accepts his body *as* his self, not seeking anything deeper within; and superficial media representations *as* reality, with nothing more real grounding it. In turn-of-the-millennium terms, Patrick's identity is his body, which he can alter and perfect according to media norms. As they watch Ronald Reagan lying on television, one of his interchangeable yuppie friends comments that the president presents himself as harmless, "but inside...," upon which Bateman comments in voiceover "but inside doesn't matter." Asked by his friends what he thinks about Reagan's inside he just says "whatever." If the murders he has committed were mere hallucinations they are not "in his mind," but exist materially, on paper—Jean, his secretary, finds gory doodling in his diary. The very last image of the film is of his face, with the camera moving in closer, this time with no facial masks being removed, and a voiceover that declares a flat, bodily immanence where introspection is no longer relevant. "There are no more barriers to cross," he explains. Turning his back to the tradition of Hollywood psychoanalysis, in which remembering a repressed trauma offers an immediate cure, he declares, "But even after admitting this, there is no catharsis. [...] I gain no deeper knowledge of myself." As the camera zooms in to an extreme close up of his eyes he clearly states, "This confession has meant nothing," adding a significant nail in Freud's coffin.

If, as suggested in this reading, the body is the self in this film, and moreover, this body-as-identity is not stable, but can be and is molded and shaped to match virtual media-generated images, it could account for the strange status of death in the film. It is never quite clear whether Patrick has murdered anyone, and in the reality of the film it would be impossible ever to know. Media representations are just as real as anything else is in Patrick's world and the body, which is one's identity, can be changed. In the circles Patrick travels, everybody seems to be more-or-less clones. They all aspire to have the same body, go to the same hairdresser, wear the same clothes, and eat at the same restaurant (the people outside these circles, the homeless man and the prostitute, are truly insignificant to the Manhattanites in the film). It is hardly surprising that it is never clear who murders whom if at all.

When, in the film, Patrick confesses to his lawyer that he murdered Paul Allen, his lawyer insists that the man he is talking to is not Patrick, that Patrick is not talented enough to have done it, and that he had lunch with Paul Allen in London ten days earlier. None of this means that Patrick did not murder Paul Allen, or that someone did not murder someone. Many people in the film confuse Patrick and others for other people and the characters truly look like clones. Did the lawyer have lunch with Allen? With someone else? Did Patrick murder Allen or someone else? Did someone else murder Allen? Is Patrick really Patrick? Since identity is the body and the inside does not matter, this too does not matter. With the return to the body, identity becomes fluid because the body can be altered. Death is meaningless and it is unclear if it ever took place.

Patrick's world and being are not easily compatible with the ways we have seen to make death meaningful in classical Hollywood. In relation the past, Patrick is not killable like the traditional gangster, because he lacks a stable identity. His body is malleable and his identity fluid. He does not need to be stopped from committing any additional murders, by being caught or killed, because it is never quite clear who he really is and whether he has committed any real murders, or only imagined he did by being immersed in virtual media images. Nor can death serve to reveal any secret truths. Acts of admitting or confessing are meaningless. Revealing a past truth—whether through death or not—is without any significance. In relation to the future, deaths are questionable in this world because no one is sure who died and if anybody, at all, has died.

A community to remember the unknown deceased, who perhaps is still alive, is difficult to imagine. The murdered victims, if there are any, are not missed. Not knowing who is who and whether anyone has died, it is also difficult to say whether death, which perhaps has never taken place, has altered any goals or obstacles. Patrick will not be caught, punished, or stopped. Like Patrick's confession, which has meant nothing, in a virtual and back-to-the-body world, death also remains meaningless by the standards we encountered in classical films.

Both *Fight Club* and *American Psycho* are not *about* CGI virtual characters, brain science, or genetic engineering, screening, and cloning and their ramifications for death. They do however enable us to think death in a cyber–cyborg age in which bodies can be abandoned as we immerse ourselves in a virtual world and in which identities are defined by a malleable body. Like the cyber and back-to-the-body discourse, the films offer worlds in which mortality is no longer certain or necessary. The films are also enigmatic, not quite explaining what has happened or how things will now proceed. If, as Deleuze suggests, film theory's role is to create the concepts which films arouse, that is, to think the unthought in films, then these films' incoherence and incompleteness is a resource we can use. Even if the worlds they portray never come into existence, especially if they never do, films can offer us a starting point for an attempt to think beyond our actual mortal ways of being.

Notes

1 The Meaning of Death in Classical Hollywood

1. Epicurus, "Epicurus to Menoeceus," trans. C. Bailey, *The Stoic and Epicurean Philosophers: The Complete Extant Writings of Epicurus, Epictetus, Lucretius, Marcus Aurelius*, ed. Whitney J. Oates (New York: The Modern Library, 1940), 30–31; and "Principal Doctrines," trans. C. Bailey, *Stoic and Epicurean Philosophers*, II, 35.
2. See Michel Foucault, *The Birth of the Clinic: An Archaeology of Medical Perception*, trans. A. M. Sheridan Smith (New York: Vintage Books, 1994), 171.
3. Martin Heidegger, *Being and Time*, trans. John Macquarrie and Edward Robinson (Oxford and Cambridge: Blackwell, 2004), §47, 283–284; Jacques Derrida, *The Gift of Death*, trans. David Wills (Chicago and London: The University of Chicago Press, 1995), 44. Death is therefore "meaningless" insofar as difference is essential to meaning, as for example has been argued about language. See, Ferdinand de Saussure, *Course in General Linguistics*, ed. Charles Bally, Albert Sechehaye, in collaboration with Albert Riedlinger, trans. Wade Baskin (New York, Toronto, and London: McGraw-Hill, 1966), 120.
4. Is it not true, Jacques Derrida asks, that "culture itself, cultures in general, is essentially, before anything, even a priori, the culture of death?" (*Aporias: Dying—Awaiting [One Another at] the "Limits of Truth*," trans. Thomas Dutoit [Stanford: Stanford University Press, 1993], 43). Dying, Arthur Schopenhauer suggests, is "to be regarded as the real aim of life," like the fruit is the aim of a plant (*The World as Will and Representation*, trans. E. F. J. Payne [New York: Dover, 1966], II: 637). Cicero, according to Michel de Montaigne, said that "to philosophize is nothing else but to prepare for death" (*The Complete Works of Montaigne: Essays, Travel Journal, Letters*, trans. Donald M. Frame [Stanford: Stanford University Press, 1967], Essay 1, 20, 56). Philosophy, Plato writes, is engaged in practicing for death ("Phaedo," *Symposium and the Death of Socrates*, trans. Tom Griffith [Ware: Wordsworth, 1997], 64a), while philosophers themselves practice death, as Simon Critchley shows in *The Book of Dead Philosophers* (London: Granta Books, 2008). In the case of non-philosophers, Blaise Pascal claims, it is in order to not think of their incurable death that they seek *divertissement* "like gambling, hunting, some absorbing show," and all the hustle and bustle that prevents them from thinking about themselves and their mortal wretchedness (*Pensées*, trans. A. J. Krailsheimer, revised edition [London: Penguin Books, 1995], §136 [Lafuma]/§139 [Brunschvicg], 38). For Heidegger the "idle talk of the 'they'" is "an evasion in the face of death—an evasion which conceals" (*Being and Time*, §52, 299).

According to Thomas Hobbes, a multitude of men unite into the great Leviathan under one sovereign who acts to ensure peace among them because the "worst of all," at a time of war of everyman against every man, is "continual fear, and danger of violent death" (*Leviathan[, or the Matter, Forme, & Power of a Common-Wealth Ecclesiasticall and Civill]*, ed. J. C. A. Gaskin [Oxford: Oxford University Press, 1998], XIII §9, 84; see also XVII §§13–14, 114). For Benedict de Spinoza the "supreme and essential mystery" in "despotic statecraft" is that this form of dominion can hoodwink the subjects to "count it not shame but highest honour to risk their blood and their lives for the vainglory of a tyrant" ("A Theologico-Political Treatise," *A Theologico-Political Treatise and a Political Treatise*, trans. R. H. M. Elwes [New York: Dover Publications, 1951], 5). Some three centuries later, Benedict Anderson is occupied with a similar mystery when he asks how the nation can make it possible for millions of people "not so much to kill, as willingly to die" (*Imagined Communities: Reflections on the Origin and Spread of Nationalism*, revised edition [London and New York: Verso, 1991], 7). He argues that nationality is superbly designed to make our deaths meaningful, to help us deal, in an age of rising secularization, with the overwhelming burden of our inescapable death by transforming fatality into continuity within the "immemorial past" and "limitless future" of the nation (11–12).

5. André Bazin, "The Ontology of the Photographic Image," *What Is Cinema?* trans. Hugh Gray (Berkeley, Los Angeles, and London: University of California Press, 2005), 9–16 and "The Myth of Total Cinema," 17–22; Edgar Morin, *Le Cinéma ou l'homme imaginaire: Essai d'anthropologie* (Genève: Éditions Gonthier, 1965); Susan Sontag, *On Photography* (New York: Dell Publishing, 1977); Roland Barthes, *Camera Lucida: Reflections on Photography*, trans. Richard Howard (New York: Hill and Wang, 1983); Pier Paolo Pasolini, *Heretical Empiricism*, ed. Louise K. Barnett, trans. Ben Lawton and Louise K. Barnett (Bloomington and Indianapolis: Indiana University Press, 1988); Laura Mulvey, *Death 24 x a Second: Stillness and the Moving Image* (London: Reaktion Books, 2006). See also Garrett Stewart, *Between Film and Screen: Modernism's Photo Synthesis* (Chicago and London: The University of Chicago Press, 1999) for a discussion of "the Bazin-Barthes line" linking photography (and sometimes cinema) and death.

6. Friedrich A. Kittler, *Gramophone, Film, Typewriter*, trans. Geoffrey Winthrop-Young and Michael Wutz (Stanford: Stanford University Press, 1999), 124–125.

7. J. David Slocum, "Violence and American Cinema: Notes for an Investigation," *Violence and American Cinema*, ed. J. David Slocum (New York and London: Routledge, 2001), 13.

8. bell hooks, "*Crooklyn*: The Denial of Death," *Reel to Real: Race, Sex, and Class at the Movies* (New York and London: Routledge, 1996), 35.

9. Richard Dyer, "White," *Film Theory: Critical Conceptions in Media and Cultural Studies*, ed. Philip Simpson, Andrew Utterson, and K. J. Shepherdson, Vol. III. (London and New York: Routledge, 2004), 213.

10. Dyer, "White," 227.

11. Steve Neale, "Masculinity as Spectacle: Reflections on Men and Mainstream Cinema," *Feminism and Film: An Anthology*, ed. E. Ann Kaplan (Oxford: Oxford University Press, 2000), 262.

12. Vito Russo, *The Celluloid Closet: Homosexuality in the Movies* (New York: Harper & Row, Publishers, 1981), 261–262.
13. Elisabeth Bronfen, *Over Her Dead Body: Death, Femininity and the Aesthetic* (New York: Routledge, 1992), 405.
14. Bronfen, *Over Her Dead Body*, xi.
15. Gilles Deleuze, "Having an Idea in Cinema (On the Cinema of Straub-Huillet)," trans. Eleanor Kaufman, *Deleuze and Guattari: New Mappings in Politics, Philosophy, and Culture*, ed. Eleanor Kaufman and Kevin Jon Heller (Minneapolis and London: University of Minnesota Press, 1998), 15.
16. Gilles Deleuze, *Cinema 2: The Time-Image*, trans. Hugh Tomlinson and Robert Galeta (Minneapolis: University of Minnesota Press, 1989), 280; see also Gilles Deleuze and Félix Guattari, *What Is Philosophy?* trans. Hugh Tomlinson and Graham Burchell (New York: Columbia University Press, 1994); Daniel Frampton, *Filmosophy* (London and New York: Wallflower Press, 2006); and D. N. Rodowick, "An Elegy for Theory," *October* 122 (Fall 2007): 91–109, esp. 101–106.
17. Deleuze, "Having an Idea in Cinema," 15.
18. Jacques Rancière, *Film Fables*, trans. Emiliano Battista (Oxford and New York: Berg, 2006), 117.
19. Deleuze, *Cinema 2*, 168. Deleuze is dealing here with ideas he has found in Artaud, Heidegger, Blanchot, and Schefer.
20. Deleuze and Guattari, *What Is Philosophy?*, 218.
21. I am therefore not following the claim that films offer argumentation that can be integrated into professional Anglo-American philosophy. For this approach, see Thomas A. Wartenberg, *Thinking on Screen: Film as Philosophy* (London and New York: Routledge, 2007) and Thomas A. Wartenberg, "Film as Philosophy," *The Routledge Companion to Philosophy and Film*, ed. Paisley Livingston and Carl Plantinga (London and New York: Routledge, 2009), 549–559.
22. This is not Deleuze's view. Being an unabashed elitist to the nth degree, he would never agree that run-of-the-mill classical Hollywood films can do this. For him, for example, only "the essence of cinema—which is not the majority of films—has thought as its higher purpose" (*Cinema 2*, 168).
23. Temporality according to Heidegger "has the unity of a future which makes present in the process of having been" (*Being and Time*, §65, 374). He calls the future, the character of having been, and the Present the "ecstases" of temporality (*die Ekstasen der Zeitlichkeit*; §65, 377). His account of both authentic and inauthentic Being links the ecstases to death. The ecstasis which has priority in primordial and authentic temporality is the future, which is the authentic Being-towards-its-end of Dasein and thus reveals itself as finite (§65, 378). Heidegger shows that it is primarily having been that grounds anxiety, which "arises out of Being-in-the-world as thrown Being-towards-death" and enables the disclosure of authentic Being-towards-death (§68, 395). The Present, in authentic temporality, is called "moment of vision" (*Augenblick*, §65, 376). It discloses the Situation and "temporalizes itself [. . .] in terms of the authentic future" (§68, 388), which as we have already noted is authentic Being-towards-death. The current Situation and "therewith the primordial 'limit-Situation' of Being-towards-death," says Heidegger, can "be

disclosed as a moment of vision which has been held on to" (§68, 400). In inauthentic temporality, the Present makes possible falling, which is one of the constitutive items of the structure of care. Heidegger takes curiosity as an example and says that in curiosity the making-present constantly leaps and runs away and is thus the condition for the possibility of distraction (§68, 398). In that Dasein flees its authentic Being-towards-death, and so, according to Heidegger, the "leaping-away" of the Present, the falling, also "has its source in that primordial authentic temporality itself which makes possible thrown Being-towards-death" (§68, 399). For a further discussion of how death grounds temporality in Heidegger, see Brent Adkins, *Death and Desire in Hegel, Heidegger and Deleuze* (Edinburgh: Edinburgh University Press, 2007), esp. 54–71.

24. Emmanuel Levinas, *God, Death, and Time*, trans. Bettina Bergo (Stanford: Stanford University Press, 2000), 21. For a discussion of the differences between Levinas and Heidegger on the issue of death and time, see Tina Chanter, *Time, Death, and the Feminine: Levinas with Heidegger* (Stanford: Stanford University Press, 2001), esp. chapter 5.

25. By the mid-1920s, according to Kristin Thompson, "classical filmmaking had reached a relative stability" (David Bordwell, Janet Staiger, and Kristin Thompson, *The Classical Hollywood Cinema: Film Style & Mode of Production to 1960* [London, Melbourne and Henley: Routledge & Kegan Paul, 1985], 231). Films made after that period, she writes, followed with technical and stylistic perfection the norms and standards that were already fully formulated, sometimes in print, by 1917. Thomas Schatz describes 1955 as "a watershed year in filmmaking history," which "marked the end of the [... major studios'] resistance to active television production" (*The Genius of the System: Hollywood Filmmaking in the Studio Era* [London: Faber and Faber, 1998], 476). By the mid-1950s, according to Bordwell, television had become the dominant mass-entertainment form and by the end of the decade, it was widely believed in the film industry that "Hollywood had reached the end of its mature existence" (Bordwell, Staiger, and Thompson, *Classical Hollywood Cinema*, 10).

26. I fully accept genre as a retrospective, unstable construct and I have used two different post-1955 critical or scholarly sources for each genre in order to form a list of classical Hollywood films which represent that genre for us today. Although I will not be able to analyze each film separately, all generalizations in this book about "classical Hollywood" deaths are meant to apply to this sample of films. For the Western, I have used the select filmography in the tenth chapter of John Belton's textbook *American Cinema/American Culture* (New York: McGraw-Hill, 1994) and the Westerns in Will Wright's *Six Guns and Society: A Structural Study of the Western* (Berkeley, Los Angeles, and London: University of California Press, 1977), which were among the top grossing films of the year they were released (Wright, *Six Guns and Society*, 29). For the gangster film, I have taken all of the gangster films mentioned in the third chapter of Dominic Strinati's *Introduction to Studying Popular Culture* (London and New York: Routledge, 2000) and all of those mentioned in the fourth chapter of Thomas Schatz's *Hollywood Genres: Formulas, Filmmaking, and the Studio System* (New York: McGraw-Hill, 1981). For the melodrama, or family melodrama, I used the select filmography in the

sixth chapter of Belton's book and all of the melodramas mentioned in the eighth chapter of Schatz's *Hollywood Genres*. Finally, the sample of war films was taken from the select filmography in the eighth chapter of Belton's book and all American war films mentioned in Lenny Rubenstein's entry "The War Film," *The Political Companion to American Film*, ed. Gary Crowdus (Chicago: Lake View Press, 1994), 455–463. In order to reduce the sample to a more manageable size and so as to make an equal effort to view the different films in the list, I have further limited it to those texts which were available at the Anda Zimand Film Archive at Tel Aviv University in early 2005, when I began this project. I will mention other films when discussing specific historical phenomena or when a point, which is discernable in the sample, could be better illustrated using a different film.

The sample of films is:

Westerns:

1. *Apache* (Robert Aldrich, 1954)
2. *Duel in the Sun* (King Vidor, 1946)
3. *Fort Apache* (John Ford, 1948)
4. *High Noon* (Fred Zinnemann, 1952)
5. *Johnny Guitar* (Nicholas Ray, 1954)
6. *The Man from Laramie* (Anthony Mann, 1955)
7. *My Darling Clementine* (John Ford, 1946)
8. *The Naked Spur* (Anthony Mann, 1952)
9. *Red River* (Howard Hawks, 1948)
10. *Shane* (George Stevens, 1953)
11. *She Wore a Yellow Ribbon* (John Ford, 1949)
12. *Stagecoach* (John Ford, 1939)

Gangster:

1. *Angels with Dirty Faces* (Michael Curtiz, 1938)
2. *The Asphalt Jungle* (John Huston, 1950)
3. *The Big Heat* (Fritz Lang, 1953)
4. *Dead End* (William Wyler, 1937)
5. *Force of Evil* (Abraham Polonsky, 1948)
6. *High Sierra* (Raoul Walsh, 1941)
7. *Jesse James* (Henry King, 1939)
8. *Key Largo* (John Huston, 1948)
9. *Little Caesar* (Mervyn LeRoy, 1930)
10. *Manhattan Melodrama* (W. S. Van Dyke II, 1934)
11. *The Petrified Forest* (Archie Mayo, 1936)
12. *The Public Enemy* (William Wellman, 1931)
13. *The Roaring Twenties* (Raoul Walsh, 1939)
14. *Scarface, the Shame of the Nation* (Howard Hawks, 1932)
15. *They Live by Night* (Nicholas Ray, 1949)
16. *White Heat* (Raoul Walsh, 1949)
17. *You Only Live Once* (Fritz Lang, 1937)

Melodrama:

1. *All I Desire* (Douglas Sirk, 1953)
2. *The Bad and the Beautiful* (Vincent Minnelli, 1953)
3. *Caught* (Max Ophuls, 1949)
4. *The Cobweb* (Vincent Minnelli, 1955)
5. *The Crowd* (King Vidor, 1928)
6. *East of Eden* (Elia Kazan, 1955)
7. *A Farewell to Arms* (Frank Borzage, 1932)
8. *Gone with the Wind* (Victor Fleming, 1939)
9. *Imitation of Life* (John Stahl, 1934)
10. *Letter from an Unknown Woman* (Max Ophuls, 1948)
11. *Madame Bovary* (Vincent Minnelli, 1949)
12. *Magnificent Obsession* (John Stahl, 1935)
13. *Magnificent Obsession* (Douglas Sirk, 1954)
14. *Mildred Pierce* (Michael Curtiz, 1945)
15. *Rebel without a Cause* (Nicholas Ray, 1955)
16. *Sunrise* (F. W. Murnau, 1927)
17. *When Tomorrow Comes* (John Stahl, 1939)

War:

1. *All Quiet on the Western Front* (Lewis Milestone, 1930)
2. *The Best Years of Our Lives* (William Wyler, 1946)
3. *The Big Parade* (King Vidor, 1925)
4. *The Desert Fox* (Henry Hathaway, 1951)
5. *Duck Soup* (Leo McCary, 1933)
6. *The Great Dictator* (Charles Chaplin, 1941)
7. *Objective, Burma!* (Raoul Walsh, 1945)
8. *Sands of Iwo Jima* (Allan Dwan, 1949)
9. *Sergeant York* (Howard Hawks, 1941)
10. *The Story of G. I. Joe* (William Wellman, 1945)
11. *Stalag 17* (Billy Wilder, 1953)
12. *A Walk in the Sun* (Lewis Milestone, 1945)

Of the films in this sample, *All I Desire*, *Sunrise*, and *Madame Bovary* will not be dealt with because they do not show or tell of any actual deaths (although the first two get very close). *Madame Bovary* is the story of the trial of Gustave Flaubert, which includes selected and relatively inoffensive scenes from his book with his voiceover narration. No deaths take place during this trial. In *Sunrise*, the Man does imagine drowning the Wife, begins to strangle the Woman from the City, and at a certain stage believes the Wife has drowned, but in the end no one dies and the film offers its viewers a happy ending (as does Murnau's *City Girl* [1930], in which a father shoots at his son, but misses).

27. Bordwell, Staiger, and Thompson, *Classical Hollywood Cinema*, 13.
28. Suffice it to think of how death functions in films that do not follow the Hollywood formula. In Carl Theodor Dreyer's *Ordet* (1955), for example, Christianity is used to motivate a miraculous event near the end of the film. Giving up causal logic, death turns out to be reversible when one of

the characters, Inger, who dies during the film, returns back to life. Before this event, nothing in the film cued us to believe this was a possibility—no supernatural options were given and her resurrection was not "realistically" motivated (David Bordwell, *The Films of Carl-Theodor Dreyer* [Berkeley, Los Angeles, and London: University of California Press, 1981], 147). Moreover, the man who commands her back to life is Johannes, who believed he was Jesus of Nazareth, because, so everybody in the film assumed, he was mad (perhaps due to the study of Kierkegaard). Yet even he goes sane before resurrecting Inger, so that her coming back to life is truly a miracle within the film's narrative. It is, as Paul Schrader writes, "unexpected, implausible" (*Transcendental Style in Film: Ozu, Bresson, Dreyer* [New York: De Capo Press, 1988], 134). As if to make things even more exacerbating, the rebirth of Inger takes place within the very sequence in which Dreyer suddenly abandons his idiosyncratic long takes and introduces Hollywood-style classical analytic editing, constructing for the first time in the film intelligible space and time responsive to the narrative (Bordwell, *Films of Carl-Theodor Dreyer,* 170). Death, then, in a Danish auteur film, can work against causality, even, or particularly, while using other Hollywood stylistic conventions. The other two directors in Schrader's book—Bresson and Ozu—are both cited by Bordwell as examples of cases where no personal narrative causality is assured (*Classical Hollywood Cinema,* 13), and the way death is meaningful in their works is likely to differ from the way it does in classical Hollywood.

29. Bordwell, Staiger, and Thompson, *Classical Hollywood Cinema,* 16.
30. Bordwell, Staiger, and Thompson, *Classical Hollywood Cinema,* 12.
31. They are usually relegated to an initiating event or an abrupt alteration of the storyline, which then resumes its personal-casual structure, and are frequently generically motivated, for instance, the romantic couple meets again by chance in the last scene (Bordwell, Staiger, and Thompson, *Classical Hollywood Cinema,* 13).
32. I have not found that death *must* have a certain event before it or after it, or that classical film is characterized by the "coincidence of death and closure" (Catherine Russell, *Narrative Mortality: Death, Closure, and New Wave Cinemas* [Minneapolis and London: University of Minnesota Press, 1995], 20).
33. Bordwell, Staiger, and Thompson, *Classical Hollywood Cinema,* 12. The priority of the plot is of course not unique to Hollywood cinema as analyzed by Bordwell, and could also be found, for example, in Aristotle's claim that in tragedy, the plot is the most important constituent element (*Poetics,* trans. James Hutton [New York and London: W. W. Norton, 1982], 1450a).
34. David Bordwell, *The Way Hollywood Tells It: Story and Style in Modern Movies* (Berkeley, Los Angeles, and London: University of California Press, 2006), 43–44. Bordwell suggests that in some films the tidiness of the classical plot can become the film's thematic core, even announcing to the characters destiny's intention or the hand of god. Bordwell's "saturation" of motifs are similar to Bellour's "symbolic blockage," in which elements "echo" each other or "rhyme" and the end might "reply" to the beginning. I will discuss Bellour in more detail in Chapter 4.
35. I will return to these in more detail in Chapter 4.
36. David Thomson, "Death and Its Details," *Film Comment* 29.5 (September–October 1993): 14. Incidentally, Gary Cooper's character dies within minutes

of the character's first appearance in *Wings* (William A. Wellman, 1927), and Jeanine Basinger offers a short list of movies in which John Wayne's characters die in *The World War II Combat Film: Anatomy of a Genre* (New York: Columbia University Press, 1986), 168.

37. Hollywood's Production Code is critical of this formula when it warns that if evil is presented alluringly and then condemned or punished "it must not be allowed to appear so attractive" that the emotions drawn to it later "forget the condemnation and remember only the apparent joy of the sin" (Second Section, "Working Principles," I note (a), qtd. in Thomas Doherty, *Pre-Code Hollywood: Sex, Immorality, and Insurrection in American Cinema 1930–1934* [New York: Columbia University Press, 1999], 351).

38. Qtd. in Gregory D. Black, *Hollywood Censored: Morality Codes, Catholics, and the Movies* (Cambridge: Cambridge University Press, 1994), 5.

39. For a history of the Code see Black's *Hollywood Censored*. An analysis of the actual work done by the administration vis-à-vis the studios, regional, and international censors, in one of the contexts most relevant to death is given in Stephen Prince, *Classical Film Violence: Designing and Regulating Brutality in Hollywood Cinema, 1930–1968* (New Brunswick, New Jersey, and London: Rutgers University Press, 2003). For an analysis of the films in the rather strange four-year period between the formal adoption of the code and its more rigorous enforcement, see Doherty's *Pre-Code Hollywood*.

40. Amendments, IV ("*Regulations re crime in motion pictures*"), 10, qtd. in Doherty, *Pre-Code Hollywood*, 366.

41. A note about my use of history might be helpful here. This creation of concepts makes use of the past—classical Hollywood films from the 1920s through the 1950s and other events and discourses, some of which were taking place at the time these films appeared. I would like to clarify that my use of the past is in the service of the creation of concepts. I do not deny that there are differences between different periods, but I am not attempting to describe vast historical changes (or "progress"), in which films are a component, or, worse, of which films are a reflection. While films existed with other practices at various times, I am unable (and not very eager) to claim that one particular realm determines all others. There is no transcendent or underlying ground (or historical "context") which is the source and guarantee of all other terms. For Deleuze, the creation of the concepts that cinema gives rise to is related to concepts that correspond to other practices. For him "beings, images, concepts, all the kinds of events" take place "at the level of the interference of many practices" with no practice, not even philosophy, the practice of concepts, having privilege over others (*Cinema 2*, 280). The term "interference" here should be understood in the sense it has in physics, the mutual action of multiple waves, whose superposition results in constructive or destructive interference, that is, in reinforced, weakened, or neutralized undulations. No one wave is the "context" in which the others take place or is known in advance to determine the others in some way. The attempt will therefore not be to force the films to conform to a single other external practice, such as the historical "moment" which films must reflect or subvert (or even a past or future moment, the residual or emergent, culture/society, cf. Raymond Williams, *Marxism and Literature* [Oxford and New York: Oxford University Press, 1977], 121–127). I will not find their

"*combinatoire*" which opens up/shuts down their formal possibilities (Fredric Jameson, *The Political Unconscious: Narrative as a Socially Symbolic Act* [Ithaca: Cornell University Press, 1981], 148). Nor will I be stipulating a subject—neither a sovereign universal "active viewer" (David Bordwell, *Narration in the Fiction Film* [Madison: The University of Wisconsin Press, 1985], 29–47) nor a viewer whose negotiated reading is the result of the way the viewer is "situated [...] within the social system" (John Fiske, *Reading the Popular* [London and New York: Routledge, 1989], 2). I will even not presuppose that the popular text *must* offer popular pleasures that "must contain elements of the oppositional" (John Fiske, *Understanding Popular Culture* [Boston: Unwin Hyman, 1989], 127). Not that any of these are a priori and by necessity wrong. I will frequently be mentioning other practices which interact with the cinematic texts, but I would not like to presuppose in advance that the films *must* be correlated in a certain way to any of these; that one realm of the social is known in advance to determine another. Saying that there is no single ground that determines all other terms does not mean that there are no historical differences. At different times, different practices take place and their interferences (that is, the beings, images, concepts, and events) can surely be different.

My goal is not to build a historical continuum, not to fill in missing details, not to put everything in order and our minds at ease. It is to find different ways of thinking, which might involve a montage of heterogeneous sources (films, philosophy, and other practices) from diverse periods. It thus resonates with some of the methodological comments Walter Benjamin has made. In his early "Epistemo-Critical Prologue" to the *Trauerspiel* book, he extols the treatise, which, like a mosaic, is made up of distinct and disparate fragments (*The Origin of German Tragic Drama*, trans. John Osborne [London: NLB, 1977], 28–29). The task of philosophy, he writes, is the representation of ideas, which takes place "in an arrangement of concrete elements," through "the medium of empirical reality." Ideas are distinct elements of phenomena which are arranged in configurations, as stars are in constellations (34). The constellations and configurations, the montages, he deals with in his later writing are not only constructed with distinct and disparate fragments, but also with fragments from diverse periods. The "different epochs of the past," he claims, "are not all touched in the same degree by the present day of the historian" (*The Arcades Project*, trans. Howard Eiland and Kevin McLaughlin [Cambridge and London: Harvard University Press. 1999], [N7a, 2], 470). He images a historian who "ceases to tell the sequence of events like the beads of a rosary" and "grasps the constellation into which his own era has entered, along with a very specific earlier one" ("On the Concept of History," *Selected Writings*, volume 4, ed. Howard Eiland and Michael W. Jennings [Cambridge and London: The Belknap Press of Harvard University Press, 2003], 4: §A, 4: 397). The elements he takes in order to construct his constellations, then, can come from various different eras and do not form one causal sequence of events or a continuum. Rather, he is concerned with an image of the past, "that wherein what has been comes together in a flash with the now to form a constellation" (*Arcades Project*, [N2a, 3], 462). My discussion will offer various "flashes" and "constellations" of heterogeneous sources from diverse periods: Henry Fonda and Hegel, John Wayne and Nietzsche, and James Dean and Plato, as they become recognizable in my present, form a constellation with my concern.

In some cases, notably Chapter 3, the constellation will be between various phenomena from the same period. The point, again, is not to put things into a larger historical context in an unproblematic fashion. Indeed, in this chapter, the crime films are *dissimilar* to other explanations of criminality from the period.

42. Stanley Cavell, *Pursuits of Happiness: The Hollywood Comedy of Remarriage* (Cambridge and London: Harvard University Press, 1981), 272–273. He then adds that he does not know "that any single person knows, or could know, all of those things" (273).

43. Stanley Cavell in conversation with Andrew Klevan, " 'What Becomes of Thinking on Film?' " *Film* as *Philosophy: Essays in Cinema after Wittgenstein and Cavell*, ed. Rupert Read and Jerry Goodenough (Basingstoke and New York: Palgrave Macmillan, 2005), 190. See also Stephen Mulhall's understanding of some films as "philosophy in action" (2) and as engaged in "a systematic and sophisticated thinking" that can critically evaluate and question (7) in *On Film* (London and New York: Rouledge, 2002). I will not be following Mulhall in giving particular attention to the way films philosophize about themselves.

44. For the meaning of "ethics" that I am referring to, see Adi Ophir, *The Order of Evils: Toward an Ontology of Morals*, trans. Rela Mazali and Havi Carel (New York: Zone Books, 2005), §8.515, 501–503.

45. Jürgen Habermas, "Consciousness-Raising or Redemptive Criticism: The Contemporaneity of Walter Benjamin," trans. Philip Brewster and Carl Howard Buchner, *New German Critique* 17 (Spring 1979): §VI, 54.

46. Peter Sloterdijk, *Critique of Cynical Reason*, trans. Michael Eldred (Minneapolis: University of Minneapolis Press, 1988), 5.

47. Slavoj Žižek, *The Sublime Object of Ideology* (London and New York: Verso, 1991), 33.

48. Slavoj Žižek, "The Spectre of Ideology," *Mapping Ideology*, ed. Slavoj Žižek (London and New York: Verso, 1994), 18.

49. Friedrich Nietzsche, "On the Uses and Disadvantages of History for Life," *Untimely Meditations*, ed. Daniel Breazeale, trans. R. J. Hollingsale (Cambridge: Cambridge University Press, 1997), §3, 76.

50. Deleuze finally lays the burden on the virtual, which at most will be actualized in the future, in a people "who do not yet exist" ("Having an Idea in Cinema," 19). This retreat to the virtual and the future has already been offered by Nietzsche who called for studying history "as the attendant of a mighty new current of life, of an evolving culture for example," ("On the Uses and Disadvantages of History for Life," §1, 66) and claimed that history will be understood only by architects of the future, that "only he who constructs the future has a right to judge the past" (§6, 94). Habermas's understanding of Benjamin's "redemptive criticism" of the past can also be read as implying that its relevance might be most acute for the future. His reading suggests that it is possible that Benjamin's rescuing and redeeming of the past will be useful at a future date, when an emancipated humanity is nevertheless still "deprived of the terms in which it is able to interpret life as good life" ("Consciousness-Raising or Redemptive Criticism," §VII, 58).

2 Two Platos: Death, Truth, and Knowledge

1. According to the Internet Movie Database, there are 807 titles with the key-word "time travel." Only eight of them are American theatrical motion pictures that fall within the time frame of classical Hollywood as I have defined it (I have not included shorts, serials, TV series episodes, and non-American films). See: <http://www.imdb.com/keyword/time-travel/?sort=release_date>, accessed 11 August 2009.

2. It can be argued that in many cases the question is hardly pressing. Whether or not death is meaningful in relation to the past, it can still be meaningful in relation to the future. Moreover, even if death is the last event in a particular storyline and therefore affects no future in that storyline, the film might still go on and deal with other storylines without brooding over the death that concluded a storyline. In Westerns, a showdown might be a story-terminating death in a storyline that has to do with a conflict between two sides. Yet other storylines in the film still remain to be settled, and the side that has won the showdown and has remained alive can play a role in them. After killing his rivals, the eponymous protagonist of *Shane* (George Stevens, 1953) still needs to part from little Joey, the young boy who admires him; in *My Darling Clementine* (John Ford, 1946), after the showdown Wyatt has a role in a second storyline in which he tells Clementine he is leaving but might return; in *Stagecoach* (John Ford, 1939), after the shooting ends, the Ringo Kid, an outlaw, leaves to his ranch across the border with Dallas, a woman with a past; and in *High Noon* (Fred Zinnemann, 1952), Will Kane has a role in a storyline in which he leaves the town with his wife.

   Yet in other cases, there are no additional storylines. Death is the conclud-ing event of the entire film and it can only be meaningful in relation to the past.

3. Plato, "Phaedo," *Symposium and the Death of Socrates*, trans. Tom Griffith (Ware: Wordsworth, 1997), 133–211.

4. Plato, "Phaedo," 82e–83a.

5. Plato, "Phaedo," 61b–61d.

6. Plato, "Phaedo," 66d.

7. Plato, "Phaedo," 79d.

8. Plato, "Phaedo," 64a, 67e, 80e.

9. For a discussion of the moment of death as a moment of truth (or at least self-understanding) in Solon, Montaigne, Hegel, and Heidegger, see Adi Ophir, *The Order of Evils: Toward an Ontology of Morals*, trans. Rela Mazali and Havi Carel (New York: Zone Books, 2005), §§9.520–9.521, 619–620; 652n24.

10. Michel Foucault, *The Birth of the Clinic: An Archaeology of Medical Perception*, trans. A. M. Sheridan Smith (New York: Vintage Books, 1994), 124.

11. Foucault, *Birth of the Clinic*, 144.

12. Qtd. in Foucault, *Birth of the Clinic*, 146.

13. If we think of death not only as an event that ends life, but also as a pos-sible presence throughout one's life, then the (living) knower and what is known can be the same person. In these cases, death serves not so much to reveal new information as to alter the truthfulness of one's own life. Death is associated with "genuineness" in Siegfried Kracauer, *The Salaried Masses: Duty and Distraction in Weimar Germany*, trans. Quintin Hoare (London and

New York: Verso, 1998), 58–59; and death is described as related to the possibility of authentic existence in Martin Heidegger, *Being and Time*, trans. John Macquarrie and Edward Robinson (Oxford and Cambridge: Blackwell, 2004), §53, 307.

14. Walter Benjamin, "The Storyteller: Observations on the Works of Nikolai Leskov," trans. Harry Zohn, *Selected Writings*, Volume 3, ed. Howard Eiland and Michael W. Jennings (Cambridge and London: The Belknap Press of Harvard University Press, 2002), §X, 3: 151. But death is also transcended in this artisan form of communication as stories are passed down from generation to generation, experience accumulates in them, and tradition survives intact, see Bernd Witte, *Walter Benjamin: An Intellectual Biography*, trans. James Rolleston (Detroit: Wayne University Press, 1991), 164–165.

15. On the centrality of attaining knowledge in the film and its foregrounding within the film's own dialogue and monologues, see Steve Neale, "Aspects of Ideology and Narrative Form in the American War Film," *Screen* 32.1 (Spring 1991): 35–57, esp. 50–53.

16. Similarly, in *Bullets or Ballots* (William Keighley, 1936), Johnny is an undercover policeman posing as a gangster. By being shot, he manages to get hold of bullets that can be traced back to the gun of another gangster and enable the police to solve two previous murders. Being shot solves the crime. And it also kills him.

17. Scott Simmon, *The Invention of the Western Film: A Cultural History of the Genre's First Half-Century* (Cambridge: Cambridge University Press, 2003), 120.

18. Claudia Gorbman, "Drums along the L. A. River: Scoring the Indian." *Westerns: Films through History*, ed. Janet Walker (New York and London: Routledge, 2001), 177–195. Gorbman discusses the paucity of musical language to designate the faceless and undifferentiated Indians in the classical Western which "stands in direct contrast to the variety of musical expression for the hero and other individualized white characters" (182).

19. Simmon, *Invention of the Western Film*, 157.

20. As Daniel Dayan shows, the Indians in the film seem to be practically blind, their gazes are "inert, emptied of all intentionality. They are trompe-l'oeil gazes, non-gazes" (Daniel Dayan, *Western Graffiti: Jeux d'images et programmation du spectateur dans La chevauchée fantastique de John Ford* [Paris: Éditions Clancier-Guénaud, 1983], 134).

21. Technically, they have not run out of bullets. Hatfield the gambler still has one bullet left, but he is about to use it in order to kill the lady on the stagecoach and save her from the proverbial "fate worse than death." We also later learn that another character, the Ringo Kid, has three bullets left, which he later uses to kill three brothers. The diminished Indian force, however, is still too large for these four bullets to make any difference.

22. Pamela Robertson, "Camping Under Western Stars: Joan Crawford in *Johnny Guitar*," *Journal of Film and Video* 47.1–3 (1995): 34.

23. John G. Cawelti, *The Six-Gun Mystique* (Bowling Green: Bowling Green University Popular Press, 1970), 60.

24. Immanuel Kant, "Critique of Practical Reason," *Practical Philosophy*, trans. and ed. Mary J. Gregor (Cambridge, New York, and Melbourne: Cambridge University Press, 1996), preface, 140–141.

25. Max Weber, *The Protestant Ethic and the Spirit of Capitalism*, trans. Talcott Parsons (London: Unwin Paperbacks, 1987), 164.

26. Simmon, *Invention of the Western Film*, 129.

27. This is developed in Gilles Deleuze's *Nietzsche and Philosophy* (trans. Hugh Tomlinson [New York: Columbia University Press, 1983]). While I believe these concepts do enable a reading that is a useful elucidation of the world of these films, it is, of course, an extremely partial application of Nietzsche's theory, since it is in the service of death-as-truth and so does not partake in Nietzsche's call for a critic of the value of truth. Nietzsche's alternative powers of falsehood will be discussed in Chapter 5, when dealing with the meaning of death in relation to the future.

28. In this sense as Grayson Cooke writes, also relying on the work of Deleuze ("Willing to Explode: The American Western as Apocalypse-Machine," *Bang Bang, Shoot Shoot! Essays on Guns and Popular Culture*, ed. Murray Pomerance and John Sakeris [Needham Heights: Simon & Schuster, 1999], 1–10), many Westerns revolve around the idea of an apocalypse-machine, "a lingering preparation for crossing the line, a calm before the storm. [...] Yet the guns do go off [... t]he explosions do happen, and the terrible truth is that they are desired" (6). Robert Warshow similarly claims in "Movie Chronicle: The Westerner" (*The Immediate Experience: Movies, Comics, Theatre & Other Aspects of Popular Culture* [Garden City: Doubleday, 1962], 135–154) that the "Westerner could not fulfill himself if the moment did not finally come when he can shoot his enemy down" but he can wait to make sure it is kept pure because "it is so thoroughly the expression of his being" (140).

29. Arthur Schopenhauer, *The World as Will and Representation*, trans. E. F. J. Payne (New York: Dover, 1966), I: §58, 322.

30. Dana Polan, *Power and Paranoia: History, Narrative, and the American Cinema, 1940–1950* (New York: Columbia University Press, 1986), 303–304.

31. Maureen Turim, *Flashbacks in Film: Memory and History* (New York and London: Routledge, 1989), 156.

32. Stanley Cavell, *Contesting Tears: The Hollywood Melodrama of the Unknown Woman* (Chicago and London: The University of Chicago Press, 1996), 171.

33. Cavell, *Contesting Tears*, 170.

34. My examples are of "postwar" films, the term Douglas Pye employs in his survey of scholarly and critical work on Westerns to designate the more complex "handling of generic conventions" ("Criticism and the Western," *The Movie Book of the Western*, ed. Ian Cameron and Douglas Pye [London: Studio Vista, 1996], 15). Richard Slotkin, however, notes that the attempt to avoid war was part of the progressive, "historical epic" version of the new wave of Westerns since the late 1930s (*Gunfighter Nation: The Myth of the Frontier in Twentieth-Century America* [New York: Atheneum, 1992], 288, 316).

35. On the (almost) "too late" in Hollywood melodramas, see Steve Neale's "Melodrama and Tears" (*Screen* 27.6 [November–December 1986]: 6–22) where he reworks Franco Moretti's discussion of "moving" literature; Linda Williams, "Film Bodies: Gender, Genre and Excess," *Feminist Film Theory: A Reader*, ed. Sue Thornham (New York: New York University Press, 1999), 267–281, esp. 279; and Linda Williams, *Playing the Race Card: Melodramas of Black and White from Uncle Tom to O. J. Simpson* (Princeton and Oxford: Princeton University Press, 2001), 30–38.

36. Thomas Elsaesser, "Tales of Sound and Fury: Observations on the Family Melodrama," *Home Is Where the Heart Is: Studies in Melodrama and the Woman's Film*, ed. Christine Gledhill (London: BFI Publishing, 2002), 61.

37. On the importance of authenticity and seeing and acknowledging the truth in this film, see Murray Pomerance, "Stark Performance," *Rebel without a Cause: Approaches to a Maverick Masterwork*, ed. J. David Slocum (Albany: State University of New York Press, 2005), 35–52.

38. There is a long Western tradition that takes the death of non-human animals as less significant than the death of humans, particularly when they are used as food. See Jacques Derrida, "The Animal That Therefore I Am (More to Follow)," trans. David Wills, *Critical Inquiry* 28.2 (Winter 2002): 369–418. For an example of a writer who is *against* animal rights, we could take Spinoza who geometrically proves that the law against killing animals "is based upon an empty superstition and womanish tenderness, rather than upon sound reason." Without in any way denying that animals are being killed or that "brutes feel," he believes that we have the right to use them "for our own pleasure" (Benedict Spinoza, *Ethics*, trans. W. H. White, revised by A. H. Stirling [Ware: Wordsworth, 2001], Part 4, Proposition 37, Scholium 1, 190).

39. To the extent that Plato incarnates falsehood and is unable to stop lying in a world that can only accept truths, the justification for his death will be dealt with in the next, third, chapter.

3 Embodying the Past

1. Slavoj Žižek, *Looking Awry: An Introduction to Jacques Lacan through Popular Culture* (Cambridge and London: The MIT Press, 1991), 21–22.

2. Peter A. French, *Cowboy Metaphysics: Ethics and Death in Westerns* (Lanham: Rowman & Littlefield, 1997), 127.

3. French, *Cowboy Metaphysics*, 129.

4. Such is the fate of those not-quite-evil characters who go straight but are nevertheless killed; their death is meaningful in other ways. Chihuahua in *My Darling Clementine* (John Ford, 1946) for example is killed exactly when she does choose to tell the truth to the good guys. Her death is hardly the end of the story; it is part of the mutual acts of revenge between the two sides and thus has meaning in relation to the future. She also becomes the victim of a bad guy, who thus proves his own killability. Her death thus contributes to the meaningfulness of his future death.

5. Robert Warshow, "Movie Chronicle: The Westerner," *The Immediate Experience: Movies, Comics, Theatre & Other Aspects of Popular Culture* (Garden City: Doubleday, 1962), 143. The other characters, the gangster's friends, rivals, and the police, as Robert Sklar notes, are all capable of "greater dishonesty and disloyalty" than the gangster (*Movie-Made America: A Cultural History of American Movies*, revised and updated [New York: Vintage Books, 1994], 181). They can change and some of them remain alive throughout the film; the deaths of those who do perish are meaningful in other ways.

6. Whether and in what sense these three films have legitimately earned this title is beyond the scope of the present study. As already noted in Chapter 1, I fully accept genre as a retrospective, unstable construct.

7. Stephen Prince, *Classical Film Violence: Designing and Regulating Brutality in Hollywood Cinema*, 1930–1968 (New Brunswick, New Jersey, and London: Rutgers University Press, 2003), 90.

8. Prince, *Classical Film Violence*, 89. As we will see later on in this chapter, the film actually lingers on for a while before ending, but it is the last event in the narrative.

9. Prince, *Classical Film Violence*, 115.

10. Thomas Leitch, *Crime Films* (Cambridge: Cambridge University Press, 2002), 35; Jack Shadoian, *Dreams & Dead Ends: The American Gangster Film*, Second Edition (Oxford and New York: Oxford University Press, 2003), 175; Martha P. Nochimson, *Dying to Belong: Gangster Movies in Hollywood and Hong Kong* (Malden and Oxford: Blackwell, 2007), 122. If not explicitly The Bomb, the ending was described at the very least as an "apocalyptic demise [...] in a towering mushroom cloud" (Thomas Schatz, *Hollywood Genres: Formulas, Filmmaking, and the Studio System* [New York: McGraw-Hill, 1981], 105).

11. Gerhard O. W. Mueller, *Crime, Law and the Scholars: A History of Scholarship in American Criminal Law*, vol. 26 of *Cambridge Studies in Criminology* (London: Heinemann, 1970), 74.

12. Mueller, *Crime, Law and the Scholars*, 79.

13. Carl N. Degler, *In Search of Human Nature: The Decline and Revival of Darwinism in American Social Thought* (New York and Oxford: Oxford University Press, 1991), parts I and II.

14. Degler, *In Search of Human Nature*, 202.

15. Degler, *In Search of Human Nature*, 197–202.

16. Degler, *In Search of Human Nature*, 188–192.

17. Degler, *In Search of Human Nature*, 203.

18. Degler, *In Search of Human Nature*, 187.

19. Qtd. in Mueller, *Crime, Law and the Scholars*, 102.

20. David E. Ruth, *Inventing the Public Enemy: The Gangster in American Culture, 1918–1934* (Chicago and London: The University of Chicago Press, 1996), 24; on the changing social beliefs about the causes of crime, and particularly biological, environmental, aspirational (free will), and psychopathological explanations, see Kirsten Moana Thompson, *Crime Films: Investigating the Scene* (London and New York: Wallflower, 2007), 6.

21. Leitch, *Crime Films*, 291.

22. Leitch, *Crime Films*, 107–108.

23. On his stardom following this film, see Thomas Schatz, *The Genius of the System: Hollywood Filmmaking in the Studio Era* (London: Faber and Faber, 1998), 138.

24. Being "yellow" is a common issue in gangster films. Proving he ain't yellow motivates Rico in *Little Caesar* to disclose his location to the police and in a rather startling turn of events *Scarface's* Tony turns out to be yellow at the very end; on this strange shift near the end of the film, see Richard Maltby, "The Spectacle of Criminality," *Violence and American Cinema*, ed. J. David Slocum (New York and London: Routledge, 2001), 117–152, 136–137. On

endocrinological theories of criminality ("something to do with the glands") see Mueller, *Crime, Law and the Scholars*, 85–86.

25. Shadoian, *Dreams & Dead Ends*, 52.

26. Shadoian, *Dreams & Dead Ends*, 51.

27. Schatz, *Hollywood Genres*, 88.

28. Richard Slotkin writes that the film's opening sequence emphasizes how "the inadequacies of his family shape" Tom's "fate," particularly the overindulgent mother and brutally authoritarian father (*Gunfighter Nation: The Myth of the Frontier in Twentieth-Century America* [New York: Atheneum, 1992], 262). This still does not explain why only one brother turned to crime and has complicated affairs with women.

29. David Bordwell, Janet Staiger, and Kristin Thompson, *The Classical Hollywood Cinema: Film Style & Mode of Production to 1960* (London, Melbourne and Henley: Routledge & Kegan Paul, 1985), 13.

30. Harold B. Segel, *Body Ascendant: Modernism and the Physical Imperative* (Baltimore and London: The Johns Hopkins University Press, 1998).

31. Peter Gay, "Pathologies," *The Bourgeois Experience: Victoria to Freud*, volume III, *The Cultivation of Hatred* (London: HarperCollins Publishers, 1994), 128–212; Sander L. Gilman, *Difference and Pathology: Stereotypes of Sexuality, Race and Madness* (Ithaca and London: Cornell University Press, 1985); Frank J. Sulloway, *Freud Biologist of the Mind: Beyond the Psychoanalytic Legend* (Cambridge and London: Harvard University Press, 1992).

32. Simon A. Cole, *Suspect Identities: A History of Fingerprinting and Criminal Identification* (Cambridge and London: Harvard University Press, 2001).

33. Cole, *Suspect Identities*, 305.

34. Despite his reputation, there are other types of criminals and other causes of crime—such as diet and the weather—in Lombroso's work. These will not be dealt with here.

35. Cesare Lombroso, *Crime: Its Causes and Remedies*, trans. Henry P. Horton (Montclair: Patterson Smith, 1968), 447.

36. Lombroso, *Crime*, 365.

37. Lombroso, *Crime*, 368.

38. Schatz, *Hollywood Genres*, 92.

39. On his "simian carriage" see also Ruth, *Inventing the Public Enemy*, 75, who quotes Pauline Kael quoting François Truffaut on how Hawks deliberately directed Paul Muni to look like a monkey (169n47).

40. Cesare Lombroso, *L'Homme criminel: Étude anthropologique et médico-légale*, traduit par G. Regnier et A. Bornet (Paris: Félix Alcan, Turin: Bocca Frères, 1887), 225.

41. Even Lew Ayres in *The Doorway to Hell* (Archie Mayo, 1930), which precedes the three "classical" gangster films.

42. Ruth, *Inventing the Public Enemy*, 26.

43. Lombroso, *Crime*, 365.

44. Lombroso, *Crime*, 366.

45. Thomas Doherty, *Pre-Code Hollywood: Sex, Immorality, and Insurrection in American Cinema 1930–1934* (New York: Columbia University Press, 1999), 146.

46. Lombroso, *L'Homme criminel*, 225.

47. Cf. the tropes of inversion and gender separatism in Eve Kosofsky Sedgwick, *Epistemology of the Closet* (Berkeley and Los Angeles: University of California Press, 1990), 86–90.
48. See Robert A. Nye, "Heredity or Milieu: The Foundations of Modern European Criminological Theory," *Isis* 67.3 (1976): 334–355, esp. 340 on the "eugenical service" of Lombrosoian criminal science. See also Daniel J. Kevles, *In the Name of Eugenics: Genetics and the Uses of Human Heredity* (Cambridge and London: Harvard University Press, 1995), 71; Martin S. Pernick, *The Black Stork: Eugenics and the Death of "Defective" Babies in American Medicine and Motion Pictures Since 1915* (New York and Oxford: Oxford University Press, 1996), 48; and Thompson, Crime Films, 8–11.
49. On Davenport, see the third chapter of Kevles's *In the Name of Eugenics*.
50. Qtd. in Garland E. Allen, "The Social and Economic Origins of Genetic Determinism: A Case History of the American Eugenics Movement, 1900–1940 and Its Lessons for Today," *Genetica* 99 (1997): 77–88, 78.
51. On the vagueness of the terms employed in eugenics, including the terms "eugenics" and "heredity," see Pernick, *Black Stork*, 50–54. In this discussion I will be emphasizing the nature aspects of eugenics.
52. Kevles, *In the Name of Eugenics*, 71.
53. Kevles, *In the Name of Eugenics*, 47.
54. Pernick, *Black Stork*, 47.
55. Allen, "Social and Economic Origins of Genetic Determinism," 79.
56. Allen, "Social and Economic Origins of Genetic Determinism," 81.
57. Allen, "Social and Economic Origins of Genetic Determinism," 80; Kevles, *In the Name of Eugenics*, 69. As Kevles writes, by World War I the unit-character doctrine and certainly the idea that in phenotypes like produced like was quite dead but somehow unaware of its demise (145).
58. Allen, "Social and Economic Origins of Genetic Determinism," 81.
59. Pernick, *Black Stork*, 129–139.
60. Pernick, *Black Stork*, 144.
61. Doherty, *Pre-Code Hollywood*, 146.
62. Their careers in crime can even be seen as an attempt to shed off their immigrant background and to become assimilated in the Protestant middle-class. For a reading which emphasizes the immigrant identities throughout the history of the genre, see Nochimson, *Dying to Belong*.
63. Lombroso, *Crime*, 158–159. The third sister was also no good.
64. Lombroso, *Crime*, 159–160.
65. The closest in the films I have studied is the Jarrett family in *White Heat*, which is said to have insanity running in it. But this film from the late 1940s is already quite distant from the heyday of American eugenics. The film's protagonist, Cody Jarrett, is always under the threat of going mad like his father, who died in an institution. Yet, his criminality seems to be encouraged by his mother who does not come from the insane side of the family. In fact, it is acknowledged by everyone, including Cody, that she is the one who keeps him sane and his extremely close relationship with her might be more amenable to a Freudian explanation, not a merely hereditary one (Dana Polan writes that *White Heat* "is explicitly psychoanalytic in its replaying of the oedipal situation as constitutive of the criminal mind" in *Power and Paranoia: History, Narrative, and the American Cinema, 1940–1950*

[New York: Columbia University Press, 1986], 177. See also Schatz, *Hollywood Genres*, 108. On Hollywood's shift to psychodynamic explanations in Westerns so as not to be perceived as making any dangerous social criticism during the postwar "Red Scare," see Slotkin, *Gunfighter Nation*, 381–382). Madness is not the cause of Cody's criminality but seems rather to mark the expiration date on it. Evans, the Treasury Department man running the investigation on Cody, feels that he is under pressure to get an undercover agent to approach him because Cody will become useless once he does go insane. The only signs of insanity so far are Cody's headaches. These, as Evans explains, were faked by him as a child in order to get his mother's attention and have since become real. Suspiciously, however, they only seem to appear when Cody is in a difficult situation he is in no other way able to alter, such as his mother's death, an attempt to kill him in jail, or signs of rebellion in his gang. His going "nuts" seems to scare all those around him into obedience and mothering him. While perhaps caused by bad blood, his insanity is also extremely effective at altering his world. Is it any coincidence that Cody truly acts in a "mad" way only at the end of the film, when the police corner him and knowing that if he is caught he will surely be executed? He blows up a chemical plant and hollers to his dead mother that he has reached the top of the world. But what would be a sane reaction of someone who has always managed to outsmart the police when he knows he cannot get away and will be put to death if he surrenders?

66. The most famous example is the "Juke" family originally introduced to the American public in Richard Dugdale's 1877 study. It was understood in the twentieth century to indicate the "hereditary nature of social pathology" although Dugdale actually explained it by a degradation in their environment (Kevles, *In the Name of Eugenics*, 71).

67. Pernick, *Black Stork*, 129. See chapter 8 of Sklar's *Movie-Made America* for a discussion that emphasizes the class and religious affiliation of the anti-Hollywood and pro-censorship groups, including the Payne Fund studies and their 1933 popular summary, *Our Movie Made Children* by Henry James Forman.

68. Gregory D. Black, *Hollywood Censored: Morality Codes, Catholics, and the Movies* (Cambridge: Cambridge University Press, 1994), 108. See also Sklar, *Movie-Made America*, 174–175.

69. Henry James Forman, *Our Movie Made Children* (New York: The MacMillan Company, 1933), 193. See also chapter XV on a "congested" area of New York City.

70. Black, *Hollywood Censored*, 109.

71. Maltby, "Spectacle of Criminality," 118.

72. Nevertheless, as Richard Maltby notes, the major film companies "consistently sought to defer public attention away from anxieties about oligopoly control and trade practices onto issues of film content" (" 'Nobody Knows Everything': Post-Classical Historiographies and Consolidated Entertainment," *Contemporary Hollywood Cinema*, ed. Steve Neale and Murray Smith [London and New York: Routledge, 1998], 21–44, esp. 27–28). So creating a scandal about organized crime films and not about the organized block-booking and vertical integration of the studio system might actually have been advantageous for the film manufacturers.

73. Kevles, *In the Name of Eugenics*, 75.
74. Especially in sterilization, see: Allen, "Social and Economic Origins of Genetic Determinism," 81; Kevles, *In the Name of Eugenics*, 116–118.
75. On the Catholic criticism of the movement which seemed to violate many of its beliefs see Kevles, *In the Name of Eugenics*, 118–119, 168; and on the absence of Jews in the American branch of the eugenics movement, 172. The Production Code Administration and the Legion of Decency are discussed in Black, *Hollywood Censored*. The influence of Jews, including the Eastern- and Central-European first- or second-generation immigrants who ran many of the studios, is discussed, for example, in Neal Gabler, *An Empire of Their Own* (London: W H Allen, 1989); William E. H. Meyer, Jr., "An American 'Precedent'? Propaganda in American Movies: The Case of the Hollywood Jews." *Literature/Film Quarterly* 27.4 (1999): 271–281; Schatz, *Genius of the System*.
76. There are of course villains who do not fit this formula even within the gangster genre. Their deaths are different, and we will discuss this further in the concluding chapter.
77. The editing does not spatially locate the phonograph in the house and it remains a somewhat mysterious presence in the sequence, see Nochimson, *Dying to Belong*, 42 and 111.
78. The two other famous early 1930s films—*Little Caesar and Scarface*—similarly end their stories with the death of their protagonists but go on for no clear narrative reason, flaunting their choice to not continue the story.

    Little Caesar does not quite end with the death of its gangster, Rico. Rather, the picture dissolves from his dying body to the billboard through which the police shot him down. It advertises the "LAUGHING SINGING DANCING SUCCESS" of Joe, Rico's friend, who abandoned crime and Rico and went straight, and Olga, the woman and dancing partner for whom Joe left Rico. The billboard, as Jack Shadoian writes, "dominates the screen in both size and light" (*Dreams & Dead Ends*, 48; see also Nochimson, *Dying to Belong*, 115). It almost seems as if the film would like to continue its story, show us how Rico's death had a good and moral effect, how it made Olga's and Joe's life together safe and successful. But there was no reason to kill Rico for that—the film showed us that the billboard and their success were already there before he died. The film, then, does not continue the story, but does bother to show us it is not doing so—the good and redeemed Joe and Olga have not been forgotten, the film could now cut to them, but does not. The death of Rico is enough.

    Similarly, after Tony is shot down in *Scarface*, the camera tilts up from his body in the gutter to a sign that could be seen from the window in Tony's apartment: "THE WORLD IS YOURS/COOK'S TOURS." Earlier in the film, he promised in a heavy Italian accent: "Some day I look at that sign and I say: 'Okay, she's mine'" (The "she" refers not only to the world but also to his interlocutor, Poppy—his boss's "expensive" girlfriend who also interests Tony). But by the end of the film he is dead. The shot of the sign indicates no potential to continue the story; it merely shows what could surely no longer happen; the future that is no longer possible—that Tony will take over the world. Something in his very destruction must be good; not in what it achieves, but in what it prevents and was indicated by his past deeds.

79. The function of this "exculpatory afterword" and the more common exculpatory preface was to deflect political heat by claiming it is the duty of the
motion picture industry to provide a tale of violence and immorality in
order to demonstrate that crime does not pay and call attention to a social
problem. Presenting the lucrative gangster film as "a public service and cau-
tionary notice" was a "transparent ploy" that seemed to fool no one, not
even the censors (Doherty, *Pre-Code Hollywood*, 154–155).

4   Melodrama and the Shaping of Desires to Come

1. G. W. F. Hegel, *Phenomenology of Spirit*, trans. A. V. Miller (Oxford, New York,
Toronto, and Melbourne: Oxford University Press, 1977), §113, 68.
2. To follow the distinction David Bordwell borrowed from Seymour Chatman,
these deaths are given as a recounting, not as an enactment (*Narration
in the Fiction Film* [Madison: The University of Wisconsin Press, 1985],
77–78).
3. I will be discussing melodramas and their strange logic in more detail
throughout this chapter.
4. E. Ann Kaplan, *Motherhood and Representation: The Mother in Popular Culture
and Melodrama* (London and New York: Routledge, 1992), 168.
5. David Bordwell, Janet Staiger, and Kristin Thompson, *The Classical Hollywood
Cinema: Film Style & Mode of Production to 1960* (London, Melbourne and
Henley: Routledge & Kegan Paul, 1985), 13.
6. It is similar to the resolution which Thomas Schatz finds in certain genres
(which he calls genres of determinate, contested space), which reduces polar
opposition by the elimination of one of the forces. See *Hollywood Genres: Formulas, Filmmaking, and the Studio System* (New York: McGraw-Hill, 1981), 32.
The difference is that Schatz is interested in the resolution, whereas our
concern here is with how the plot goes on and the death is meaningful in
relation to the future.
7. Who is a former major holding the Medal of Honor, a fact which does not
change his mind. See Douglas Pye, "Genre and History: Fort Apache and
The Man Who Shot Liberty Valance," *The Movie Book of the Western*, ed. Ian
Cameron and Douglas Pye (London: Studio Vista, 1996), 116.
8. The Dancing Kid is shot by Emma Small who is extremely interested in both
Vienna and the Kid, but, at least ostensibly, her interest is in killing them,
not kissing them. In any case, she too is dead by the time Johnny and Vienna
do kiss at the end of the film.
9. One of the three types of Westerns that Will Wright identifies during the
period we are dealing with is the vengeance variation (*Six Guns and Society:
A Structural Study of the Western* [Berkeley, Los Angeles, and London: University of California Press, 1977], 29). For revenge in war films, see Dana Polan,
Power and Paranoia: History, Narrative, and the American Cinema, 1940–1950
(New York: Columbia University Press, 1986), 143.
10. Edward Gallafent, "Four Tombstones 1946–1994," *The Movie Book of
the Western*, ed. Ian Cameron and Douglas Pye (London: Studio Vista,
1996), 302. This is in contradistinction to the "psychopathic" murders in
the 1990s versions of the story, which, according to Gallafent, lack adequate

logical or emotional reasons—they have "no narrative relationship to the central confrontation [...] or no relationship to any discernable cause" (304).

11. They do end up joining Holliday and the Earps, in fact, impersonating them to confuse the Clantons, but this is not mentioned in the dialogue and modern audiences (myself included), "accustomed to having action plots spelled out more bluntly and reinforced with dialogue, often fail to notice the scheme at all" (Scott Simmon, *The Invention of the Western Film: A Cultural History of the Genre's First Half-Century* [Cambridge: Cambridge University Press, 2003], 258). I will return to this incident in Chapter 5.

12. For more examples of revenge after the death of comrades, see Polan, *Power and Paranoia*, 143.

13. Dominick LaCapra, "Trauma, Absence, Loss," *Critical Inquiry* 25 (Summer 1999): 703.

14. LaCapra, "Trauma, Absence, Loss," 708.

15. I would like to thank Yael Ben-Tzvi for pointing out the relevance of these two Frank Capra films to me.

16. Dana Polan sees this as an example of a more general notion of equivalence and the possibility of exchange (*Power and Paranoia*, 70 and 141; see also 72 on the narrative figure of the "second-in-command").

17. Steve Neale, "Aspects of Ideology and Narrative Form in the American War Film," *Screen* 32.1 (Spring 1991): 50. Actually, the lieutenant is at first only wounded, and they only later learn for certain that he has died.

18. Gilles Deleuze and Félix Guattari, *Anti-Oedipus: Capitalism and Schizophrenia*, trans. Robert Hurley, Mark Seem, and Helen R. Lane (Minneapolis: University of Minnesota Press, 1983), 24; see also Adi Ophir, *The Order of Evils: Toward an Ontology of Morals*, trans. Rela Mazali and Havi Carel (New York: Zone Books, 2005), §6.001, 257.

19. Mary Ann Doane, *The Desire to Desire: The Woman's Film of the 1940s* (Basingstoke and London: Macmillan Press, 1987), 9.

20. Ernest Jones, *Sigmund Freud: Life and Work*, Vol. 2, *Years of Maturity 1901–1919* (London: The Hogarth Press, 1955), 468; Sigmund Freud, "Some Psychical Consequences of the Anatomical Distinction between the Sexes," *The Standard Edition of the Complete Psychological Works of Sigmund Freud*, ed. and trans. James Strachey (London: The Hogarth Press and The Institute of Psycho-Analysis, 1953–1974), 19: 243–258. Incidentally, for Freud a woman simply lacks a penis. On desire and demand in relation to the phallus, absence, and loss or lack in Lacan, see LaCapra, "Trauma, Absence, Loss," 708n20.

21. Joan Copjec, "More! From Melodrama to Magnitude," *Endless Night: Cinema and Psychoanalysis, Parallel Histories*, ed. Janet Bergstrom (Berkeley, Los Angeles, and London: University of California Press, 1999), 258.

22. Doane, *Desire to Desire*, 171.

23. Christine Gledhill, "Between Melodrama and Realism: Anthony Asquith's *Underground* and Kind Vidor's *The Crowd*," *Classical Hollywood Narrative: The Paradigm Wars*, ed. Jane Gaines (Durham and London: Duke University Press, 1992), 152.

24. Gledhill, "Between Melodrama and Realism," 158.

25. Gledhill, "Between Melodrama and Realism," 153.

26. Gledhill, "Between Melodrama and Realism," 164.

27. Linda Williams, *Playing the Race Card: Melodramas of Black and White from Uncle Tom to O. J. Simpson* (Princeton and Oxford: Princeton University Press, 2001), 22–23.

28. Rick Altman, "Dickens, Griffith, and Film Theory Today," *Classical Hollywood Narrative: The Paradigm Wars*, ed. Jane Gaines (Durham and London: Duke University Press, 1992), 26.

29. Raymond Bellour, *The Analysis of Film*, ed. Constance Penley, trans. Mary Quaintance, Ben Brewster, Diana Matias, Maureen Turim, Bertrand Augst, Hillary Radner, Nancy Huston, and Inge Pruks (Bloomington and Indianapolis: Indiana University Press, 2000), 14.

30. Bellour, *Analysis of Film*, 238.

31. Bellour, *Analysis of Film*, 192. Symbolic blockage is a form of repetition which is combined with narrative change—neither the same again nor something completely new. While these repetitions, according to Bellour, might seem only to halt the narrative, in fact, they are the very same elements which construct it. Moreover, they sometimes also reproduce it by offering a mise-en-abîme of the developing narrative.

32. Daniel Dayan, *Western Graffiti: Jeux d'images et programmation du spectateur dans La chevauchée fantastique de John Ford* (Paris: Éditions Clancier-Guénaud, 1983), 12.

33. Dayan, *Western Graffiti*, 232.

34. Dayan, *Western Graffiti*, 234.

35. Williams, *Playing the Race Card*, 197.

36. Helen Taylor, *Scarlett's Women: Gone with the Wind and Its Female Fans* (New Brunswick: Rutgers University Press, 1989), 106. See also 150.

37. Rhett has good reason to believe so. Earlier in the film, Rhett probably rapes Scarlett and, having been "pleasurably ravished," she wakes up smiling (Williams, *Playing the Race Card*, 200; on this troubling sequence, see also Taylor, *Scarlett's Women*, 129–137). She has finally experienced something directly—not wanting something because the Wilkersons want it, but because she herself has enjoyed it. She has no way of dealing with this new pleasure and quickly hides it from Rhett. At this stage, she is still unable to understand that telling him she does want him might make him stay, so she pretends to be offended by his conduct. Presumably, she believes that the best way to attract him is to pretend that *she* doesn't give a damn.

38. The character of Pearl's mother has no name, but it is interesting to note that the savage squaw is played by Viennese ballerina, Max Reinhardt disciple, and English countess, Tilly Losch.

39. Robin Wood, "Duel in the Sun: The Destruction of an Ideological System," *The Movie Book of the Western*, ed. Ian Cameron and Douglas Pye (London: Studio Vista, 1996), 193.

40. Laura Mulvey, "Afterthoughts on 'Visual Pleasure and Narrative Cinema' Inspired by King Vidor's *Duel in the Sun* (1946)," *Feminist Film Theory: A Reader*, ed. Sue Thornham (New York: New York University Press, 1999), esp. 127–129.

41. In his summary of the film Will Wright even claims Laura Belle is Scott's sister (*Six Guns and Society*, 37).

42. Wood, "Duel in the Sun," 189.

43. Copjec, "More!". The similarity between the two King Vidor films, *Stella Dallas* and *Duel in the Sun*, has been described by Laura Mulvey ("Afterthoughts," 128–9).

44. Copjec, "More!", 262.

45. Copjec, "More!", 263.

46. Copjec, "More!", 266. In Copjec's reading, the last shot of Stella Dallas smiling and walking away could be read as a feeling of the Kantian sublime (as testimony of a sense of the supersensible necessary for ethical action) or Lacanian love (as presence of the real in the symbolic), and her ability to find a place for herself *within* society. This is not typical of melodramas.

47. Or perhaps her father from seeing them, in which case the couple to protect would also be her parents, not only her mother and her lover.

48. While I have attempted to account for the deaths in the films, this is hardly an exhaustive analysis of the desires in the text, particularly that of Lewt. Should we desire to extend the psychoanalytic diagnoses of characters in this film, we might label Lewt a pervert. He performs "horse tricks," which include having a half-breed watch him stick his horse's head between his thighs from behind and then giving her the horse. Sexology, to the best of my knowledge, has yet to coin a proper Greek–Latin term for such a horse-related anal-cranial form of exhibitionism and gift giving. More specifically, he seems to be a "moral masochist" who desires nothing more than to have his father, who only orders him to enjoy, punish him. He goes about committing every unthinkable outrage, including attempted fratricide, so that his father would do so, but it is only Pearl who finally does punish him for his crimes by shooting him, initially in the thigh. He agrees with her that she "had to do it" and can finally say that he loves her since he is no longer bound exclusively to enjoy himself, but can, now, even commit to a woman who happens to play the role of a punishing father. On different forms of masochism, perversion, and their relation to gender instability—all relevant for understanding Lewt as well as Pearl—see Kaja Silverman, "Masochism and Male Subjectivity," *Male Trouble*, ed. Constance Penley and Sharon Willis (London and Minneapolis: University of Minnesota Press, 1993), 33–64.

5   Cults of the Dead and Powers of the False

1. Maurice Halbwachs, *On Collective Memory*, ed. and trans. Lewis A. Coser (Chicago and London: The University of Chicago Press, 1992), 73.

2. Jean-François Lyotard, *The Differend: Phrases in Dispute*, trans. Georges van den Abbeele (Minneapolis: University of Minnesota Press, 1988), §156, 100.

3. G. W. F. Hegel, *Phenomenology of Spirit*, trans. A. V. Miller (Oxford, New York, Toronto, and Melbourne: Oxford University Press, 1977), §452, 271. For the wider context of these statements within Hegel's thoughts on death in relation to nature, the family, and the state, see Edith Wyschogrod, *Spirit in Ashes: Hegel, Heidegger, and Man-Made Mass Death* (New Haven and London: Yale University Press, 1985), esp. 107–113, 126–132 and Brent Adkins, *Death and Desire in Hegel, Heidegger and Deleuze* (Edinburgh: Edinburgh University Press, 2007), part II, esp. chapter 5.

4. Scott Simmon, *The Invention of the Western Film: A Cultural History of the Genre's First Half-Century* (Cambridge: Cambridge University Press, 2003), 112. See also Robert Warshow, "Movie Chronicle: The Westerner," *The Immediate Experience: Movies, Comics, Theatre & Other Aspects of Popular Culture* (Garden City: Doubleday, 1962), 135–154, esp. 137 and 140.

5. In the World War II combat film the "need to remember and discuss home, and the dangers involved in doing so" have become a generic requirement (Jeanine Basinger, *The World War II Combat Film: Anatomy of a Genre* [New York: Columbia University Press, 1986], 62).

6. Cf. Georg Wilhelm Friedrich Hegel, *The Philosophy of History*, trans. J. Sibree (Mineola: Dover, 2004), 33; Wyschogrod, *Spirit in Ashes*, 80.

7. Richard Slotkin claims the film is the most influential of the "outlaw Westerns" (*Gunfighter Nation: The Myth of the Frontier in Twentieth-Century America* [New York: Atheneum, 1992], 295), which adopted "the 'populist' perspective of those victimized by technological and industrial progress and treated their outlaw-heroes as social bandits" (286). That is, the film characterizes Jesse's criminal career as that of an "armed representative of 'the People'" (299).

8. Adi Ophir, *The Order of Evils: Toward an Ontology of Morals*, trans. Rela Mazali and Havi Carel (New York: Zone Books, 2005), §1.101, 48.

9. Ophir, *Order of Evils*, §2.001, 89.

10. Ophir, *Order of Evils*, §2.214, 106.

11. Simmon suggests that the genre actually owes quite a bit to the values of the Old South, such as honor, individualism, and a vigilante tradition of local justice. The Western's justification of violence, however, has to do with looking forward and bringing the nation together; it shows itself as owing nothing to, and clearly differentiated from, those who turn back, divide the nation, and opt for traditionalism (Simmon, *Invention of the Western Film*, 147).

12. Peter A. French, *Cowboy Metaphysics: Ethics and Death in Westerns* (Lanham: Rowman & Littlefield, 1997), 115.

13. Bob Baker, "Shane through Five Decades," *The Movie Book of the Western*, ed. Ian Cameron and Douglas Pye (London: Studio Vista, 1996), 214–220, 215.

14. Steve Neale, "'The Story of Custer in Everything But Name?': Colonel Thursday and *Fort Apache*," *Journal of Film and Video* 47.1–3 (1995): 26–32, 30. Neale is summarizing an analysis of the film by Peter Lehman.

15. Slotkin, *Gunfighter Nation*, 338.

16. Douglas Pye, "Genre and History: Fort Apache and The Man Who Shot Liberty Valance," *The Movie Book of the Western*, ed. Ian Cameron and Douglas Pye (London: Studio Vista, 1996), 111–122, 117.

17. Slotkin, *Gunfighter Nation*, 342.

18. John G. Cawelti, *The Six-Gun Mystique*. (Bowling Green: Bowling Green University Popular Press, 1970), 61.

19. V. F. Perkins, "Johnny Guitar," *The Movie Book of the Western*. ed. Ian Cameron and Douglas Pye (London: Studio Vista, 1996), 221–228, 224.

20. Jane Tompkins, *West of Everything: The Inner Life of Westerns* (New York and Oxford: Oxford University Press, 1992), 49.

21. Simmon, *Invention of the Western Film*, 259.

22. Simmon, *Invention of the Western Film*, 258.

23. Tompkins, *West of Everything*, 27.
24. Tompkins, *West of Everything*, 34.
25. Tompkins, *West of Everything*, 28.
26. Tompkins, *West of Everything*, 36–39. Her description of the Western as anti-Christian has been challenged; see, for example, Simmon, *Invention of the Western Film*, 124–130.
27. Tompkins, *West of Everything*, 39.
28. Tompkins, *West of Everything*, 42.
29. Tompkins, *West of Everything*, 35.
30. Tompkins, *West of Everything*, 34.
31. Tompkins, *West of Everything*, 32.
32. Tompkins, *West of Everything*, 39.
33. Tompkins, *West of Everything*, 45.
34. Tompkins, *West of Everything*, 35.
35. Tompkins, *West of Everything*, 38.
36. Tompkins, *West of Everything*, 44, italics mine.
37. One such attempt, which critically deals with Tompkins's work and attempts to develop a new, non-Christian account of what Western heroes give a damn about, is Peter A. French's *Cowboy Metaphysics*.
38. For a different reading of the Western in light of Nietzsche's work, see French, *Cowboy Metaphysics*, 92–96.
39. Friedrich Nietzsche, *Beyond Good and Evil: Prelude to a Philosophy of the Future*, trans. Helen Zimmern (Mineola: Dover Publications, 1997), §203, 69–70.
40. Nietzsche, *Beyond Good and Evil*, §211, 83.
41. Friedrich Nietzsche, *On the Genealogy of Morals and Ecce Homo*, trans. Walter Kaufmann and R. J. Hollingdale (New York: Vintage Books, 1989), III §24, 152.
42. Gilles Deleuze, *Nietzsche and Philosophy*, trans. Hugh Tomlinson (New York: Columbia University Press, 1983), 95.
43. Deleuze, *Nietzsche and Philosophy*, 96.
44. Deleuze, *Nietzsche and Philosophy*, 184.
45. Deleuze, *Nietzsche and Philosophy*, 102.
46. Nietzsche, *Genealogy of Morals*, III §25, 153.
47. D. N. Rodowick, *Gilles Deleuze's Time Machine* (Durham and London: Duke University Press, 1997), 134.
48. Rodowick, *Gilles Deleuze's Time Machine*, 136.
49. This is discussed in chapters 5 and 6 of Rodowick's *Gilles Deleuze's Time Machine*.
50. Gilles Deleuze, *Cinema 2: The Time-Image*, trans. Hugh Tomlinson and Robert Galeta (Minneapolis: University of Minnesota Press, 1989), 132.
51. Deleuze, *Cinema 2*, 137.
52. Deleuze, *Cinema 2*, 140.
53. Deleuze, *Cinema 2*, 140.
54. Nietzsche, *Beyond Good and Evil*, §211, 83.
55. Deleuze, *Cinema 2*, 152.
56. Deleuze, *Cinema 2*, 150; see also 217–224.
57. It has often been noted that "Western movies do not provide a reliable record of America's Western past" (Edward Buscombe and Roberta E. Pearson, Introduction, *Back in the Saddle Again: New Essays on the Western*, ed. Edward

Buscombe and Roberta E. Pearson [London: BFI Publishing, 1998], 6). For a discussion of the historiographic function of the Western as well as the period in which it is set, see Janet Walker, "Westerns through History," *Westerns: Films through History*, ed. Janet Walker (New York and London: Routledge, 2001), 1–24. Although overall for the films dealt with here the "West" belongs to the past, it should be noted, as Walker mentions, that early turn-of-the-century Westerns could have been contemporary with the events they depicted. In addition, 1930s B-Westerns, as Richard Slotkin (*Gunfighter Nation*, 273–277) and Scott Simmon show (*Invention of the Western Film*, esp. 150–170), are surreally set in a "purposely odd and ambiguous" historical era (150), mixing the modern with the "Old" west. All the Westerns dealt with here, however, are post-1939 A-films.

58. On the "hodgepodge of justifications" for expansionism termed "Manifest Destiny" see Simmon, *Invention of the Western Film*, esp. 141–148.

59. Deleuze admits "that it was the neo-Western" that first demonstrated the break-up of the American people, no longer "the melting-pot of peoples past or the seed of a people to come" (*Cinema 2*, 216).

60. I am alluding, of course, to the famous line in *The Man Who Shot Liberty Valance* (John Ford, 1962), in which, as Thomas A. Wartenberg writes, "two fundamental social institutions of our society—the legal order and the press" are shown as "linked in their adherence to deception over truth" (*Thinking on Screen: Film as Philosophy* [London and New York: Routledge, 2007], 6).

61. Ophir, *Order of Evils*, §2.001, 89.

62. Ophir, *Order of Evils*, §2.230, 108.

63. A rather extreme and odd case is the ending of *Gabriel over the White House* (Gregory La Cava, 1933), in which president Hammond's death somehow concludes the signing of a covenant of peace amongst the nations of the world.

64. Lyotard, *Differend*, §156, 100.

65. Lyotard, *Differend*, Plato Notice §1, 20.

66. Lyotard, *Differend*, Plato Notice §1, 20–21.

67. Lyotard, *Differend*, §160, 105.

68. Sigmund Freud, *Totem and Taboo*, *The Standard Edition of the Complete Psychological Works of Sigmund Freud*, ed. and trans. James Strachey (London: The Hogarth Press and The Institute of Psycho-Analysis, 1953–1974), 13: 142.

69. Cathy Caruth shows the traumatic presence of Freud's own story in the book, see her *Unclaimed Experience: Trauma, Narrative, and History* (Baltimore and London: The Johns Hopkins University Press, 1996), 10–24.

70. Sigmund Freud, *Moses and Monotheism*, *The Standard Edition of the Complete Psychological Works of Sigmund Freud*, ed. and trans. James Strachey (London: The Hogarth Press and The Institute of Psycho-Analysis, 1953–1974), 23: 3–137

71. Freud, *Moses and Monotheism*, 81.

72. Freud, *Moses and Monotheism*, 52.

73. Freud, *Moses and Monotheism*, 48.

74. Freud, *Moses and Monotheism*, 107.

75. Freud, *Moses and Monotheism*, 39. This tribe that traveled in the desert additionally joined with kindred tribes who were not in Egypt and they thus

became the Jewish people. This union would later split again into the kingdom of Judah and the kingdom of Israel (37–38).

76. A different connection between Westerns and psychoanalysis and trauma is offered in Janet Walker's "Captive Images in the Traumatic Western: *The Searchers, Pursued, Once Upon a Time in the West,* and *Lone Star*," *Westerns: Films through History,* ed. Janet Walker (New York and London: Routledge, 2001), 219–251.

77. While I have relied on Freud, the works of additional thinkers that I will not be exploring in detail here can also be helpful in elaborating the ideas in this chapter. Slavoj Žižek, for example, could be used to theorize the false exclusion. He defines ideological fantasy as representing in a positive element the inherent impossibility of the fullness of society, transforming the a priori closure/impossibility into an empirical obstacle, such as blaming the "Jewish plot" (Žižek, "Class Struggle or Postmodernism? Yes, Please!" Judith Butler, Ernesto Laclau and Slavoj Žižek, *Contingency, Hegemony, Universality: Contemporary Dialogues of the Left* [London and New York: Verso, 2000], 90–135, 100–101).

René Girard's account of the scapegoat also has many similarities to the issues discussed here, and, in fact, he frequently returns to Freud's work, especially *Totem and Taboo.* Nevertheless, I find his work less useful for my purpose primarily because for him the scapegoat sacrifice functions to "quell violence within the community and to prevent conflicts from erupting," that is, to prevent vengeance which is "an interminable, infinitely repetitive process" (*Violence and the Sacred,* trans. Patrick Gregory [Baltimore: The Johns Hopkins University Press, 1979], 14). My interest, however, is not in how violence could be channeled to a safe outlet so as not to upset the social equilibrium, but how an intermediary death might function in relation to the future, how it does contaminate and unsettle the community; what happens when no ritual to "purify" violence (36) exists. In addition, although Girard claims that scapegoating is "the generative principle of mythology, ritual, primitive religion, even culture as a whole" ("Generative Scapegoating" and "Discussion," *Violent Origins: Ritual Killings and Cultural Formations,* ed. G. Hamerton-Kelly [Stanford: Stanford University Press, 1987], 106), that it contributes to "social unity" (90), and is "the very basis of cultural unification" (*Violence and the Sacred,* 302), he also assumes that "a single, solitary group" (249) already exists; indeed, according to him groups were present even before humans—in "animal sociality" (*Things Hidden since the Foundation of the World,* in collaboration with Jean-Michel Oughourlian and Guy Lefort, trans. Stephen Bann and Michael Metteer [Stanford: Stanford University Press, 1987], 91), so it is not quite obvious to me in what sense the violence he describes generates the community. Furthermore, Girard repeatedly insists on the unanimity of the mob violence in which an "entire community" vents "its fury on a single individual" arbitrarily chosen from within the community and even believes that this is reminiscent of "the frontier 'justice' of American Westerns" (*Violence and the Sacred,* 299), whereas the films I am dealing with, including American Westerns, do not as a rule include such acts of unanimous lynching and the victims at times really are to some extent at least outsiders. The films could perhaps be analyzed with Girard's tools as "myths" which offer "clues" to the real event which they disguise, but such a hermeneutics of suspicion is not within the scope of the present work. Nevertheless, as J. David Slocum notes, Girard's ideas about sacrifice, scapegoating, and mimesis have been fruitful in discussions of violence in American cinema, see Slocum, "Violence and American Cinema: Notes for an Investigation," *Violence and American Cinema*, ed. J. David Slocum (New York and London: Routledge, 2001), 1–34, esp. 13–14, 29n50, 29n51; see also Dana Polan, *Power and Paranoia: History, Narrative, and the American Cinema, 1940–1950* (New York: Columbia University Press, 1986), esp. 61–62; and Christopher Sharrett, "Sacrificial Violence and Postmodern Ideology," *Mythologies of Violence in Postmodern Media*, ed. Christopher Sharrett (Detroit: Wayne State University Press, 1999), 413–434.

Finally, Thomas Hobbes argues that the sovereign is essential for the survival of the covenant but excluded from it—the sovereign, unlike the subjects, never lays down the rights everyone has before the institution of the commonwealth and therefore maintains the right to use violence in order to punish (*Leviathan[, or the Matter, Forme, & Power of a Common-Wealth Ecclesiasticall and Civill]*, ed. J. C. A. Gaskin [Oxford: Oxford University Press, 1998], XXVIII §2, 205–206). Unfortunately, Hobbes's sovereign insists on staying alive, as do the subjects, and is therefore less useful than Freud for my present discussion.

78. Will Wright, *Six Guns and Society: A Structural Study of the Western* (Berkeley, Los Angeles, and London: University of California Press, 1977), 32. See also Slotkin on the idea that is "deeply rooted" within the ideological traditions of American liberalism of establishing a just society by the removal "of a relatively small class of evil men" (*Gunfighter Nation*, 601).

79. French, *Cowboy Metaphysics*, 138.

80. Cawelti suggests several variations on how this happens (*Six-Gun Mystique*, 46–47).

81. Cawelti, *Six-Gun Mystique*, 47–49.

82. Walter Benjamin, "Critique of Violence," trans. Edmund Jephcott, *Selected Writings*, volume 1, ed. Marcus Bullock and Michael W. Jennings (Cambridge and London: The Belknap Press of Harvard University Press, 1996), 1: 242.

83. Benjamin, "Critique of Violence," 238.

84. Benjamin, "Critique of Violence," 241.

85. Baker, "Shane through Five Decades," 220. It is no wonder commentators on the film sought for explanations elsewhere, particularly, Shane and Marion, Joe Starret's wife, being in love (e.g. Wright, *Six Guns and Society*, 47).

86. Wright, *Six Guns and Society*, 47.

87. Benjamin, "Critique of Violence," 241.

88. Benjamin, "Critique of Violence," 241.

89. Benjamin, "Critique of Violence," 239.

90. Jacques Derrida, "Force of Law: The 'Mystical Foundations of Authority,'" trans. Mary Quaintance, *Cardoza Law Review* 11.5–6 (1990): 997.

91. French, *Cowboy Metaphysics*, 28.

92. Wright, *Six Guns and Society*, 46.

93. Simmon, *Invention of the Western Film*, 147.

94. Slotkin, *Gunfighter Nation*, 392. In addition to the personal element, Slotkin offers professional, social, and the "red-blooded" principles of "manhood" as justifications for Kane's decision to face Miller.

6 A Perpetual Present: Death and the War Film

1. This was done either by depicting modern wars, or by emphasizing the modern aspects in earlier wars but in historical films which were made after the Great War. The battle against the Apaches is a senseless massacre (of the whites, not the apaches) in *Fort Apache* (John Ford, 1948) and the Civil War becomes mass-murder hell in *Gone with the Wind* (Victor Fleming, 1939; on how the war in the film resonates with later wars, see Helen Taylor, *Scarlett's Women:* Gone with the Wind *and Its Female* Fans [New Brunswick: Rutgers University Press, 1989], 210–219). I will not be limiting my discussion to overt battle films or scenes of battle, but dealing with the entire chaotic world in which modern warfare take place.
2. Edith Wyschogrod, *Spirit in Ashes: Hegel, Heidegger, and Man-Made Mass Death* (New Haven and London: Yale University Press, 1985), 1; see also 52–57 on modern war in contradistinction to traditional war.
3. Peter Sloterdijk, *Critique of Cynical Reason*, trans. Michael Eldred (Minneapolis: University of Minneapolis Press, 1988), 420.
4. Robert Baird, "*Hell's Angels* above *The Western Front*," *Hollywood's World War I: Motion Picture Images*, ed. Peter C. Rollins and John E. O'Connor (Bowling Green: Bowling Green University Popular Press, 1997), 88–89.
5. Michael T. Isenberg, "The Great War Viewed from the Twenties: *The Big Parade*," *Hollywood's World War I: Motion Picture Images*, ed. Peter C. Rollins and John E. O'Connor (Bowling Green: Bowling Green University Popular Press, 1997), 50.
6. This possibility is especially accessible in the case of aerial combats, see Baird "*Hell's Angels* above *The Western Front*"; Thomas Doherty, *Projections of War: Hollywood, American Culture, and World War II* (New York: Columbia University Press, 1993), 94–98; Guy Westwell, *War Cinema: Hollywood on the Front Line* (London and New York: Wallflower, 2006), 19. In many aspects, however, these films still depict the world of modern warfare like other war films.
7. Jeanine Basinger, *The World War II Combat Film: Anatomy of a Genre* (New York: Columbia University Press, 1986), 62.
8. Basinger, *World War II Combat Film*, 73.
9. Anton Kaes, "The Cold Gaze: Notes on Mobilization and Modernity," *New German Critique* 59 (Spring-Summer 1993): 111. On the incompatibility of subjectivity with modern warfare, see also Bernd Hüppauf, "Experiences of Modern Warfare and the Crisis of Representation," *Hollywood and War: The Film Reader*, ed. J. David Slocum (New York and London: Routledge, 2006), 57–67. Hüppauf argues that anti-war films attempt to revitalize obsolete subjectivity and experience. I will offer a different reading of classical Hollywood war films, including anti-war films.
10. Pierre Sorlin, "Cinema and the Memory of the Great War," *The First World War and Popular Cinema: 1914 to the Present*, ed. Michael Paris (New Brunswick: Rutgers University Press, 2000), 16. This was not, according to Sorlin, necessarily the only and exclusive concern of all of these films which also knew how to convey the excitement and pleasure of war, for example by enjoying camaraderie, commanding a unit, confronting danger, and particularly the personal skill and thrill of aerial battles. The films,

according to Sorlin, were ambivalent and so reflected the debate within American public opinion on the US involvement in the war (14–17). Michael T. Isenberg suggests that it was mostly elitist literature and art that was "intensely critical of the war and of America's role in it," whereas more popular media, including motion pictures, "did not advance beyond the common sentimentality of daring heroism and noble sacrifice" ("Great War Viewed from the Twenties," 40; see also 54–55 on the American ambivalence). On the tension between the two attitudes to war in American films, and a challenge to the attempt to divide films using a clear dichotomy of "romanticism" vs. "realism," see Baird "*Hell's Angels* above *The Western Front.*"

11. Richard Slotkin, *Gunfighter Nation: The Myth of the Frontier in Twentieth-Century America* (New York: Atheneum, 1992), 314.
12. Slotkin, *Gunfighter Nation*, 323.
13. Thomas Schatz, "World War II and the Hollywood 'War Film,'" *Refiguring American Film Genres: History and Theory*, ed. Nick Browne (Berkeley, Los Angeles, and London: University of California Press, 1998), 91.
14. Schatz, "World War II," 107. In addition these films suspended the formation of the (hetero-)sexual couple. The example Schatz gives here is *Casablanca* (Michael Curtiz, 1942). On the group in war films, see also Robert Warshow, "Movie Chronicle: The Westerner," *The Immediate Experience: Movies, Comics, Theatre & Other Aspects of Popular Culture* (Garden City: Doubleday, 1962), 153.
15. For a critical discussion of the bombing of civilians in these films, wee George H. Roeder, Jr., "War as a Way of Seeing," *Hollywood and War: The Film Reader*, ed. J. David Slocum (New York and London: Routledge, 2006), 70–72.
16. Isenberg, "Great War Viewed from the Twenties," 46.
17. Paul Virilio, *War and Cinema: The Logistics of Perception*, trans. Patrick Camiller (London and New York: Verso, 1992).
18. Baird "*Hell's Angles* above *The Western Front*," 93. See also Westwell, *War Cinema*, 20–21.
19. Basinger, *World War II Combat Film*, 70; see also 45–50.
20. Dana Polan, *Power and Paranoia: History, Narrative, and the American Cinema, 1940–1950* (New York: Columbia University Press, 1986), 142.
21. Polan, *Power and Paranoia*, 213.
22. Doherty, *Projections of War*, 103–104.
23. Doherty, *Projections of War*, 110.
24. Isenberg, "Great War Viewed from the Twenties," 48.
25. Polan, *Power and Paranoia*, 70.
26. Doherty, *Projections of War*, 139–148.
27. Basinger, *World War II Combat Film*, 51.
28. Basinger, *World War II Combat Film*, 63–67.
29. Doherty, *Projections of War*, 98. On the "forgotten man" of World War I in the cinema see also Andrew Kelly, "The Greatness and Continuing Significance of *All Quiet on the Western Front*," *The War Film*, ed. Robert Eberwein (New Brunswick, New Jersey, and London: Rutgers University Press, 2005), 28.
30. Annette Insdorf, *Indelible Shadows: Film and the Holocaust*, third edition (Cambridge and New York: Cambridge University Press, 2003), 59.
31. Polan, *Power and Paranoia*, 60.

32. On the inevitability of Southern Defeat in the film, see Melvyn Stokes, "*Gone With the Wind* (1939) and the Lost Cause: A Critical View," *The New Film History*, ed. James Chapman, Mark Glancy, and Sue Harper (Basingstoke: Palgrave Macmillan, 2007), 13–26, esp. 19.

33. Baird "*Hell's Angles* above *The Western Front*," 94.

34. Steve Neale, "Aspects of Ideology and Narrative Form in the American War Film," *Screen* 32.1 (Spring 1991): 50.

35. Neale, "Aspects of Ideology," 51.

36. This disparity between verbal commentary and the images on the screen constitutes the double-layered structure required in order to produce irony, see Sarah Kozloff, *Invisible Storytellers: Voice-Over Narration in American Fiction Film* (Berkeley, Los Angeles, and London: University of California Press, 1988), 109–112.

37. Unless we read it, as Jeanine Basinger does, as a "postwar reminder" to the audience that "we must not ever let them die in memory" (*World War II Combat Film*, 149).

38. Robert Sklar, *Movie-Made America: A Cultural History of American Movies*, revised and updated (New York: Vintage Books, 1994), 96.

39. Carl Schmitt, *The Concept of the Political*, trans. George Schwab (New Brunswick: Rutgers University Press, 1976), 26.

40. Schmitt, *Concept of the Political*, 35.

41. Schmitt, *Concept of the Political*, 46.

42. Virilio, *War and Cinema*, 5.

43. As Andrew Kelly points out, this was an American film which depicted the Germans as equal and having the same values, ("Greatness and Continuing Significance," 24).

44. Doherty, *Projections of War*, 196; on the concentration camp footage in this context, see 247–250.

45. Qtd. in Doherty, *Projections of War*, 122.

46. Lawrence H. Suid, *Guts & Glory: The Making of the American Military Image in Film*, revised and expanded edition (Lexington: The University Press of Kentucky, 2002), 76–78. On the flexibility in actually implementing the directive, see for example Suid's discussion of the off-screen atrocities in Lewis Milestone's 1944 *The Purple Heart* (82). On the continuation of the policy after the war, see Suid, *Guts & Glory*, 97–102.

47. Ilan Avisar, *Screening the Holocaust: Cinema's Images of the Unimaginable* (Bloomington and Indianapolis: Indiana University Press, 1988), 110.

48. Neale, "Aspects of Ideology," 40.

49. Neale, "Aspects of Ideology," 44.

50. The positive portrayal of a Nazi general in an American film is in itself, of course, a way to confuse friend and enemy. On the less than mild reactions to *The Desert Fox*, see Suid, *Guts & Glory*, 162–163.

51. Stokes, "*Gone With the Wind*," 20.

52. Schmitt, *Concept of the Political*, 38.

53. Carl Schmitt, *Political Theology: Four Chapters on the Concepts of Sovereignty*, trans. George Schwab (Cambridge: MIT Press, 1985), 5.

54. Gilles Deleuze and Félix Guattari, *A Thousand Plateaus: Capitalism and Schizophrenia*, trans. Brian Massumi (Minneapolis and London: University of Minnesota Press, 1987), 351.

55. Deleuze and Guattari, *Thousand Plateaus*, 352.
56. Deleuze and Guattari, *Thousand Plateaus*, 418.
57. Deleuze and Guattari, *Thousand Plateaus*, 358.
58. Deleuze and Guattari, *Thousand Plateaus*, 448. They claim that the war machine does not necessarily have war as its object and that war results only when the nomadic war machine collides with States and cities opposing it (*Thousand Plateaus*, 416–417).
59. Deleuze and Guattari, *Thousand Plateaus*, 380–387.
60. Deleuze and Guattari, *Thousand Plateaus*, 381.
61. Deleuze and Guattari, *Thousand Plateaus*, 380.
62. Deleuze and Guattari, *Thousand Plateaus*, 385.
63. Deleuze and Guattari, *Thousand Plateaus*, 382.
64. Deleuze and Guattari, *Thousand Plateaus*, 381.
65. On the disorientation and limited views, politically and spatially, in war films, see Westwell, *War Cinema*, esp. 33–34, 51–55, 109–110.
66. Sorlin, "Cinema and the Memory of the Great War," 21.
67. Virilio, *War and Cinema*, 70.
68. Doherty (*Projections of War*, 284) quotes Gustav Hasford's 1979 novel *The Short Timers* as the source exposing Wayne's "solar confusion." See also Slotkin, *Gunfighter Nation*, 523–524 and Suid, *Guts & Glory*, 256.
69. On the stalemate in battle in this film, see John Whiteclay Chambers II, "*All Quiet on the Western Front* (U.S., 1930): The Antiwar Film and the Image of Modern War," *World War II, Film, and History*, ed. John Whiteclay Chambers II and David Culbert (New York and Oxford: Oxford University Press, 1996), 18–19.
70. On the filming of the legendary parade sequences, see Thomas Schatz, *The Genius of the System: Hollywood Filmmaking in the Studio Era* (London: Faber and Faber, 1998), 37.
71. Gregory D. Black, *Hollywood Censored: Morality Codes, Catholics, and the Movies* (Cambridge: Cambridge University Press, 1994), 90.

7   Conclusions: The Ends of Classical Death

1. For a critical view on the supposed impossibility of representing the Holocaust particularly in the cinema, see Lawrence Baron, *Projecting the Holocaust into the Present: The Changing Focus of Contemporary Holocaust Cinema* (Lanham: Rowman & Littlefield Publishers, 2005), esp. 1–22.
2. Anton Kaes, "Holocaust and the End of History: Postmodern Historiography in Cinema," *Probing the Limits of Representation: Nazism and the "Final Solution,"* ed. Saul Friedlander (Cambridge and London: Harvard University Press, 1992), 207.
3. Jean-François Lyotard, *The Differend: Phrases in Dispute*, trans. Georges Van Den Abbeele (Minneapolis: University of Minnesota Press, 1988), §2, 4.
4. Lyotard, *Differend*, §2, 3.
5. Miriam Bratu Hansen, "*Schindler's List* Is Not *Shoah*: The Second Commandment, Popular Modernism, and Public Memory," *Critical Inquiry* 22 (Winter 1996): 301. However, an awareness of the problematic status of such an attempt or its impossibility can be represented, for example in Lanzmann's

own cinematic work. See for example Shoshana Felman's reading of *Shoah* as dealing with the problem of testimony, "The Return of the Voice: Claude Lanzmann's *Shoah,*" *Testimony: Crises of Witnessing in Literature, Psychoanalysis and History*, ed. Shoshana Felman and Dori Laub (New York: Routledge 1992), 204–283.

6. On the cinematic response of Jewish filmmakers immediately after the war in Europe, see Ira Konigsberg, *"Our Children* and the Limits of Cinema: Early Jewish Responses to the Holocaust," *Film Quarterly* 52.1 (Fall 1998): 7–19; on atrocity photographs and Holocaust memory, see Barbie Zelizer, *Remembering to Forget: Holocaust Memory through the Camera's Eye* (Chicago: The University of Chicago Press, 1998); and on the concentration camp newsreel footage and its reception, see Thomas Doherty, *Projections of War: Hollywood, American Culture, and World War II* (New York: Columbia University Press, 1993), 247–250.

7. Ilan Avisar, *Screening the Holocaust: Cinema's Images of the Unimaginable* (Bloomington and Indianapolis: Indiana University Press, 1988), 116. Lawrence Baron discusses attempts by Hollywood and television to address the Holocaust before this film, but defines a "Holocaust film" in a different way from Avisar and others, see Baron, *Projecting the Holocaust into the Present*, chapter 2 and Rev. of *Imaginary Witness: Hollywood and the Holocaust* in *Film & History: An Interdisciplinary Journal of Film and Television Studies* 35.1 (2005): 72–74. Baron nevertheless agrees this is "the first American film to deal with the Holocaust itself" (74). See also Caroline Joan (Kay) S. Picart and David A. Frank, *Frames of Evil: The Holocaust as Horror in American Film* (Carbondale: Southern Illinois University Press, 2006), 23.

8. Annette Insdorf, *Indelible Shadows: Film and the Holocaust*, third edition (Cambridge and New York: Cambridge University Press, 2003), 3; this would change in the last decades of the century. By the beginning of the third millennium Holocaust films were so numerous that Insdorf could claim that they "constitute a veritable genre" (245).

9. Annette Insdorf claims the film fits "the bristling new material of the Holocaust into an old narrative form" (*Indelible Shadows*, 6).

10. Omer Bartov, "Spielberg's Oskar: Hollywood Tries Evil," *Spielberg's Holocaust: Critical Perspectives on* Schindler's List, ed. Yosefa Loshitzky (Bloomington and Indianapolis: Indiana University Press, 1997), 47.

11. For the idea that the "unrepresentable" can be altered to become compatible with a representative regime, see Jacques Rancière, *The Future of the Image*, trans. Gregory Elliott (London and New York: Verso, 2007), 117. Rancière is in general skeptical of the idea of the "unrepresentable."

12. Lyotard, *Differend*, §2, 3–4; §§24–27, 13–14.

13. Lyotard, *Differend*, §§152–160 and Hegel notice, 86–106.

14. Edith Wyschogrod, *Spirit in Ashes: Hegel, Heidegger, and Man-Made Mass Death* (New Haven and London: Yale University Press, 1985), 65. Wyschogrod however argues that Hegel does provide resources for theorizing contemporary death worlds.

15. The term "universe of the cinema" appears in Primo Levi, *The Drowned and the Saved*, trans. Raymond Rosenthal (London: Abacus, 2005), 123.

16. See Robert Horton, Introduction, *Billy Wilder: Interviews*, ed. Robert Horton (Jackson: University Press of Mississippi, 2001), xvi.

17. Sander Lee, "Scapegoating, the Holocaust, and McCarthyism in Billy Wilder's *Stalag 17*," *Senses of Cinema* 5 (April 2000) <http://www.sensesof cinema.com/contents/00/5/stalag.html>, accessed 11 August 2009.
18. Levi, *Drowned and the Saved*, 63.
19. Levi, *Drowned and the Saved*, 64.
20. Again, *I* am using the films to elaborate a certain idea, not claiming that the filmmakers at the time were knowingly trying to address the claims by Lyotard or Levi.
21. Jacques Rancière, *Film Fables*, trans. Emiliano Battista (Oxford and New York: Berg, 2006), 169.
22. I am indebted to Thomas Elsaesser for his generosity and help which enabled me to view Schlöndorff's documentary.
23. For those more interested than I in historical contexts, symptomatic readings, and auteur studies, it might be worthwhile to note that an argument could be made that for Wilder himself *Ace in the Hole* was—consciously or not—connected to the Nazi atrocities. In interviews in Schlöndorff's and Grischow's series, Wilder talks about shooting an army film at the liberated Nazi camps at the end of World War II (the name of the film is not mentioned in the program, but Wilder directed the 1945 *Death Mills*). "I have never forgotten one image," Wilder tells Schlöndorff, "a dying man—the only one still moving. He was looking at the camera. He turns, gets up slowly, and falls over dead. [...] the look of this dying man—shattering!" Recall his choice to have both Leo and Tatum look directly at the camera when they die in *Ace in the Hole*.

   On the gaze of the near-dead in photographs of the camps, see also Barbie Zelizer's *Remembering to Forget*, esp. 114–118. I have borrowed the term "near-dead" from her work. See also on the return of the gaze in the case of the dead in Karsten Witte, "Was haben Kinder, Amateure, Sterbende gemeinsam? Sie Blicken zurück: Traversen zum Tod im Film," *Kino und Tod: zur filmischen Inszenierung von Vergänglichkeit*, ed. Ernst Karpf (Marburg: Schüren, 1993), 25–51. On the near-dead, or almost dead, as bearing witness, see Giorgio Agamben, *Remnants of Auschwitz: The Witness and the Archive*, trans. Daniel Heller-Roazen (New York: Zone Books, 1999).

   In addition, both the German concentration camp documentary and *Ace in the Hole* were badly received by their audience. Wilder tells Schlöndorff that the Americans believed they should show the films of the concentration camp to as many Germans as possible. Afraid the Germans would not believe his film—especially since it was made by a Jew from Hollywood—they decided to preview it in Würzburg, where it was clear that the audience was unwilling to view the atrocity footage accompanied by narration blaming the German people for their indifference and cooperation with the Nazi regime. "There were 500 in the audience," Wilder recalls of the preview screening, "at the end, only about 75." The way he understands the failure of *Ace in the Hole* in the United States seems applicable to the German viewers as well. "It affronted the people who saw the picture," he explains. "They say '[...] I don't want to [...] be told that I am a son of a bitch, that we are bad people, that that we are very cruel'". It could therefore be argued that for Wilder, at least retrospectively, *Ace in the Hole* ended up being related to an earlier attempt to deal with the Holocaust.

24. In an interview with Cameron Crowe, Wilder mentions that his mother, her husband (his stepfather, whom he had never met) as well as his grandmother were taken to a concentration camp (Cameron Crowe, *Conversations with Billy Wilder* [New York: Alfred A. Knopf, 1999], 183) and that he was later told that his mother had died at Auschwitz (184).
25. Lyotard, *Differend*, §156, 100.
26. Lyotard, *Differend*, §157, 100.
27. Lyotard, *Differend*, §157, 100–101.
28. Lyotard, *Differend*, §157, 101; see also §159, 103–104.
29. Lyotard, *Differend*, §157, 101.
30. Lyotard, *Differend*, §158, 102.
31. Lyotard, *Differend*, §158, 103.
32. An attitude that, historically, can be increasingly discerned among Holocaust films since the 1960s, in some cases following Arendt's argument about the "banality" of Nazi evil. See A. D. Moses, "Structure and Agency in the Holocaust: Daniel J. Goldhagen and His Critics," *History and Theory* 37.2 (May 1998): 194–219 and Picart and Frank, *Frames of Evil*, 17ff and 127.
33. During World War II, Wilder himself made a war film which fits the description in Chapter 6—*Five Graves to Cairo* (1943). It features a tank that keeps rolling on despite the death of almost its entire crew; a British corporal who becomes a British spy by impersonating a German spy who impersonates a neutral waiter; a French chambermaid whose allegiance seems to shift and change throughout the film; civilian activities like archeology serving the military; and of course a map of Egypt especially printed for German Field Marshal Rommel, but in English, a fact which holds the key to the "five graves"—the German name for Egypt, *Ägypten*, does not have five letters. On the last point, see Herbert G. Luft, "A Matter of Decadence," *The Quarterly of Film Radio and Television* 7.1 (Autumn 1952): 63.
34. Thomas Elsaesser, "A German Ancestry to Film Noir? Film History and Its Imaginary," *Iris* 21 (Spring 1996): 129–143; see also Thomas Elsaesser, "Ethnicity, Authenticity, and Exile: A Counterfeit Trade? German Filmmakers and Hollywood," *Home, Exile, Homeland: Film, Media, and the Politics of Place*, ed. Hamid Naficy (New York and London: Routledge, 1999), 120.
35. Avisar, *Screening the Holocaust*, 110.
36. On the "facile distortion" of positing "a one-to-one analogy between the Harlem ghetto in 1965 and the camps of the early forties" in *The Pawnbroker*, see Insdorf, *Indelible Shadows*, 28.
37. See Insdorf, *Indelible Shadows*, 170–173 on this complex film within a wider context of (mostly non-American) Holocaust-related films that offer ambiguous identities.
38. This television series, of course, is not a theatrical feature film, but often appears within discussions about film, and particularly Hollywood, and the representation of the Holocaust.
39. Described by Lawrence Baron in 2005 as "the most graphic cinematic portrayal of the gassing facility at Birkenau to date" (*Projecting the Holocaust into the Present*, 253).
40. As noted in Chapter 3, eugenics was a racist movement, which enjoyed warm ties with colleagues in Germany. Hollywood found ways of circumventing certain aspects of the racist potential in its films (it clearly was

racist toward African Americans and First Americans). In the case of some gangster films as noted in Chapter 3, while the criminal protagonists are "ethnically" marked, their ethnic background is clearly shown as *discouraging* crime—for example by including an Italian or Irish mother or Catholic priest who disapproves of crime.

Another interesting example can be found in war films. The films' most unabashed and genocidal racism seems to be reserved for the Japanese enemy. As Thomas Schatz writes, the majority of these dramas "depicted the Japanese enemy as not only uncivilized but essentially inhuman—a view that pervaded the American media and mindset in general" (Thomas Schatz, "World War II and the Hollywood 'War Film,'" *Refiguring American Film Genres: History and Theory*, ed. Nick Browne [Berkeley, Los Angeles, and London: University of California Press, 1998], 113). In *Objective, Burma!* (Raoul Walsh, 1945), one group of soldiers encounters a second group that was attacked by the Japanese. It seems that they were tortured and mutilated—the gruesome results of the encounter with the Japanese remain off screen. One American officer is still alive when the group finds him and he begs them to kill him. An aging journalist who accompanies the forces then voices his feelings, referring to the Japanese as "degenerate, moral idiots" and "stinking little savages" and calling to "wipe them off the face of the earth" (the racial diatribe is quoted in John Belton, *American Cinema/American Culture* [New York: McGraw-Hill, 1994], 177). The men prepare for the arrival of the Japanese soldiers, whom they sometimes refer to as "monkeys." The Americans then efficiently butcher their racial inferiors. The Japanese soldiers proved they were degenerate and subhuman; there is no dealing with them except by wiping them off the face of the earth, which is indeed what the American soldiers are committed to doing in these films.

Yet while Hollywood clearly was racist, it was uncomfortably so. In the context of the war, explains Richard Slotkin, the traditional values of democracy and equality "constituted the ideological rationale for our armed opposition to the totalitarian and racist systems of Nazi Germany and Imperial Japan" (*Gunfighter Nation: The Myth of the Frontier in Twentieth-Century America* [New York: Atheneum, 1992], 320). That the films themselves were also racist, in particular toward the Japanese savage enemy and the minorities in the multi-ethnic platoon whose deaths are particularly gruesome (Jeanine Basinger, *The World War II Combat Film: Anatomy of a Genre* [New York: Columbia University Press, 1986], 75; Slotkin, *Gunfighter Nation*, 319, 322), was part of the Hollywood war film's successful integration of the contradictory pressures in "America's war-fighting ideology" which "contained a potent racist element and at the same time required an explicit disavowal of racism" (Slotkin, *Gunfighter Nation*, 320. See also 366ff on the "pro-Indian" Western).

Was then a film like *Objective, Burma!* at all concerned that it was claiming the Americans were racially superior to the Japanese while Americans in Hollywood and elsewhere considered themselves morally superior to the racist Nazis? During the battle against the Japanese soldiers, one American throws a grenade ("a pineapple") while shouting "mazal tov!" a phrase he had already used earlier in the film. In another anti-Japanese film, *Sands of Iwo Jima* (Allan Dwan, 1949), a wounded soldier still has time to utter his Shma' Yisra'el prayer before dying and leaving John Wayne to add the amen. In other words, Hollywood films attempted to justify their attitude toward the Japanese by having them commit such heinous atrocities that they must remain off camera. In addition, they made a point of showing that the Americans were not racist like the Nazis, that is, not anti-Semite; rather, the Jews were part of the nation, fighting and dying like all other Americans, even using Hebrew phrases while praying, and then receiving John Wayne's blessing. Even at their racist worst, when describing the "Nips" as degenerate monkeys, Hollywood films were still trying to appear non-racist, in this case at least toward Jews.

41. Erving Goffman, *The Presentation of Self in Everyday Life* (Garden City: Doubleday Anchor Books, 1959), 101.
42. Goffman, *Presentation of Self in Everyday Life*, 114.
43. Frank J. Sulloway, *Freud Biologist of the Mind: Beyond the Psychoanalytic Legend* (Cambridge and London: Harvard University Press, 1992), 437–438; Richard LaPiere, *The Freudian Ethic* (New York: Duell, Sloan and Pearce, 1959), 44.
44. Although love, a South American cruise, and a makeover could also help. This treatment was similar to Breuer and Freud's late-nineteenth-century cathartic method. See David Bordwell, Janet Staiger, and Kristin Thompson, *The Classical Hollywood Cinema: Film Style & Mode of Production to 1960* (London, Melbourne and Henley: Routledge & Kegan Paul, 1985), 20–21; Mary Ann Doane, *The Desire to Desire: The Woman's Film of the 1940s* (Basingstoke and London: Macmillan Press, 1987), esp. chapter 2; Glen O. Gabbard and Krin Gabbard, *Psychiatry and the Cinema*, Second Edition (Washington and London: American Psychiatric Press, 1999), esp. 27ff; E. Ann Kaplan, "Melodrama, Cinema and Trauma," *Screen* 42.2 (2001): 201–205; Dana Polan, *Power and Paranoia: History, Narrative, and the American Cinema, 1940–1950* (New York: Columbia University Press, 1986), 176–191; Marc Vernet, "Freud: Effets spéciaux/Mise en scène: U.S.A.," *Communications* 23 (1975): 223–234; Janet Walker, *Couching Resistance: Women, Film, and Psychoanalytic Psychiatry* (Minneapolis and London: University of Minnesota Press, 1993).
45. These killers, or potential killers, are curable and therefore no longer killable—they remain alive at the end of the film (although the convict is caught by the police). Less extreme is Raven in *This Gun for Hire* (Frank Tuttle, 1942), who undergoes an unofficial talking cure by a woman he befriends in which he tells of a childhood event which might explain his murderous tendencies. He is not cured of being a killer, but he does manage to divert his violence to patriotic ends. While he still dies, his death is also meaningful in relation to the future: the woman is there next to him and can remember him and the fact that he has helped his country.
46. The cult of the dead in *Jesse James* was dealt with in Chapter 5.
47. Their death concludes the events in the film, but it does not end it. Jo dies and then Eddie does, but the film continues and the dead characters go on. The deceased Eddie now hears the dead priest he killed earlier addressing him and telling him he is finally free. His "cult," then, includes not only the baby but also the dead themselves.

48. Jack Shadoian, *Dreams & Dead Ends: The American Gangster Film*, Second Edition (Oxford and New York: Oxford University Press, 2003), 62–63.
49. I am indebted to Doron Galili, among many things, for introducing me to some of these films and discussing them with me.
50. Tony Balio, *Grand Design: Hollywood as a Modern Business Enterprise 1930–1939*, Vol. 5 of *History of the American Cinema* (New York: Charles Scribner's Sons, 1993), 292; David E. Ruth, *Inventing the Public Enemy: The Gangster in American Culture, 1918–1934* (Chicago and London: The University of Chicago Press, 1996), 145; Kirsten Moana Thompson, *Crime Films: Investigating the Scene* (London and New York: Wallflower, 2007), 18–19.
51. He does alter his looks though—he "fixes" his face medically not to be easily recognized. But, ridiculing Lombroso, even with a changed face he is still no less the crook and killer he always has been.
52. Although poverty is continually shown, it is clear that it does not determine one's fate. Jerry did manage to grow up honest coming from the same circumstances. In addition, when the kids are given money by Rocky they do not abandon their errant ways, but rather go out to drink and gamble and refuse to listen to Jerry. Giving money to the poor is no solution!
53. See also Thomas Schatz, *Hollywood Genres: Formulas, Filmmaking, and the Studio System* (New York: McGraw-Hill, 1981), 100–101 on the "outrageous" twist and "fancy narrative footwork" in this film; and Martha P. Nochimson, *Dying to Belong: Gangster Movies in Hollywood and Hong Kong* (Malden and Oxford: Blackwell, 2007), 48 and 115–117 on the deceptiveness and ambiguity of this film. Moreover, if influence were as important as Jerry says, and Rocky was always willing to help others, was he really such a bad influence on the boys?
54. There are other films that feature a criminal who is not born bad, but rather born a decent "sucker" on the wrong side of the law, and whose death is tragic and troubling. Blackie in *Manhattan Melodrama* (W. S. Van Dyke, 1934) is a decent gangster, whose childhood friend Jim is a decent lawyer and later governor. His death leads to an aporia. At the end of the film, Blackie insists on being executed because he is bad and will not let Jim pardon him. Acting against his own criminal nature, and making sure the law is obeyed, indicates that perhaps he was not born bad, that he can change, and that in fact there is no reason to kill him. By insisting on being executed he no longer deserves to be executed; however, had he tried not to be executed he would have deserved to be. He ceases to be killable if and only if he agrees to be killed by law. He is ultimately executed, but this is no longer enough to conclude the entire film, which ends with Jim resigning from his post for having wanted to pardon him and reuniting with the woman he loves.

    Bart in *Gun Crazy/Deadly Is the Female* (Joseph H. Lewis, 1950) is apparently born with an incurable fetish for guns and with a talent for shooting, but he is not bad; in fact he harbors a reluctance to kill any living being or hurt anyone, acquired at an early age. He is also incurably attracted to Laurie, who *is* bad and much to his dismay and surprise does kill (and is happy to give a multitude of reasons for doing so—"because I had to, because I was afraid, because they would have killed you, because you're the only thing I've got in the whole world, because I love you.") At the end, after being involved in countless armed robberies which she demanded, and several murders which she committed, both are trapped in a foggy swamp with Bart's two childhood friends approaching to arrest them. Laurie threatens to shoot them and Bart, stuck in a double bind in which he is unable to stop her from killing but does not want to be involved in harming anyone, shoots *her* dead. He is then hit by a bullet, probably shot by one of his friends who heard his gun in the fog, and dies.

55. This Christian symbolism was pointed out in the television documentary *A Personal Journey with Martin Scorsese through American Movies* (Martin Scorsese and Michael Henry Wilson, 1995).

56. Dudley Andrew, "Film Noir: Death and Double Cross over the Atlantic," *Iris* 21 (Spring 1996): 29.

57. Andrew, "Film Noir," 23.

58. Jeff's death in *Out of the Past* is meaningful in relation to the future—his friend makes sure his memory is distorted, so that another woman who loves him is able to go on with her life with another man, incorrectly believing that Jeff meant to leave her.

59. I will be assuming that overall many American films have retained the character-centered linear causal storylines of classical Hollywood. Although I know of no one who would claim that a 1995 Hollywood film looks like a 1925 film, how exactly "new Hollywood" or "new new Hollywood" differs from classical Hollywood has been a matter of considerable debate. See for example Justin Wyatt, *High Concept: Movies and Marketing in Hollywood* (Austin: University of Texas Press, 1994); Steve Neale and Murray Smith, ed., *Contemporary Hollywood Cinema* (London and New York: Routledge, 1998); Kristin Thompson, *Storytelling in the New Hollywood: Understanding Classical Narrative Technique* (Cambridge and London: Harvard University Press, 1999); Warren Buckland and Thomas Elsaesser, *Studying Contemporary American Film: A Guide to Movie Analysis* (London: Arnold, 2002); David Bordwell, *The Way Hollywood Tells It: Story and Style in Modern Movies* (Berkeley, Los Angeles, and London: University of California Press, 2006), esp. 1–18; Warren Buckland, *Directed by Steven Spielberg: Poetics of the Contemporary Hollywood Blockbuster* (New York and London: Continuum, 2006); and Thomas Schatz, "Studio System," *Schirmer Encyclopedia of Film*. Ed. Barry Keith Grant. Vol. 4 (New York: Schirmer Reference, 2007). 169–176.

60. This is far from a complete historical "context" of death at the period, which should include other factors such as the end-of-the-world fantasies as the year 2000 approached and the 11 September 2001 terrorist attacks against the United States. Moreover, much of the change was not actually taking place. It was only a promise, a possibility for the future, a "virtual" change.

61. Nicholas Mirzoeff, *An Introduction to Visual Culture* (London and New York: Routledge, 1999), 101–126.

62. Rose Marie San Juan and Geraldine Pratt, "Virtual Cities: Film and the Urban Mapping of Virtual Space," *Screen* 43.4 (Autumn 2002): 252–254.

63. Sergio Sismondo, "Reality for Cybernauts," *Postmodern Culture* 8.1 (1997): §19.

64. Jacques Choron, *Death and Western Thought* (New York: Collier Books, 1963), 26. According to Simon Critchley, the "contemporary obsession

with 'near-death' or 'out-of-body' experiences" was spawned by Raymond Moody's book *Life after Life* in the mid 1970s (*The Book of Dead Philosophers* [London: Granta Books, 2008], xxii).

65. Choron, *Death and Western Thought*, 25.

66. Choron, *Death and Western Thought*, 26. See also Mary M. Litch, *Philosophy through Film* (New York and London: Routledge, 2002), 69–70.

67. Michele Pierson, "No Longer State-of-the-Art: Crafting a Future for CGI," *Wide Angle* 21.1 (January 1999): 37.

68. William Gibson, *Neuromancer* (London: Voyager HarperCollins Publishers, 1995), 85.

69. Gibson, *Neuromancer*, 97. Not unlike many of the undead in Hollywood, even the already-dead McCoy Pauley can still die, and asks the protagonist to be "erased" when it is all over (130 and 246).

70. Yvonne Spielmann, "Expanding Film into Digital Media," *Screen* 40.2 (Summer 1999): 131; Philip Rosen, *Change Mummified: Cinema, Historicity, Theory* (Minneapolis and London: University of Minnesota Press, 2001), 318, 333–349.

71. Warren Buckland, "Between Science Fact and Science Fiction: Spielberg's Digital Dinosaurs, Possible Worlds, and the New Aesthetic Realism," *Screen* 40.2 (Summer 1999): 178.

72. A. O. Scott, "Now, Which of You Are Dead?" *The New York Times*, 10 Aug. 2001, East Coast late ed.: E.1. It is particularly reminiscent of Henry James's 1898 *The Turn of the Screw* (New York: Dover Publications, 1991).

73. His first feature film, *Tesis/Thesis* (1996), is set in a film school where snuff videos are made; his next feature, *Abre los ojos*, shows a film crew in its opening credits; and his the film that followed *The Others*, *Mar adentro/The Sea Within/The Sea Inside* (2004) opens with a voice asking an unseen addressee to relax and imagine a movie screen.

74. Barbara Creed, "The Cyberstar: Digital Pleasures and the End of the Unconscious," *Screen* 41.1 (Spring 2000): 79.

75. Creed, "The Cyberstar," 84.

76. Creed, "The Cyberstar," 85.

77. Gregory T. Huang, "The New Face of Hollywood," *Technology Review* 107.7 (Sep 2004): 68.

78. Leslie A. Kurtz, "Digital Actors and Copyright—From The Polar Express to Simone," *Santa Clara Computer and High-Technology Law Journal* 21.4 (May 2005): 785.

79. Noël Burch, *Life to Those Shadows*, trans. and ed. Ben Brewster (Berkeley and Los Angeles: University of California Press, 1990), 12.

80. Huang, "New Face of Hollywood," 73.

81. David Lavery, "From Cinespace to Cyberspace: Zionists and Agents, Realists and Gamers in *The Matrix* and *eXistenZ*," *Journal of Popular Film and Television* 28.4 (Winter 2001): 152.

82. Carl N. Degler, *In Search of Human Nature: The Decline and Revival of Darwinism in American Social Thought* (New York and Oxford: Oxford University Press, 1991), 216; see part III for a more general discussion of the causes and shifts in the social sciences. For a discussion of the shift in American psychiatry, see Allan Young, *The Harmony of Illusions: Inventing Post-Traumatic Stress Disorder* (Princeton: Princeton University Press, 1995),

94–107, 269–272. For a discussion of the attempt by genetics to break its association with eugenics, see Barry Barnes and John Dupré, *Genomes and What to Make of Them* (Chicago and London: The University of Chicago Press, 2008), esp. 176–177.

83. On the importance of culture in sociobiology see Degler, *In Search of Human Nature*, chapter 13.

84. Elizabeth A. Wilson, "Neurological Preference: LeVay's Study of Sexual Orientation," *SubStance* 29.1 (2000): 23, 37n1.

85. Simon LeVay, "A Difference in Hypothalamic Structure between Heterosexual and Homosexual Men," *Science* 253 (30 Aug. 1991): 1034.

86. LeVay, "Difference in Hypothalamic Structure," 1034, 1036.

87. Simon LeVay, *The Sexual Brain* (Cambridge and London: MIT Press, 1993), xiii; Simon LeVay, *Queer Science: The Use and Abuse of Research into Homosexuality* (Cambridge and London: MIT Press, 1996), esp. 67–85.

88. Abi Berger, "The Rise and Fall of Viagra," *British Medical Journal* 317 (19 Sep. 1998): 824.

89. Samuel H. Barondes, "Thinking about Prozac," *Science* 263 (25 Feb. 1994): 1102.

90. Peter D. Kramer, *Listening to Prozac* (New York: Viking, 1993), 15.

91. Jennifer Hansen, "Listening to People or Listening to Prozac? Another Consideration of Causal Classifications," *Philosophy, Psychiatry & Psychology* 10.1 (2003): 58.

92. Barondes, "Thinking about Prozac," 1102; for a similar shift from impotence as an emotional or psychological problem to "erectile dysfunction" as a physiological problem which coincided with the success of Viagra, see Barbara L. Marshall, " 'Hard Science': Gendered Constructions of Sexual Dysfunction in the 'Viagra Age,' " *Sexualities* 5.2 (2002): 131–158, esp. 136–137.

93. Barondes, "Thinking about Prozac," 1103.

94. On the essentialist discourse on genomes, see Barnes and Dupré, *Genomes*, 246–257. They find the essentialist approach misleading.

95. Simon A. Cole, *Suspect Identities: A History of Fingerprinting and Criminal Identification* (Cambridge and London: Harvard University Press, 2001), 308.

96. Cole, *Suspect Identities*, 287–302.

97. Barnes and Dupré, *Genomes*, 142. These claims were scientifically unwarranted. For a detailed discussion of how a statistical study of twins based on a postal questionnaire was over-interpreted by the researchers and the media and ended up with headlines claiming that for some women infidelity is irresistible because it is "in her genes," see Barnes and Dupré, *Genomes*, 153–163.

98. Qtd. in Leslie Roberts, "Genome Project Under Way, at Last," *Science* 243 (13 Jan. 1989): 167.

99. James D. Watson and Norton Zinder, "Genome Project Maps Paths of Diseases and Drugs," *The New York Times* 13 Oct. 1990, late ed.—final: 1.24.

100. Barnes and Dupré, *Genomes*, 153–155.

101. Cole, *Suspect Identities*, 310.

102. Donna Haraway, "A Manifesto for Cyborgs: Science, Technology, and Socialist Feminism in the 1980s," *Socialist Review* 80 (1985): 66.

103. Evelyn Fox Keller, "From Secrets of Life to Secrets of Death," *Secrets of Life, Secrets of Death: Essays on Language, Gender and Science* (New York and London: Routledge, 1992), 39.

104. Mary Z. Pelias and Nathan J. Markward, "The Human Genome Project: Truth and Consequences," *Emory Law Journal* 49.3 (Summer 2000): 838.

105. Jean Baudrillard, *The Vital Illusion*, ed. Julia Witwer (New York: Columbia University Press, 2000), 3.

106. Baudrillard, *The Vital Illusion*, 27.

107. Otto Rank, *The Double: A Psychoanalytical Study*, trans. Harry Tucker Jr. (Chapel Hill: The University of North Carolina Press, 1971), 85.

108. Rank, *Double*, 78–80.

109. Martin Heidegger, *Being and Time*, trans. John Macquarrie and Edward Robinson (Oxford and Cambridge: Blackwell, 2004), 289.

110. Heidegger, *Being and Time*, §50, 295.

111. Heidegger, *Being and Time*, §50, 294.

112. Heidegger, *Being and Time*, §47, 283.

113. Heidegger, *Being and Time*, §47, 284.

114. Barnes and Dupré, *Genomes*, 2, 14, 42–44.

115. J. Hoberman, "Designer Genes," *The Village Voice* (28 Oct. 1997): 84.

116. Jackie Stacey, "Masculinity, Masquerade, and Genetic Impersonation: *Gattaca*'s Queer Visions," *Signs* 30.3 (Spring 2005): 1855.

117. Stacey, "Masculinity, Masquerade, and Genetic Impersonation," 1856.

118. Stacey, "Masculinity, Masquerade, and Genetic Impersonation," 1855–1856.

119. There is no clear narrative reason for this act, but he is already suicidal when Vincent meets him. Mark Jeffreys claims that Jerome "finds purpose only by sacrificing himself to an able-bodied man's dreams and then immolating himself in a garbage incinerator" ("Dr. Daedalus and His Minotaur: Mythic Warnings about Genetic Engineering from J. B. S. Haldane, François Jacob, and Andrew Niccol's *Gattaca*," *Journal of Medical Humanities* 22.2 (2001): 144), that he must perish "so that the more truly human 'Godchild' hero of the movie can fulfill his spiritual destiny and literally ascend into the heavens" (138). Jackie Stacey argues that in the suicide scene the "improvised kinship tie between Vincent and Jerome is given symbolic permanence" because it is a confirmation of the foreverness of their shared future ("Masculinity, Masquerade, and Genetic Impersonation," 1869). We might also use Nietzsche's recommendation as explanation for why the elite man of the future chose to kill himself. "I commend to you my sort of death, voluntary death that comes to me because *I* wish it," he writes. For a man who has an heir and a goal, this death will come "at the time most favourable to his goal and his heir" (Friedrich Nietzsche, *Thus Spoke Zarathustra: A Book for Everyone and No One*, trans. R. J. Hollingdale [London: Penguin Books, 1969], "Of Voluntary Death," 97).

120. See Jonathan Eig, "A Beautiful Mind(fuck): Hollywood Structures of Identity," *Jump Cut: A Review of Contemporary Media* 46 (2003) <http://www.ejumpcut.org/archive/jc46.2003/eig.mindfilms/text.html>, accessed 11 August 2009; David Bordwell, *The Way Hollywood Tells It*, 72–103; Thomas Elsaesser, "The Mind-Game Film," *Puzzle Films: Complex Storytelling in Contemporary Cinema*, ed. Warren Buckland (Chichester: Wiley-Blackwell, 2009), 13–41.

121. This is also true for the film to which *Vanilla Sky* is a remake, *Abre los ojos* (Alejandro Amenábar, 1997). Thomas Elsaesser has even proposed a category of "post-mortem films," in "Real Location, Fantasy Space, Performative Place: Double Occupancy and Mutual Interference in European Cinema," *European Film Theory*, ed. Temenuga Trifonova (New York and London: Routledge, 2009), 58–61.

122. Stacy Thompson claims these images "seem to have been shot by a microscopic 'virtual camera,'" see: "Punk Cinema," *Cinema Journal* 43.2 (Winter 2004): 62.

123. Asbjørn Grønstad, "One-Dimensional Men: Fight Club and the Poetics of the Body," *Film Criticism* 28.1 (Fall 2003): 15.

124. Grønstad, "One-Dimensional Men," 19n11. This computer-generated imagery has frequently been commented upon. See also, for example, John McCullough, "Tedium and Torture: *Fight Club*, Globalization and Professionals in Crisis," *CineAction* 65 (January 2005): 50 and Thompson, "Punk Cinema," 63.

125. For a more detailed reading of *Fight Club* in relation to the *Doppelgänger* motif, see Lihi Nagler, "Singling Out the Double: Objectivity, Subjectivity and Alterity in Kieślowski's *The Double Life of Véronique*," *Post Script: Essays in Film and the Humanities* 22.3 (Summer 2003): 10–11.

126. Thompson, "Punk Cinema," 63.

127. The film constantly draws attention to its being a film—the narrator addresses the viewers directly and Tyler inserts frames of pornographic films into mainstream feature films, including, so it seems at the end, the film we are now watching, *Fight Club*. We know, especially if we are watching it on video, that this tampering with the film is also simulated.

128. McCullough, John. "Tedium and Torture," 46.

129. Jaap Kooijman and Tarja Laine, "*American Psycho*: A Double Portrait of Serial Yuppie Patrick Bateman," *Post Script: Essays in Film and the Humanities* 22.3 (Summer 2003): 47.

130. Richard Porton, "American Psycho," *Cineaste* 25.3 (June 2000): 43, 45; Linda S. Kauffman, "American Psycho," *Film Quarterly* 54.2 (Winter 2000/2001): 41.

131. Jaap and Laine, "American Psycho," 54.

132. Porton, "American Psycho," 44.

133. Gavin Smith, "American Psycho," *Film Comment* 36.2 (2000): 72.

Index

Note: Page numbers followed by n refer to notes.